TECHNOLOGY AND DESIGN

For CCEA GCSE

SUZANNE HAGAN

Reviewed by Raymond Moffatt

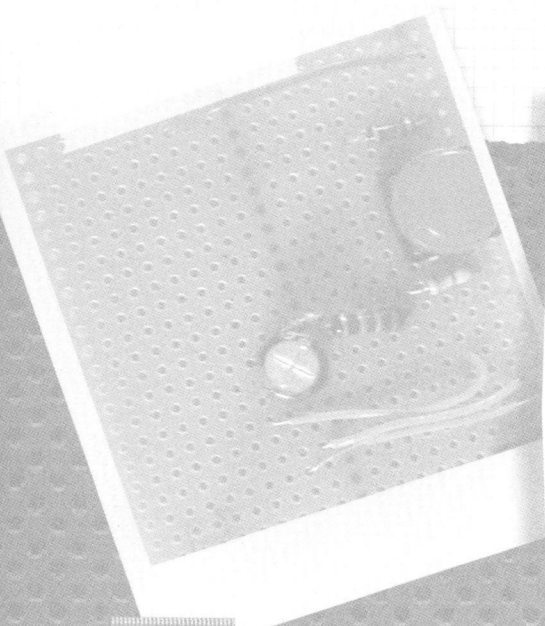

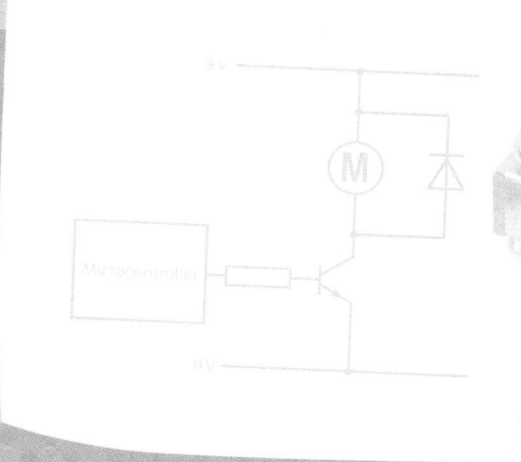

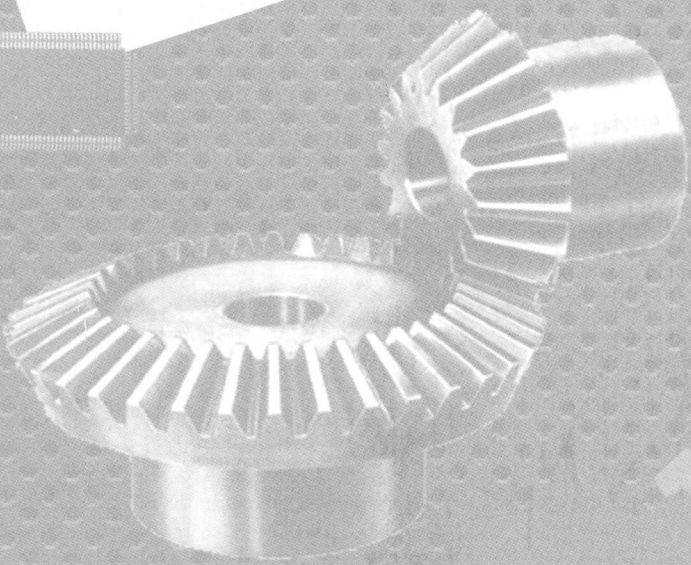

COLOURPOINT
EDUCATIONAL

©2012 Suzanne Hagan and Colourpoint Creative Ltd

ISBN: 978 1 78073 020 2

First Edition
Reprinted, 2013, 2015, 2017, 2019, 2022

Layout and design: April Sky Design, Newtownards
Printed by: GPS Colour Graphics Ltd, Belfast

The Author

Suzanne Hagan studied A Level Technology & Design at Saint Catherine's College, Armagh. She pursued her love of the subject at the University of Ulster, Jordanstown where she graduated in 1999 after completing a BSc. (Hons) 2:1 in Technology & Design and a Diploma in Industrial Studies with Distinction. After completing her PGCE in Technology & Design at UUJ, she now has over 15 years experience teaching the subject. Suzanne is currently employed in both Newbridge Integrated College, Banbridge and Drumragh Integrated College, Omagh.

Acknowledgments

Thanks must go to a number of people for their help, support and encouragement with the production of this book. Firstly, to my wonderful husband Conor, our three daughters, and my mother and father for all their support, understanding, encouragement and patience throughout the writing process. Also a special word of thanks to Rachel Irwin at Colourpoint for her guidance and time.

COLOURPOINT EDUCATIONAL

Colourpoint Educational
An imprint of Colourpoint Creative Ltd
Colourpoint House
Jubilee Business Park
21 Jubilee Road
Newtownards
County Down
Northern Ireland
BT23 4YH

Tel: 028 9182 0505
E-mail: sales@colourpoint.co.uk
Web site: www.colourpointeducational.com

Publisher's Note: This book has been written to help students preparing for the GCSE Technology and Design specification from CCEA. While Colourpoint Educational and the authors have taken every care in its production, we are not able to guarantee that the book is completely error-free. Additionally, while the book has been written to closely match the CCEA specification, it is the responsibility of each candidate to satisfy themselves that they have fully met the requirements of the CCEA specification prior to sitting an exam set by that body. For this reason, and because specifications and guidance notes change with time, we strongly advise every candidate to avail of a qualified teacher and to check the contents of the most recent specification for themselves prior to the exam. Colourpoint Creative Ltd therefore cannot be held responsible for any errors or omissions in this book or any consequences thereof.

Health and Safety: This book describes practical work that is either useful or required for the course. These must **only** be carried out in a school setting under the supervision of a qualified teacher. It is the responsibility of the school to ensure that students are provided with a safe environment in which to carry out the work. Students should never carry out the work described unsupervised.

CONTENTS

FOREWORD

The main purpose of this book is to help you succeed at CCEA GCSE Technology and Design. Technology and Design is an interesting subject to study as it is all about thinking creatively and constructing learning through experiences. It will provide you with opportunities to combine practical and intellectual skills with an understanding of aesthetic, technical, cultural, health, social, emotional, economic, industrial and environmental issues. The subject will teach you how to evaluate present and past designs and technologies, and about their uses and effects. It will help you develop as a discriminating user of products, and become confident at practical work and problem solving, both individually and as part of a team. By applying creative thinking you will learn to be innovative, which will also improve your self-esteem.

Learning and undertaking activities in GCSE Technology and Design will help you build on the NI curriculum objectives you achieved in Technology and Design Key Stage 3 to:

- develop as individuals.
- develop as contributors to society.
- develop as contributors to the economy and the environment.

The CCEA revised specification for GCSE Technology and Design is divided into five units:

Unit 1: Technology and Design Core (Compulsory) 20%
Unit 2: Systems and Control (Optional) 20%
Unit 3: Product Design (Optional) 20%
Unit 4: Design Assignment (Controlled Assessment) 20%
Unit 5: Design Project (Controlled Assessment) 40%

This text book follows the structure of the specification, divided into the five units and covering the whole examined course. Each unit provides the content for the course, along with questions and activities, a list of key words and past paper questions so you can assess your learning as you progress through the course. This layout is designed to help you learn in class with your teacher and peers, at home independently and also serve as a useful revision resource at exam time.

Unit 1: Technology and Design Core
This unit is **compulsory**. You will study (a) manufacturing, (b) electronics, (c) mechanical control systems, (d) computer control systems and (e) pneumatic systems and control. Knowledge and understanding of each of these control systems is essential when considering the design and manufacture of products. With this in mind, Unit 1 has been broken down further into these five sub-sections (a–e).

Unit 2: Systems and Control
This unit is **optional**. You will study (a) electronic and

microelectronic control systems or (b) mechanical and pneumatic control systems. This unit has been divided into two clear sub-sections (a & b) so follow the option your school has chosen for you to study. This unit will provide you with more in-depth knowledge and understanding of control systems than is necessary for Unit 1. This will help you consider using such control systems when designing and manufacturing products to solve design problems during this course.

Unit 3: Product Design

This unit is **optional**. You will study (a) designing and innovation, (b) materials, components and fabrication, (c) manufacturing practices and (d) social responsibility of product design and market influences. Product design is complex and involves all of these areas, so it is more than just sketching a concept and hoping it can be manufactured. This unit will give you all the information you need to develop your knowledge and help you understand product design.

Unit 4: Design Assignment (Controlled Assessment)

This unit is **compulsory**. You will complete a design assignment to demonstrate your ability to design a product under controlled conditions. You will be assessed on your knowledge, skills and ability to plan, carry out research, produce sketches of ideas, design and evaluate.

The information and guidance provided in this section will help you to understand what is expected and get you started on the design assignment. It is designed as support material, to be used alongside the guidelines of your teacher, suggesting possible layouts and tips to help you succeed in this unit. It also contains a useful activity on time management, requiring you to plan and organise your time, so that the work is completed with the 15 hours available.

Unit 5: Design Project (Controlled Assessment)

This unit is **compulsory**. You must demonstrate your ability to design and manufacture a product in either (a) product design or (b) systems design under controlled conditions. This section can be used as a visual checklist of the requirements of your design portfolio, showing you what needs to be included to achieve highly in this unit. It has been presented in a format to help keep you focused on the tasks, helping you manage your time and allowing you to check where you are and what you still need to do. As with Unit 4, it is designed to be used in conjunction with the guidelines of your teacher but should provide guidance and support to get you started.

We hope you enjoy this book and that it helps to accelerate your learning in Technology and Design. We want it to spark a passion for the subject within you, so you begin to consider the further paths of study and careers this subject could open to you.

LIFE-LONG SKILLS

By helping to make the GCSE course in Technology and Design more manageable, enjoyable and fun, we hope that by the time it is finished we will have helped prepare you for further learning opportunities and career choices.

By studying GCSE Technology and Design you will develop the following skills that employers want:

Further learning

This GCSE Technology and Design text book has been written to support the CCEA specification and will help prepare you for the study of Technology and Design related courses at a more advanced level, for example, AS and A2 Technology and Design, and BTEC Nationals in Engineering and/or Manufacturing. A key feature of this specification is that it allows students to develop transferable skills which will benefit them in vocational training and employment.

Employability skills

- Analytical and research skills
- Problem solving, reasoning and creativity

- Computer and technical literacy
- Flexibility and adaptability
- Interpersonal skills
- Planning and organisational skills
- Leadership/management skills
- Teamwork

It is simple enough to list a range of skills. However, if you were asked to give examples of how Technology and Design will or has helped you achieve these employability skills, could you answer? The table opposite provides some answers that could be very useful in an interview.

I hope this information on employability skills will be beneficial to you in the future. It may even be useful now if you are applying for a part-time job and have to go for an interview. Often questions at interviews ask you to give examples or explain a time when you have shown a certain skill. Although this information is not needed as part of your Technology and Design course, it is important that the subject feeds into life-long skills for employability and learning for life and work in future years.

SKILLS	EXAMPLES OF HOW T&D HELPED YOU ACHIEVE THESE SKILLS
Communication skills	The only way to explain a solution to a design problem in T&D is to have good communication skills. Therefore I am competent at writing and speaking effectively to communicate thoughts, opinions and ideas. I am also good at listening, because in T&D it is essential to understand other people's design ideas and solutions.
Analytical and research skills	I have learned how to assess situations, seek multiple views, gather information and identify key issues to be addressed.
Problem solving, reasoning and creativity	I can find solutions to problems using my creativity and reasoning, combined with available information and resources. The design projects I completed in T&D required me to research and analyse relevant areas associated with the problem, such as existing products, possible materials and manufacturing techniques. The research provided inspiration, while the analysis gave valuable information on which features worked and which did not in existing products. These combined skills allowed me to develop a range of innovative and creative design solutions. Each solution then had to be evaluated to decide on a final idea for development and manufacturing. This required me to give detailed reasons for my choice, discussing the advantages and disadvantages of each solution.
Computer and technical literacy	I have used ICT regularly for Internet research, word processing, Computer Aided Designing, graphics and presentation of work. T&D lessons helped me become very competent at using a variety of software packages. For CAD work I am proficient at using Solidworks and Techsoft 2D design, which are excellent skills that I could take into industry. Also T&D gave me lots of experience of using Microsoft Word, Excel, Publisher, Powerpoint and Photoshop during class work, homework and controlled assessments.
Flexibility and adaptability	I have developed the ability to manage multiple tasks during projects, set priorities and adapt ideas to complete projects. Project work in T&D was demanding and required me to be working at different tasks simultaneously to ensure completion. Often I had to be flexible with regards to time, sometimes using lunch times and after school to complete tasks. My adaptability was evident when I took advice from teachers and technicians about material choices or processes for project work, at times changing an idea to suit the resources or time available. This is a skill any employer would like to see in an employee.
Interpersonal skills	I have developed the ability to work with all my peers, inspiring them to participate in group work and avoid conflict. In design lessons it was important to share ideas in groups by brainstorming. This working with peers helped build my mutual respect for the opinions of others and ideas even if I did not agree with them. In practical lessons we had to share resources, tools and equipment when manufacturing. If a number of pupils all needed to use the CNC machines at the same time we had to be patient and co-operative, helping each other complete tasks.
Planning and organisational skills	I have the ability to design, plan, organise and implement projects and tasks within allotted timeframes. The design projects I completed in T&D demanded a high level of individual time planning. I have the skills now to use a Gantt chart, within which tasks to be completed are plotted against periods of time. This time management skill could be applied to a wide range of jobs. I am now competent at organising my resources for a task, arriving prepared with everything I need to complete it and ensuring that I use my time wisely to get project work started and completed to a high standard of finish.
Leadership/ management skills	I feel I can take charge in group work and manage my peers if necessary during project work or lead them effectively in team situations. Group projects in T&D were great for developing leadership and management skills, as they gave me the opportunity to work with people with different personalities. I developed motivational techniques to help my group engage in project work and have had to develop my time management skills to get tasks completed within set timeframes. T&D also taught me to be a manager of myself, as our projects were individual and unique, so it was my responsibility to motivate myself to organise what I needed for a project in terms of time, materials, machinery and human resources.
Teamwork	I have the ability to work with others efficiently in a positive and productive way. In some situations in T&D good teamwork was the only way to ensure that projects were completed. Teams usually consisted of my peers, the technician and the teacher, and good communication skills were developed to ensure everyone pulled together.
Multicultural skills	I have the ability to demonstrate and exercise a sensitivity and awareness to other people and cultures in the classroom and when designing products.

UNIT 1

TECHNOLOGY AND DESIGN CORE

TECHNOLOGY AND DESIGN CORE

This unit is compulsory for all students.
In this chapter you will be studying:

- Manufacturing
- Electronics
- Mechanical control systems
- Computer control systems
- Pneumatic control systems

1A MANUFACTURING

MANUFACTURING

RANGE OF MATERIALS AND THEIR GENERAL, PHYSICAL, AESTHETIC AND STRUCTURAL CHARACTERISTICS

Remember – many of the materials we use in T&D are becoming scarce, try to avoid waste and use them sensibly.

If you are to be successful at Technology and Design (T&D) you will need to know what materials are available and how they behave when worked. This section will help you to recognise and get to know some of the main materials used in T&D.

Selecting a material

Think carefully about the materials you choose to use in your project work. Your final choice will depend on a number of factors and you should be able to make a good choice if you consider the following:

- Intended use
- Availability
- Economics
- Properties
- Manufacturing Method
- Function of finish

These factors are looked at in more depth in 3B Materials, Components and Fabrication, page 123.

Material Properties

Materials have some of the properties below which help a designer choose that material for a specific job:

- Strength
- Hardness
- Brittleness
- Toughness
- Plasticity
- Durability
- Pliability
- Malleability
- Elasticity
- Ductility
- Heat conductivity
- Electrical conductivity
- Corrosion-resistant

These factors are looked at in more depth in 3B Materials, Components and Fabrication, page 123.

ACTIVITY

Find out about the material properties to the left and write a definition for each.

Wood

Wood is produced naturally as trees grow. Wood is the only important material that we can grow more of. It is a renewable material, so we need never run out.

Unfortunately trees are being used up faster than they are being replaced. We need to avoid waste so that we can conserve some for the future.

Softwood	Hardwood
Most softwood trees are coniferous (bear cones), usually have needle-like leaves and are evergreen, for example, cedar, pine and yew.	Most hardwood trees have broad leaves and are deciduous (shed leaves each year), for example, mahogany, beech, oak and elm.
Softwoods are fast growing, reaching maturity by 30 years, so they are easily replaced, making them usually cheaper than hardwoods and better for the environment. They grow in colder climates.	Hardwoods are slow growing, reaching maturity by 100 years, so are more expensive than softwoods.
There are several types of pine but most are pale yellow with brown streaks. • Redwood, also known as Scots pine, is fairly strong, stable and polishes well but knotty. • Parana pine is hard and more expensive than Redwood. It is straight grain and almost knot free.	• Mahogany is reddish brown with a generally straight grain. It machines and polishes well. • Beech is a pale, pinky cream timber with smooth texture and straight grain. It is hard and strong. • Oak is a rich, light brown wood with straight grain. It is heavy and strong. • Elm is a light, reddish brown colour with grain that interlocks. It resists splitting and resists decay when permanently wet.
Uses: • Redwood (Scots pine) is used for constructional work and joinery including outdoor decking, furniture and fencing. • Parana pine is used for interior joinery such as staircases, doors and built in furniture.	Uses: • Mahogany is used for cabinets, furniture, musical instruments, doors, exterior of boats and yachts. • Beech is used for mallets. • Oak is used for construction including furniture, staircases and handrails. • Elm is used for furniture, water troughs, barrels, piles for sea defences, coffins, boxes, crates and pallets.

Timber is prone to **defects**, which can sometimes cause difficulties when it is being worked. If left unprotected the strength of the wood can be weakened by insect and fungal attack. The following are some common timber defects:

- *Dry rot*
- *Insect attack*
- *Shrinkage*
- *Wet rot*
- *Splits*
- *Knots*

Consider the **natural characteristics** when choosing wood for a specific purpose:

- *Grain pattern:* the growth ring marks visible on the surface.
- *Colour:* different tree species differ greatly in colour.
- *Texture:* surface and cell texture varies with different species.
- *Workability:* some are easier to work with than others.
- *Structural strength:* weak to very strong.

CHECK YOUR LEARNING

1. List six possible defects that timber could be prone to.
2. What difficulty can defects in timber cause?
3. What five natural characteristics should be considered when choosing wood for a specific purpose?

Man-made Boards

Man-made boards are made from the waste produced when the trunks and branches of trees are cut into planks.

Advantages:

- Man-made boards are available in large sizes of uniform thickness as they are not restricted by the tree size in the way that solid wood is.
- They are not prone to defects like solid wood and are not affected by humidity.
- They can be used with veneers to improve their appearance. A veneer is a thin layer of real wood used to cover the boards. It also gives a board more strength.
- They do not have a grain structure.
- They are more easily worked than natural wood.
- They can be easily joined with knock down (KD) fittings. KD fittings are often used as the joining method for kitchen units and self-assembly furniture. They are designed to easily join two pieces of material using basic tools such as screw drivers, hammers and mallets.

ACTIVITY

Make a copy of the table below.

Complete the table to summarise the characteristics of softwoods and hardwoods.

Type of wood	Description	Growth rate	No. of years to grow	Cost	Examples
Softwood					1. 2. 3.
Hardwood					1. 2. 3.

Name	Qualities	How are they made?	Uses
MDF	• Medium Density Fibreboard. • Popular quality board. • Cost effective. • Smooth surface. • Finishes well. Paint can be applied without the need for an undercoat or primer.	• Composed of fine wood dust and resin pressed into a board. • Can be worked, shaped and machined easily. • Available in water and fire-resistant form.	• Used in the building and furniture trades.
Chipboard	• Cheap but not strong. • Usually veneered (covered) with a hardwood or plastic.	• Produced by compressing wood particles together with glue.	• Inexpensive furniture, cupboard backs, shelving.

Plywood	• Very strong for its weight and thickness, compared to solid wood.
	• Appearance can be improved with a veneer of good quality wood.
		• Odd numbers of layers that are glued with their grain at 90° to each other making it very strong.
		• Different grades suit a variety of situations:
		  1. Marine plywood is moisture resistant.
		  2. Weather and boil proof plywood.
		  3. Boil resistant plywood.
		  4. Interior plywood.
			• Building work, general construction, boat building, furniture making.

Blockboard and Laminboard	• Both of similar construction. • Cheap substitute to plywood when a thicker but not as strong board is required.	• Strips of softwood such as pine or spruce are glued side by side and sandwiched between two veneers for added strength and aesthetics. • Blockboard strips are 5–7 cm. • Laminboard strips are 7–25 mm.	• Shelving, worktops and furniture backs.
Hardboard	• It is not as strong as the other boards.	• Made from pulped wood fibres. The pulp is put under pressure until the fibres bond to produce a tough board that is smooth on one side and rough on the other.	• Furniture such as cupboard panels, tops, doors and drawer bottoms, shoe heels, jigsaw puzzles, toys, chalkboards, advertising signs, billboards, shop displays and shop fittings.

1. What are man-made boards?
2. List six man-made boards.
3. Explain the advantages of man-made boards over solid wood.
4. What do the letters MDF represent?
5. Describe MDF.
6. Explain why plywood has strength.
7. Describe how blockboard and laminboard are made and how they are different.
8. Explain how chipboard is made.
9. What is a veneer?

Sketch

- Sketch and render an image of each man-made board.
- Sketch in 3D images of 3-ply plywood and 9-ply plywood.

Metal

Some metals are pure and others are alloys. Alloys are two or more metals combined to produce a new material with different properties. There are two basic metal groups:

1. **Ferrous** (contain iron): Generally tend to corrode (rust) so need some form of protection against corrosion. Almost all are magnetic.

2. **Non-ferrous** (do not contain iron): and will therefore not corrode.

	Name	Properties	Uses
FERROUS METALS	**Mild Steel** *An alloy of iron and carbon*	• The most common ferrous metal and the softest one. • Quite a cheap and strong metal so it is used frequently in T&D. • Rusts easily and cannot be hardened or tempered.	• Used for nuts and bolts, screws, stool legs, washing machines and car bodies.
	Stainless steel	• A hard metal that will not rust but is more expensive.	• Used for sinks, kettles, medical equipment, and cutlery.
NON-FERROUS METALS	**Aluminium**	• Light, soft, easily shaped and silvery in colour. • Conducts heat and electricity well. • Corrosion resistant but expensive. • Polishes well.	• Used for window frames, saucepans, cooking foil and aircraft.

	Copper	• Tough but easily shaped and soldered, as relatively soft, malleable and ductile. • Conducts heat and electricity well. • Quite expensive.	• Used for water pipes, wires and cisterns.
NON-FERROUS ALLOY	**Brass** *An alloy of 65% copper and 35% zinc*	• Heavy, quite hard and quite strong. • Yellow in colour, looks good. • Malleable and ductile. • Corrosion resistant.	• Used for electrical parts, door handles, bathroom fittings and accessories.

CHECK YOUR LEARNING

1. Explain what an alloy is.
2. Complete the following sentences:
   a) Ferrous metals contain _____.
   b) Metals that do not contain iron are_____.
   c) Metals that do not rust are _____.
   d) _____metals are usually magnetic.
3. Do you agree or disagree with the following statements?

   a) Metals are only available in one shape and size.
   b) Alloys can be classified as both ferrous and non-ferrous metals.
   c) Ferrous metals do not contain iron and are not magnetic.
   d) Brass is a ferrous metal used to make drinks cans.

ACTIVITY

Make a copy of the table below. Complete the table to summarise the following metals.

Metal	Ferrous or non-ferrous?	Uses	Properties
Stainless steel			
Copper			
Aluminium			
Mild steel			
Brass			

Plastic

Plastics are available in different forms, including powders, granules, pellets, extruded mouldings, liquids, film, sheets, rods and tubes. They have high resistance to corrosion and decay so do not need a protective surface finish. Wet and dry paper can be used to remove scratches, followed by the polishing machine.

ACTIVITY

Collect samples of as many products made of plastic as you can. Try to identify what they are as well as the reasons why that particular material has been used for this product.

Thermosetting	Thermoplastics/thermoforming
When thermosetting plastics 'set' they cannot be softened, shaped or moulded by reheating. They cannot be reshaped or recycled because of the three dimensional cross-linking of the molecules within these plastics. This arrangement makes a very strong bond between the molecules. • Cannot be recycled. • Resist heat and fire well. • Undergo significant chemical change when heated making them hard and rigid.	Thermoplastics (also knows as thermoforming plastics) can be reheated, allowing them to be shaped and moulded in different ways. The molecular bonds are weak and are weakened further when reheated, which allows reshaping. These plastics are made up of 'long chain monomers'. • Can be recycled. • Do not resist heat well. • Do not undergo significant chemical change when heated.
Melamine: is a heat resistant polymer used for tableware, worktops, electrical installations, synthetic resin paints, and decorative laminates.	**Acrylic** (perspex): is a hardwearing, transparent or opaque plastic. It can be coloured with pigments and will shatter if treated roughly. It is used for display signs, baths, roof lights and machine guards.
Polyester resin: is a mixture of resin and hardener that polymerises at room temperature and is often reinforced with glass fibre. It is used in car bodies and boats, glass reinforced plastic GRP castings and encapsulations. It is non-recyclable.	**Rigid polystyrene:** is a light but strong plastic available in sheets and softens at about 95°C. It is used in schools for vacuum forming.

ACTIVITY

Make a copy of the table below.
Complete the table to summarise the characteristics of thermosetting and thermoforming plastics.

Type of plastic	Description	Examples	Uses
Thermosetting		1.	
		2.	
Thermoforming		1.	
		2.	

CHECK YOUR LEARNING

1. Why are casings for most electrical equipment made from plastic rather than metal?
2. Explain why a designer might choose polypropylene as a material for a food container.
3. What are the advantages of vacuum formed plastic food containers over cardboard or tinned packaging?

EXAM STYLE QUESTIONS

State the name of a suitable material for the following products and give two reasons for your suggestion:

1. Washing up bottle
2. Bicycle frame
3. Spade handle

TOOLS, PROCESSES AND TECHNIQUES

Marking out

Rule: is used for measuring and checking measurements. The marks start at the edge of the rule to allow measurements to be taken from the edge or end of a piece of material.

Scriber: is used for marking out metal.

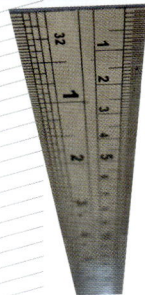

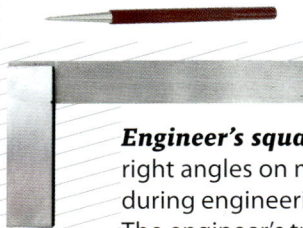

Engineer's square: is used to mark out and test right angles on materials for cutting or shaping during engineering and metalworking projects. The engineer's try square is set accurately to 90° and is composed of two parts, the stock and the blade. They are usually made from bright mild steel with the blade being hardened and tempered so that it resists damage.

Try square: is used for marking lines at right angles to the edge of a piece of wood and checking the squareness of edges and corners.

The woodworker's try square is composed of two main parts, the stock and the blade, which are riveted together at 90°. The blade is made from hardened and tempered steel which makes is resistant to damage. A brass face is added to the stock to ensure a straight edge.

Marking knife: will cut marks across the fibres when marking out wood to give a clean cut when sawing or chiselling.

OHP pen: is useful for marking on plastic.

Spring dividers: are used like a compass for drawing circles, dividing lengths and transferring measurements from a rule to material.

Dents

Marking out holes with a dent before drilling helps the drill bit from slipping off the centre during drilling. A dent is made to the centre of a hole to be drilled either by hand or on the drilling machine.

Centre punch: is used for **metal**. The centre punch is made from mild steel with the point ground to 90°, hardened and tempered so that it withstands impact with the material it is marking.

Bradawl: is used for **wood**.

Drilling

Drilling is used to make circular holes between 1 mm and 60 mm in size.

Pillar drill

Twist drill bit: Used to drill small holes (1–13 mm).

13

Countersink drill bit: is used after drilling to taper the end of the hole. This allows the screw head to sit flush below the surface of all materials.

Forstner bit: is used for large holes in wood only (6–32 mm).

Hole saw: is used for very large holes in wood or acrylic.

Pedestal polisher

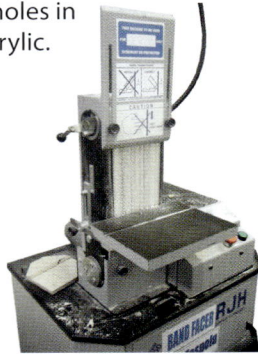

Band facer

Sawing

Tenon saw: is used to cut straight lines in wood. The stiffened back prevents the saw making a deep cut.

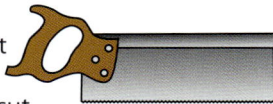

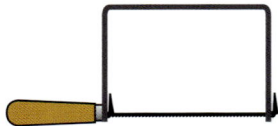

Coping saw: is used to cut curves in wood or plastic. The teeth of the saw blade point towards the handle.

Hacksaw: is used to cut straight lines in metal or plastics. The blade can be held in tension by tightening the wing nut.

Junior hacksaw: is used to cut straight lines in thin sheet metal or plastics. Used for light work.

Files

Files have small teeth to cut away material.

Single cut: is used for finish-filing, draw-filing and sharpening tools, and smoothing the edges of sheet metal. It has rows of parallel teeth cut at 65° angles to each other.

Double cut: is used for rough work and the fast removal of material. It has a second set of teeth that crisscross to form a diamond pattern.

File types

End view   Face

Flat: is used for general work.

Round: is used for filing out holes.

Half-round: is used for filing out internal curves.

File grades

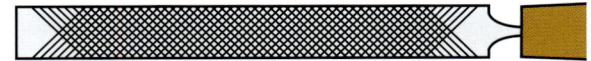

Second cut: is used for roughing out hard metals and plastics and finishing soft metals and plastic.

Smooth cut: is used for finishing cuts and draw filing.

Filing techniques

Cross filing and draw filing are the two basic techniques used to produce a straight edge on a piece of metal or plastic.

Cross filing: is used to remove the waste material. The length of the file from the tip to the handle is pushed downwards and forwards across the edge to allow the teeth of the file to cut into the material.

Draw filing: is used to finish a material as it gives a smoother cut than cross filing. The file is held by both hands close to the edge of the material and is pulled backwards and pushed forward.

Chisels

Chisel: is used for removing small amounts of waste wood, often between two saw cuts to make joints and for shaping. The chisel can be pushed by hand or hit with a wooden mallet. It is made from tool steel, which is hardened and tempered and has a handle made of beech, ash or plastic. The blade has a pointed tang to fit into the handle.

Bevel: edged chisel is slightly undercut making it easy to push into corners. It is normally used for finishing dovetail joints. When shaping, the bevel edge of the chisel is kept next to the wood. This prevents making a cut too deep and is useful for levering out waste wood.

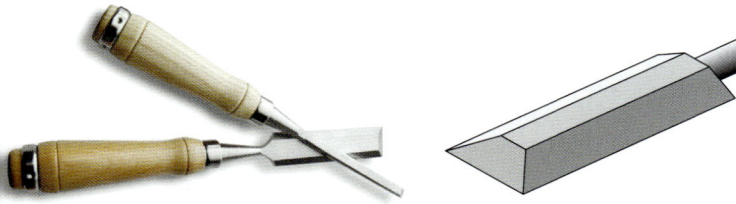

APPROPRIATE METHODS OF JOINING

Permanent joining methods

Metals can be joined by riveting, soldering, brazing and mig welding.

Riveting

Two or more pieces of metal can be joined permanently with rivets. Rivets are made from soft metals that are malleable such as aluminium, copper, brass or iron, and they withstand shear stresses. The length of the rivet will be determined by the thickness of material to be joined. The material of the job is drilled with the correct hole sizes and the rivet is passed through. The tail is usually shaped using a hammer. For a flat head rivet, work is supported on a flat surface and the tail shaped. For round head rivets a tool known as a rivet set and snap is required to help shape the tail into a rounded head.

Round-head rivet

A ball pein hammer is used to form the head of the rivet and the final shape is created using a rivet set and snap tool.

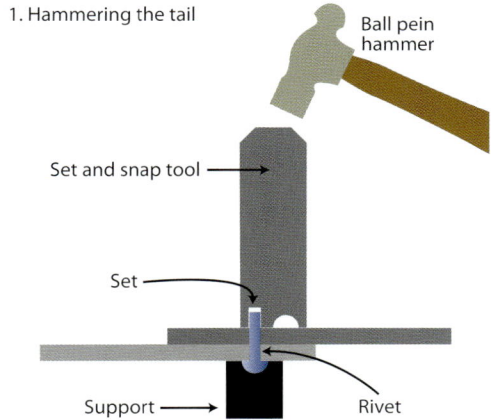

1. Hammering the tail

- Ball pein hammer
- Set and snap tool
- Set
- Support
- Rivet

2. Shaping the rivet

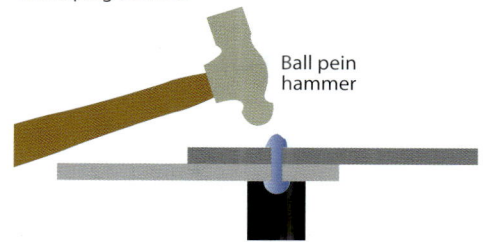

- Ball pein hammer

The small hole is the **set** which is used first to support the head while the tail is hammered. The other hollow, known as the **snap**, is used to create the final rounded head shape.

3. Making the final rounded head

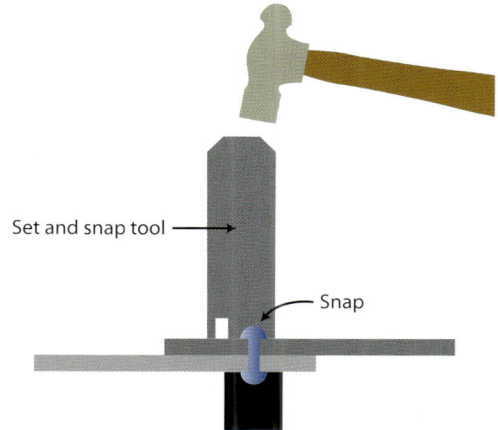

- Set and snap tool
- Snap

Pop rivet

A rivet gun is used to pull the stem of the pop rivet causing the malleable material of the head to spread and the stem to break off leaving just the head behind.

Countersunk rivet

A countersunk rivet has two finished flat sides. It is inserted in a countersunk hole, hammered down with the ball pein, and then finished with the flat hammer and smoothed with a file.

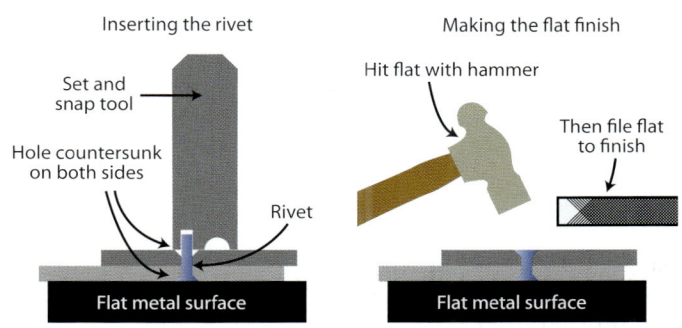

Inserting the rivet

- Set and snap tool
- Hole countersunk on both sides
- Rivet
- Flat metal surface

Making the flat finish

- Hit flat with hammer
- Then file flat to finish
- Flat metal surface

ACTIVITY

In the workshop join pieces of metal using different rivet types to become familiar with the processes involved in this permanent method of joining.

Other materials of different thicknesses can be securely joined using plastic rivets. This is an example of a button type plastic rivet that gives a neat finish, is non-conducting, and will not corrode or tarnish.

Soft soldering

Soft soldering is a relatively low temperature process. Solder is an alloy of tin and lead. Flux is applied to the joint to clean it then the components to be joined are heated until the solder 'runs'. The joint is made when the solder cools and solidifies. A soldering iron or blow torch is used in light applications such as joining electrical connections and plumbing joints.

Brazing (hard soldering)

Brazing is used for heavier applications such as joining mild steel, as the joint is much stronger. The brass bonding alloy (solder) melts at a much higher temperature than soft soldering.

Mig welding

Mig welding is a permanent method of joining two pieces of metal. The gas used in mig welding is argon. The argon keeps the join clean and prevents oxidisation. Generally used for mild steel but also aluminium sheet metal.

How to mig weld:
1. Clamp the pieces to be joined.
2. Fix an earth clamp to the work.
3. Current passes along the thin steel wire so bring the wire close to the join. An electric arc will jump across the join and heat the metal to a high enough temperature to cause the surface of the metal and the wire to melt and fuse together.
4. The fusing together is made possible because of the flow of **argon** gas around the weld join during welding.

Safety: Use a mig welding mask as the bright arc will damage your sight (welders flash). Wear long leather gloves and an apron as hot molten metal and sparks can burn you and your clothes.

Wood joints

Joints are often glued to make them secure and permanent. Accurately measured and marked out joints are essential if a joint is to fit and hold together.

Butt joint: This is the simplest of joints but the weakest. Two pieces of wood are glued, butted and nailed together. The nails should be punched below the surface to improve the appearance. This joint is used on the corner of boxes and frames.

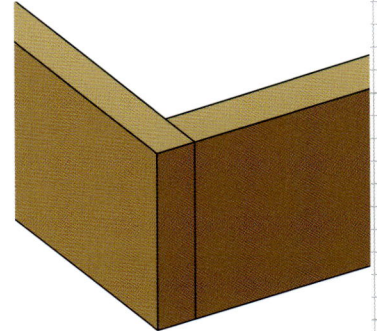

Dowel joint: Two pieces of wood are jointed with two or more round dowels. The joint is glued and cramped, and left to set. This joint is used for making frames and joining man-made boards.

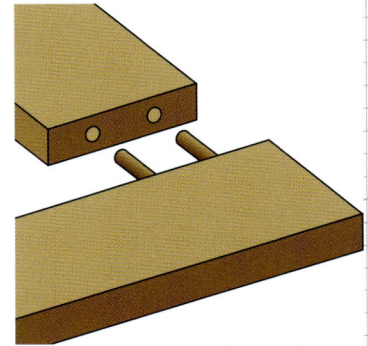

Adhesives

PVA (Polyvinyl Acetate): is a white and creamy, easy to use glue for wood. There are two types: Interior and Exterior.

Contact adhesive: is rubber based and gives a very strong bond. It is applied to both surfaces that are kept apart for 10 minutes until tacky, when sticking will be instant on contact with each other.

Araldite: is the trade name for Epoxy resin. Equal parts of two substances are mixed together. It will stick metal to wood, wood to plastic – almost anything. It takes about 15 minutes to harden and is expensive.

Tensol: is Acrylic Cement used to join plastics. It is a watery, clear liquid that is not very strong but is ideal for joints that will not get knocked about.

Superglue: is a thin, clear liquid that will give a very strong bond when pressure is applied.

Semi-permanent joining methods

When assembling products it is often cheaper to buy standard components from suppliers than to manufacture them individually.

The following are standard components to join wood semi-permanently:

Wood screws

These give a strong fixing between wood as the threads pull the pieces of wood against each other. Pilot and clearance holes are often needed. There are different types of wood screw:

Countersunk screws: have their heads below the surface.

Round head screws: have their heads above the surface.

Nails

Nails are the quickest way to join pieces of wood. They can be used alone or with glue, have a straight shank and no threads, and are hammered into wood. A nail punch should be used to drive the head of a nail below the surface. The punch has a hollow end to grip the nail head. Nails are quicker to use than screws but the joint is not as strong. There are different types of nail:

Panel nail

Oval nail

Wire nail

Nail punch

Nuts and washers, bolts and self-tapping screws

Bolts: have straight shanks and are used with washers and nuts. They have square or hexagonal heads and are tightened with a spanner. They are usually made from brass, steel or stainless steel, and are self finished or plated.

Washers: are usually under the **nuts** to spread pressure and protect materials.

Self tapping screws: have hardened threads that cut their own threaded holes in hard plastic and thin metals.

Nut on a bolt

Washer

Self tapping screw

CHECK YOUR LEARNING

1. What is the solder used in brazing a mixture of?
2. Why is flux used?
3. At around what temperature does solder melt?
4. List the safety equipment that should be worn during mig welding.
4. What do the letters PVA represent?
5. What is a washer used for?

PRODUCTION METHODS

Wasting

Wasting changes both the size and shape of ***resistant materials***.

- ***Machining:*** is a form of wasting as it removes small amounts of material at a time, for example, sawing.
- ***Shearing:*** is a form of wasting as it cuts the material to shape.

Fabrication

Fabrication is the joining of pieces using the most appropriate method.

Types of fabrication methods for different materials

	Wood	Plastic	Metal
Screws	✓	✓	✓
Bolts	✓	✓	✓
Threading		✓	✓
Rivets	✓	✓	✓
Pop Rivets			✓
Nails	✓		
Adhesives	✓	✓	✓
Joints	✓		
Knock down fittings	✓		
Soldering, Brazing, and Welding			✓

CHECK YOUR LEARNING

1. Explain the term 'wasting' as a production method.
2. State two forms of wasting and explain each.
3. Explain the term 'fabrication' as a production method.

ACTIVITY

Copy the table opposite.

Complete the table by stating three fabrication methods for wood, plastic and metal.

Material	Fabrication methods		
Wood			
Plastic			
Metal			

MOULDS AND JIGS

Jigs, moulds and templates save time and are used widely in industrial production processes to **increase speed** and **efficiency**.

Templates

A strong, hard-wearing template can be used repetitively to reproduce any number of identical shapes from an original pattern. They are easy to make, simple to use and afterwards components can be checked for accuracy against the template.

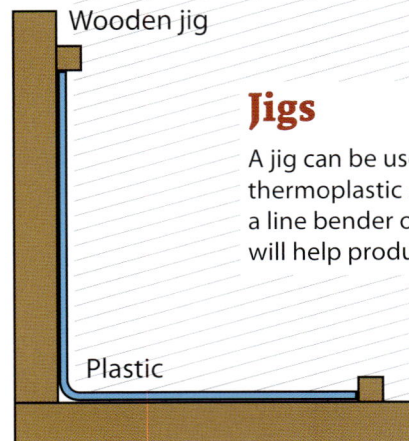

Wooden jig

Jigs

A jig can be used when line bending a thermoplastic sheet such as acrylic on a line bender or strip heater. The jig will help produce accurate angles.

Plastic

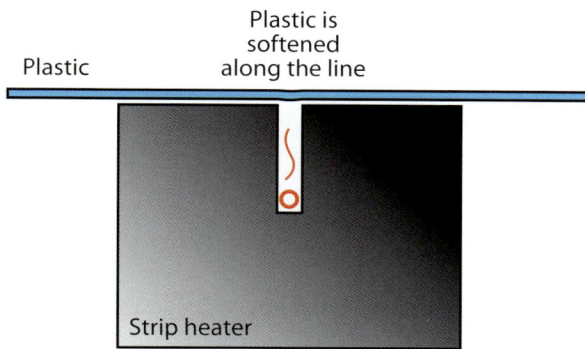

Plastic

Plastic is softened along the line

Strip heater

Moulds

Moulds are used in processes such as vacuum forming, compression moulding and blow moulding. If an accurate mould is made, detailed 3D plastic shapes can be formed with it repeatedly.

In vacuum forming a sheet of thermoplastic is clamped and heated until it is soft. A mould is then placed into the vacuum former and the air is sucked out from around it. This either pulls the plastic over or into the mould. The mould must have tapered sides to allow it to be removed from the formed thermoplastic sheet.

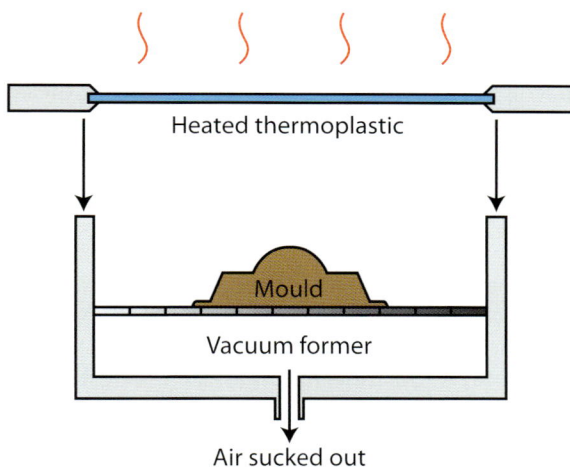

Heated thermoplastic

Mould

Vacuum former

Air sucked out

CHECK YOUR LEARNING

1. Why are templates, jigs and moulds used widely in industrial production processes?
2. State three processes that use moulds.
3. State an application for using a jig in the school workshop.

CAD AND CAM

CAD

CAD stands for **computer-aided design.** It is particularly good for producing **working drawings** and **3D computer models**.

Although CAD systems are relatively expensive they have a number of advantages over manual drawing methods:

- They produce high quality and consistent drawings.
- Information can be easily stored electronically and transmitted, for example, e-mailed.
- Complex assembly drawings can be produced more quickly once the user gets used to the package.
- Standard parts can be accessed from a library, reducing the time it takes to draw them.
- Changes to drawings can be easily made and instantly seen on screen.
- Components are dimensioned automatically with most CAD packages.
- Solid modelling allows the product to be viewed from various angles and a 3D image gives a more realistic view than a 2D image.
- Images can be scanned into the system or photos imported, which is beneficial to project work.

CAD is not a substitute for freehand sketching, which is quick and essential at the initial design and development stages of a design project.

CAM

CAM stands for **computer-aided manufacture**. It is a process that converts drawings produced by CAD into actual products.

CAM involves a **range of machines**, most commonly lathes, routers, milling machines and laser cutters. These machines are **controlled by a computer** that guides the machine through an entire manufacturing process – computer numerical control **(CNC)**.

CNC Machine	Materials cut	Applications
Laser Cutters	• Plastic • Wood card	• Intense beam of light used to cut. • No clamping of material required. • Simple and complex shapes can be cut.
Lathes	• Wood • Metal • Nylon	• Accurate and complex shapes produced that would be difficult to produce using hand operated lathes.
Milling Machines	• Acrylic/plastic • Wood • Metal	• Produce flat and complex curved shapes. • In industry fine tolerances can be worked to.
Routers	• Foam • Wood • Metal	• Similar to milling machines but using softer materials. • Can cut 2D and 3D shapes. • Used for block modelling.

Initial set up costs are high but once the system is programmed the advantages are considerable:

- Machines can work 24/7 with little human intervention.
- They ensure products are produced accurately and consistently.
- They are reliable.
- They are flexible as they can be reprogrammed.

CHECK YOUR LEARNING

1. What do the letters CAD and CAM represent?
2. Explain the advantages of using CAD over manual drawing methods.
3. List a range of machines CAM involves.
4. How are these machines controlled?
5. Explain the advantages of using CAM.
6. Explain the applications of four CNC machines and include the materials they cut.

Generating CAD drawings

All lines in a CAD drawing are called vectors and these give the coordinates that a CNC machine needs. Most CNC machines have their own software to convert these coordinates into 'toolpaths' to steer the cutter. This 'Post Processing' software needs to accept data that any CAD package can produce. This 'common format' is called DXF so you need to export your file in this format.

CNC machines use a drive motor for each axis of travel and these need careful control to create accurate shapes such as angles and curves. The DXF file will be converted into a series of left-right tool movements and, if the post processor is working well, these should result in smooth curves. Laser cutters are usually both CNC machines and printers. This means they can use DXF files to cut and score lines and they can use bitmap data to engrave images. When engraving, the laser scans from side to side, firing the laser as it goes. This process is called 'rastering'.

Two popular software packages for CAD in schools are **TechSoft 2D Design** and **SolidWorks**. The processes for generating design files on each package are explained on pages 21 and 22.

Process for generating a file using TechSoft 2D Design

Open 2D Design package
File
New
Save as: Part name

Use tools to sketch part to be cut out on CNC machine

File save as DTD (Design Tools Drawing) file
File Export

File name: Part name
Save as type DXF file

Save

OK

A design file (DXF) has now been created that will be recognised by the post processing software for the CNC machine and will allow manufacturing to start. For laser cutters, this post processing software is often part of the machine's Print Driver. In schools, files are usually exported to a memory pen, to transfer them to a PC connected to a CNC machine. The designs are then imported into the CNC machine's post processing software, which allows colours to be selected to represent the parts of the designs to engrave (raster), cut or both.

However, saving CAD drawings as DXF files also has some disadvantages. This DXF format cannot handle all the information, which can cause some of it to be lost and the design to be simplified. Drawings may include pixel images or bitmaps, which are simply clouds of tiny dots on the screen that our eyes and brains translate into pictures. They do not contain vectors so cannot be included in DXF files and used to drive a CNC machine. CAD drawings may, however, contain filled areas such as text, which are defined by a fill-boundary. These fills can be included in DXF files. Different versions of DXF files are available, so check with your teacher that you have selected the best type for the CNC machine you are outputting to. If the right DXF format is chosen and the post processor of the CNC machine is working well, the result should be the cutting of smooth curves.

Another method that your school may choose to use is to save your CAD drawing as a DTD (Design Tools Drawing)

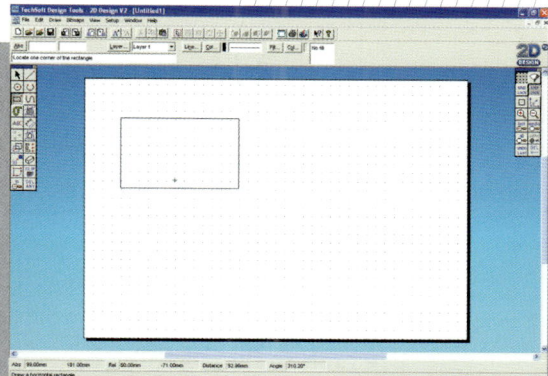

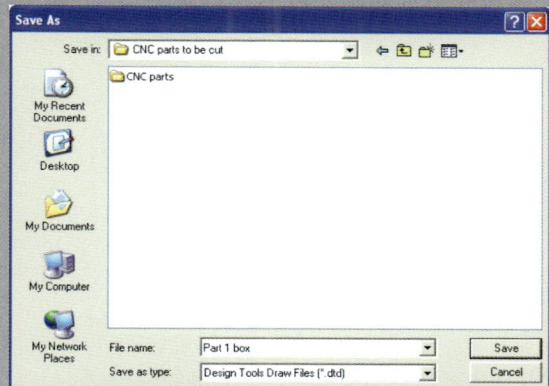

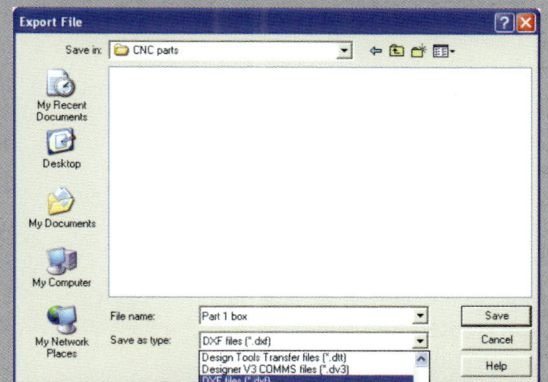

file, which can be directly output to certain CNC machines that are supported by TechSoft 2D Design. Schools using TechSoft 2D Design and outputting to TechSoft CNC machines will always be able to follow this route because post-processing software is built-in. Output to a TechSoft laser cutter is through 'File – Print' to the dedicated Windows print driver. This driver lets you select the colours to be used and whether to engrave (raster) or cut (vector), or both. Because 2D Design files (.dtd) and TechSoft LaserCAM print drivers support both vector and bitmap data, it is possible to output engraved fills, photo-images and cut data in one operation.

Your teacher will advise you on which method is used in your school.

Process for generating a file using SolidWorks

Open SolidWorks package
File
New
Save as: Part name
Save as type: Part

Use tools to sketch part to be cut out on CNC machine

File
New
Drawing
Custom sheet size
OK

Model View

Double click on part to open

Save as: Part 1
Save as type: DXF

A design file (DXF) has now been created that will be recognised by the software of the CNC machine and allow manufacturing to start.

Dassault Systemes SolidWorks Corp. All associated trademarks attributed to Dassault Systemes SolidWorks Corp.

ACTIVITY

Produce a simple 2D CAD drawing using each of the design packages on pages 21 and 22. Practice will be essential for you to become competent with the functions of each package.

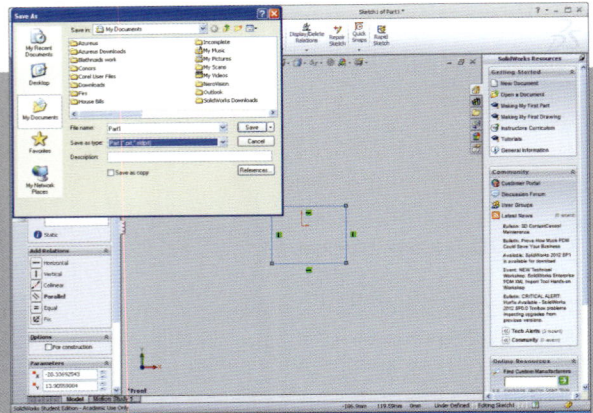

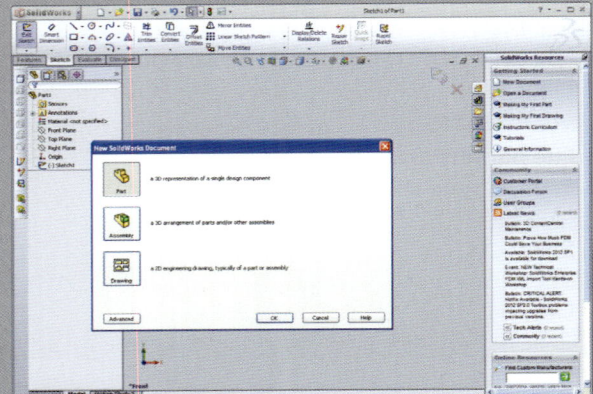

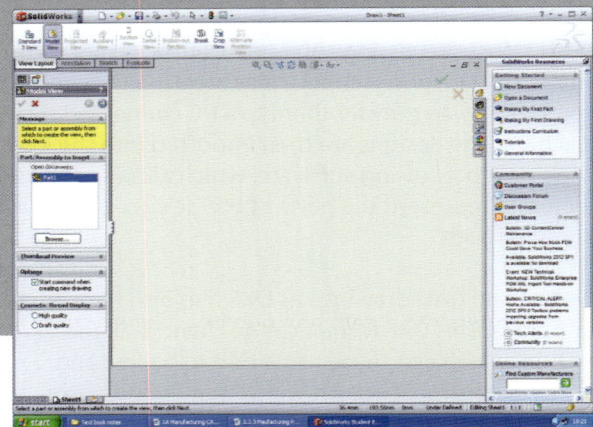

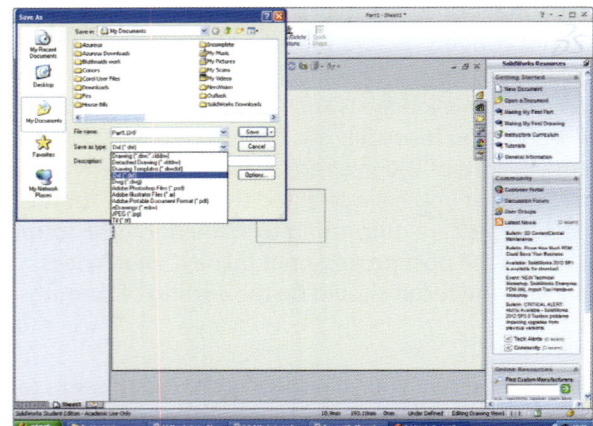

If your school has a CNC machine, such as a laser cutter or milling machine, get your teacher or technician to give a whole class demonstration of how to use it. Now get familiar with it by practicing generating CAD drawings that are saved as DXF files and can be manufactured by a CNC machine.

FINISHING TECHNIQUES

Surface finishes give protection and aesthetic appeal. They can be applied by brushing on, spraying or using a cloth.

Metal

Paint: A primer is needed if painting steel to form a chemical bond with the metal surface. Hammerite is available in a variety of colours and finishes. It will give the metal a durable top coat that dries quickly, giving protection.

Polishing: can be done by hand or using a buffing machine. When using the buffing machine, abrasive polish is applied to the machine's wheel and the metal is held against the spinning wheel until the surface finish required is achieved.

Plastic dip coated: Metal is coated in a thin coating of plastic. An oven is used to evenly heat the metal to 180°C then it is plunged into a very fine powder, which acts as a liquid as air is passed through it. It is returned to the oven so the plastic fuses to the metal, giving a smooth finish.

Galvanising: is coating steel with zinc to prevent rusting or corrosion. The zinc forms a barrier against corrosion, which stops the steel underneath from coming into contact with water or moisture in the air. A thick layer of zinc is applied to the steel by passing it through a molten bath of zinc at 460°C. The zinc forms a bond with the steel, forming an iron-zinc alloy. The zinc also forms a zinc oxide when it comes in contact with the air, which further helps prevent corrosion.

Wood

Paint: will colour and protect wood. Emulsion is water based so does not protect against water but it is cheap. Polyurethane paint is waterproof and tougher but much more expensive.

Polyurethane varnish: is available in a range of colours or clear. It seals and protects, giving a smooth surface finish.

Preservative stains: enhance the appearance of the grain but need a varnish applied on top to protect the wood. Available in natural and bright colours.

Oil: maintains appearance and some offer protection.

Plastic

Polishing: The cut edges of hard plastics like acrylic can be smoothed using wet and dry paper then polished to remove fine scratches. Polish can be applied by hand with a cloth or on the polishing machine.

MATERIAL EFFICIENCY

Material efficiency is an important consideration when designing and manufacturing products. It is a description of how materials are used, projects constructed or processes carried out to use or waste less of a certain material. For example, making a usable item out of thinner stock, such as 3 mm acrylic instead of 5 mm acrylic, increases the material efficiency of the manufacturing process and could reduce cost. Accuracy when measuring and marking out materials in the workshop also reduces material wastage during manufacture.

Use the Internet to research other ways of reducing material wastage to help increase resource efficiency, reduce pollution and increase profits.
Present your findings on an A4 information sheet.

DESIGNERS

When studying theory on manufacturing you need to obtain a working knowledge of the design process that enables the design and manufacture of a final product.

The design process

Design is ongoing and responsive to changing needs, trends and technological developments. Like designers in industry, you as a T&D pupil must engage in the design process.

Problem identification
↓
Design brief
↓
Research and analysis
↓
Specification
↓
Initial Ideas/concept sketches
↓
Development of ideas
↓
Select final idea
↓
Design development/working drawings
↓
Plan of action
↓
Manufacture
↓
Final evaluation/modifications

Problem identification

When attempting to solve a problem in T&D you must clearly define the problem and try to explain why you think it is necessary for a new product. New products are needed because:

- There is a problem with the current product.
- Improvement with performance is needed.
- A gap in the market exists.

We call this background information the **problem identification/situation**.

Design brief

The next step in attempting to solve a problem is to clearly explain, in detail, how we intend to create a solution. This is called the **design brief**. It is a statement usually beginning: "Design and make _____"

Research and analysis

Research and analysis are essential in the design process before any initial ideas/concepts are started. It allows you to check if people will actually want the product; help you find out people's likes and dislikes about existing products; and find out about materials, manufacturing techniques and standard components that could affect costs. It is important to analyse your research, which means you need to decide how to use the information to help your designing. Pick out the useful information, explain how it will impact on your designs and state how you will now move the process forward.

Specification

Now you need to create a list of everything the solution should do or have in order for you to begin designing your initial concepts. This list is called a specification. A product designer must be able to develop a specification by looking at the following factors:

1. Function
2. Form
3. Ergonomics
4. Anthropometrics
5. Cost
6. Competition
7. Environment
8. Materials
9. Manufacture

When writing a specification the factor must be stated and justified with a reason why it needs to be considered.

For example:

"Ergonomics: The product should be designed to be ergonomic so it is comfortable for the person to use continually without pain or injury."

Initial ideas/concept sketches

Initial ideas/concepts can be explored by:

Brainstorming/thought shower: This means discussing the problem and solutions in a group to come up with the best ideas.

Research: this means using different sources of media to find out more about the problem and existing solutions.

For example:
- The Internet.
- Questionnaires to identify target groups and market trends.
- Disassembling a product to look at how it was made and how it works.

Sketches: These should be freehand, quickly rendered and annotated drawings of initial ideas about how to solve the problem.

Development of ideas

To enable a designer to select an idea or concept for development, they need to **evaluate** each of their initial ideas against the design specification. This will ensure that their chosen idea meets all the design requirements. Development involves taking an idea or concept further by considering a range of possibilities for shape, form, style, materials, finish, colour, dimensions and manufacturing processes. By making design decisions throughout this process, a **final idea** should be produced.

Annotating a concept

To annotate a concept or idea means to add written notes and explanations to the drawing. Annotation gives the reader more information about the designer's thoughts that would not be apparent from the drawing alone.

Annotating a concept ...

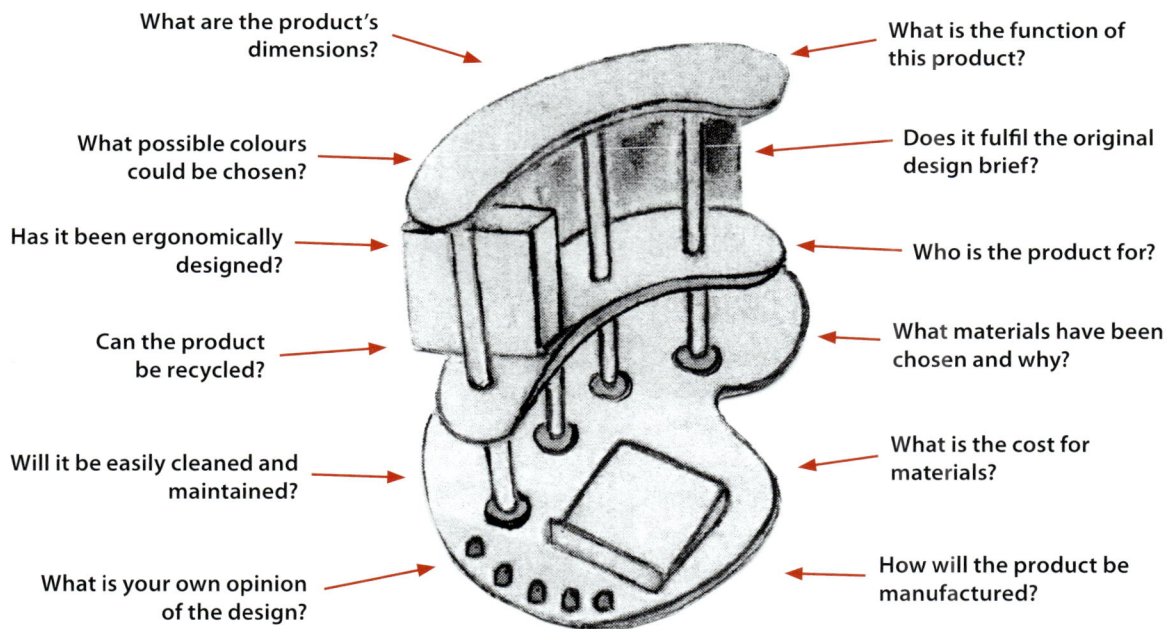

What are the product's dimensions?

What possible colours could be chosen?

Has it been ergonomically designed?

Can the product be recycled?

Will it be easily cleaned and maintained?

What is your own opinion of the design?

What is the function of this product?

Does it fulfil the original design brief?

Who is the product for?

What materials have been chosen and why?

What is the cost for materials?

How will the product be manufactured?

Use the key points above to help you annotate your own design ideas. Sometimes it is useful to refer back to your specification and to comment with notes on how the design idea has met each of the specification points. This will help the reader fully understand your design idea.

The annotation on each concept should help you make judgements and score each concept confidently. Sometimes a final idea may be a combination of features from a few concepts. As long as the designer justifies the reasons for choosing a feature this is fine. A table of scoring like this below may be useful. Each specification point is given a score out of 10 and the final score is tallied out of 100. The final score of each concept is then compared. The concept that scores the highest should be selected for development.

Concept /Idea Number	Function /10	Form /10	Ergonomics /10	Anthropometrics /10	Cost /10	Competition /10	Environment /10	Materials /10	Manufacture /10	Fun factor /10	Score /100	Comment
1												
2												
3												
4												

Select final idea

The scoring used for evaluating also provides points to help you write a statement justifying the reasons for the selection of your final idea. The final idea selected should be sketched and a statement written about the reasons it was chosen for development, its advantages and disadvantages.

Design development/working drawings

Design development requires more detailed sketches of the final solution, including dimensioned drawings to aid manufacture, a prototype, material selection and methods of manufacture.

Plan of action

The design is now ready to be manufactured, so ideally all potential problems with the design should have already been solved. A plan of action helps plan the manufacturing tasks, organise the resources and prioritise the tasks. A Gantt Chart (top right) is a planning tool that can be used to ensure good time management of manufacturing tasks. The tasks to be completed are allocated periods of time on the chart. Some tasks can be completed simultaneously whilst others are dependent on previous tasks being completed before they can begin.

An example of a Gantt Chart

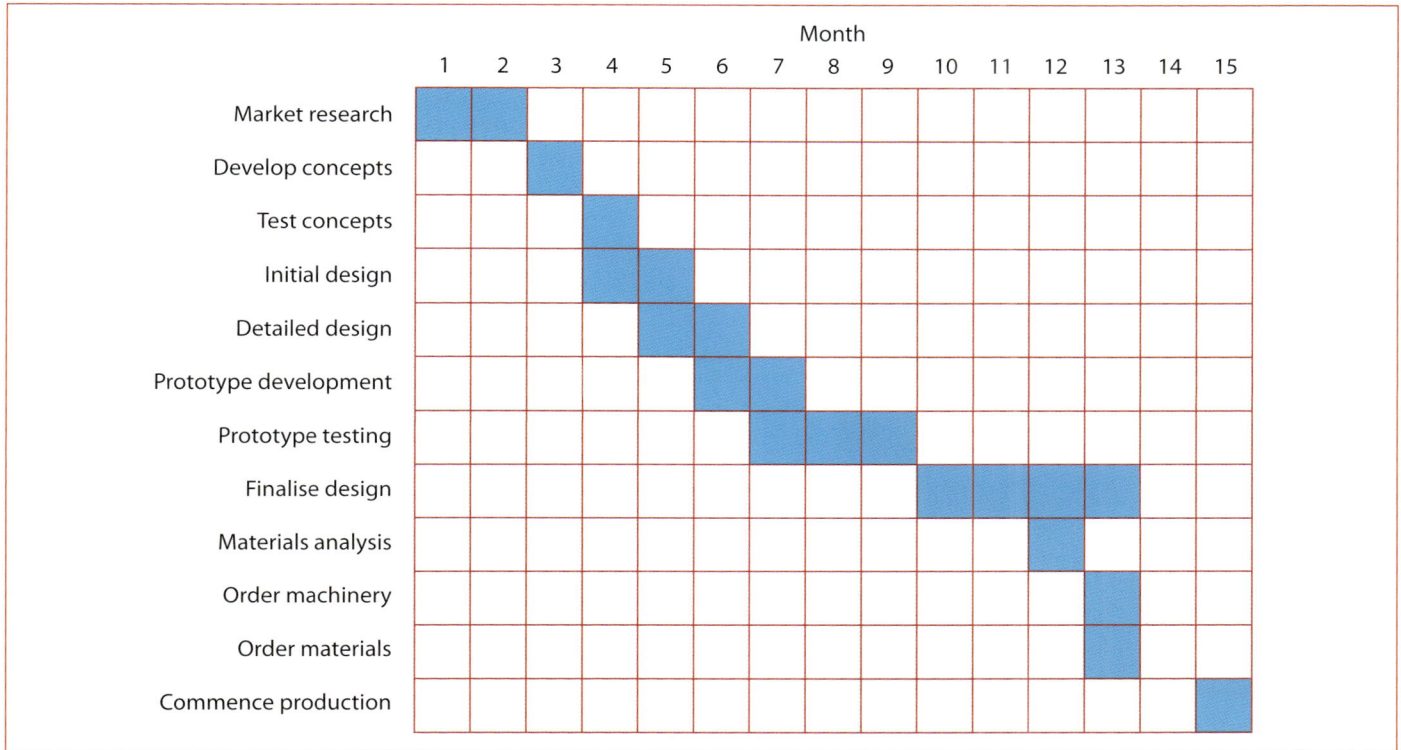

	1	2	3	4	5	6	7	8	9	10	11	12	13	14	15
Market research	■	■													
Develop concepts			■												
Test concepts				■											
Initial design					■										
Detailed design						■									
Prototype development							■								
Prototype testing								■	■						
Finalise design										■	■	■	■		
Materials analysis												■			
Order machinery													■		
Order materials													■		
Commence production															■

Manufacture

The manufacturing process can start using the selected method of production. It will have to be assembled and tested for final quality before distribution.

Final evaluation/modifications

The manufactured product will then need to be evaluated against the original design specification and consumer research conducted on their views and opinions. This allows the cycle of modifications and future design developments to begin.

As a product designer yourself, you will be engaging in the Design Cycle as you complete Unit 5, The Design and Manufacture task, worth 40% of your GCSE in T&D. As you attempt Unit 5 the requirements of each stage of the Design Cycle will become much clearer and you will have a better understanding of how designers in the real world work to produce highly successful and desirable products. This will also help you with the terminal exam.

Select a designer such as Steve Jobs or James Dyson and discuss the design process in relation to the products they designed.

Steve Jobs, former CEO of Apple Inc

www.jamesdysonfoundation.com

James Dyson, inventor of the Dual Cyclone bagless vacuum cleaner

EMERGING TECHNOLOGIES

Rapid developments are being made in **new materials**, as they have properties that allow them to be used in exciting and original applications. Smart materials react and change their properties in response to inputs, for example, heat, light or electrical current. This makes them ideal for safety applications such as giving off a warning of heat.

Smart Textiles and Pigments

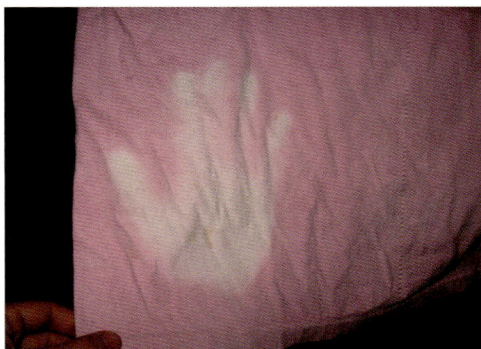

Thermochromic pigments: change colour with temperature and can be added to polymers. These are used in kettles and heat warning patches in baby food products.

Phosphorescent pigments: absorb light energy and release it when it is dark. These are used in signage that is visible in the dark, for example, clock hands and fire exit signs if mixed with ink and acrylic paint, and novelty shapes such as planets and stars for children's' bedrooms if added to polymers.

Nano technology

Nano technology is all about being small – 'nano' means one billionth of something. Materials are manipulated on the molecular or atomic level to give them new properties and functions by combining plastic and nano-sized fibres of clay.

New properties include being lighter; more resistant to scratches and dents; stiffer, less brittle and less porous; more recyclable and flame retardant; better electrical conductors; and easier to paint.

NEWS

NANOCOMPOSITES: COMING TO A STORE NEAR YOU

In 2001, Toyota started using nanocomposites to make bumpers for their cars. In 2002, General Motors (GM) made nanocomposite "step-assists" – external running boards that help people get into and out of cars – an option on the 2002 Chevrolet Astro and the GMC Safari.

Source: 'The Future of Automotive Plastics', PR Newswire, in Nanocomposites: coming to a store near you, University of Wisconsin - Madison, http://mrsec.wisc.edu/Edetc/IPSE/educators/, accessed 23 September 2011

WORD BOX

COMPOSITE
A composite is any material that is made up of one or more components.

Self cleaning glass

Self cleaning glass is a specific type of glass with a surface which keeps itself free of dirt and grime through natural processes. The glass is coated with a thin film of titanium dioxide, which has high catalytic properties, chemical stability and low price. The cleaning occurs in two stages:

1. ***Photocatalytic stage:*** The organic dirt on the glass is broken down using ultraviolet light from the sun, making it hydrophilic (which means 'loves water', as the particles are usually charged or have polar side groups that will attract water).

2. *Hydrophilic stage:* Rain washes away the dirt, leaving almost no streaks as hydrophilic glass spreads the water evenly over its surface.

However, titanium dioxide based glass will not decompose thick non-transparent deposits such as paint, silicon or construction dust.

Uses: Windows, doors, conservatories, glass roofs and skylights can look clearer and cleaner all year round when self cleaning glass is used. Also used for PDA screens or computer monitors where fingerprints are unwanted.

Other uses of nano technology include:

- Food packaging with anti-microbial agents.
- Sports clothing that use feedback from your body by measuring your fitness levels and creating individual training programmes.
- Cosmetics with UV protection.
- Protective clothing for use in extreme sports or military applications that can sense, react and absorb an impact or collision.

ACTIVITY

Using the information in this section as a starting point, carry out some independent research on emerging technologies.

Produce a Powerpoint presentation that could be used to teach other pupils in your class, including appropriate images to enhance your information.

HEALTH AND SAFETY

It is important that you are aware of health and safety issues when you are manufacturing in the workshop. Keeping yourself, others and the working environment a safe place is essential, so think health and safety at all times in T&D.

Wear appropriate protective clothing

- Always wear an apron and sensible shoes.
- Roll up your sleeves, tuck your tie in and tie long hair back.

- Always use eye protection, goggles or a face mask.
- Use strong protective gloves to protect yourself from hazardous material.
- If material is hot, wear protective gloves, an apron and a face mask.
- When casting wear thick all-body suits, face visors, gauntlets and spats.

Be careful with machinery and tools

- Never use a machine without permission.
- Carry sharp tools close to your body and facing downwards.
- Replace all tools after use.
- Only one person should work at a machine at a time, inside the marked safety area.
- Remove any loose items (for example, chuck key).
- Secure work safely, clamp work securely for drilling.
- Ensure the guard is in place before starting a machine like a lathe or drilling machine.
- Do not leave machines unattended while still on.
- Do not adjust a machine unless it is turned off.
- Report any damage to the teacher.
- Know where the Emergency Stop buttons are.
- Know where the First Aid kit is kept.

Take responsibility for yourself in the workshop

- Report all accidents to the teacher.
- Keep your bench area tidy. Remember a clean working area is a safe working area.
- Wipe up spillages immediately to avoid slippages.
- Never run, fool about or throw things in the workshop.

Safety signs

Safety signs identify the dangers they warn against and are divided into four categories:

- Hazard signs
- Prohibition signs
- Mandatory signs
- Safe Condition signs

Hazard signs

Hazard signs indicate a specific source of potential harm. Hazard signs are printed in black on a yellow background and are triangular in shape.

Prohibition signs

Prohibition signs indicate behavior that is forbidden. The prohibited activity is represented in black on white, with a red circle and diagonal stripe superimposed.

Mandatory signs

Mandatory signs identify a particular course of action that must be taken. They are represented in white on a solid blue circle.

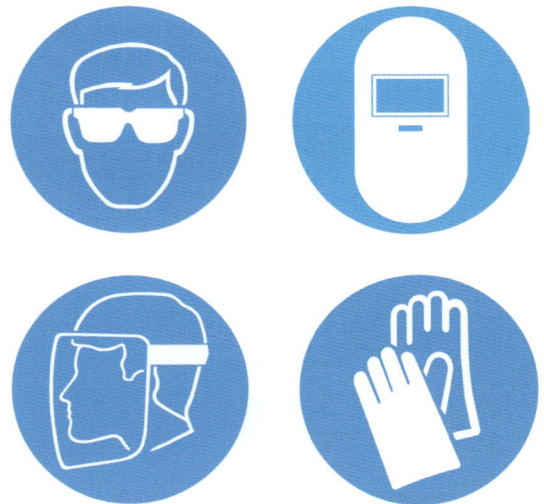

Safe condition signs

Safe condition signs indicate the presence of a safety facility and are usually represented in white on a solid green square.

Emergency stop sign

The sign used to indicate the location of an emergency stop button is represented in white on a solid red square.

Potential hazards

There are potential hazards in activities you undertake in the workshop, in the products you manufacture and in your working environment, so think health and safety at all times in T&D.

Handle materials and waste with care

- Only use hazardous materials were necessary.
- If moving long lengths of metal or timber, be aware of the possible hazard to others.
- Make sure materials are safe to handle, deburr or degrease metal before starting.
- Dispose of waste properly.
- Store material safely so it cannot fall or slide causing injury to anyone.
- Clear dust and debris with a brush not your hands.

Risk assessment

To minimise potential hazards in the workshop a risk assessment will have been carried out by the department. Risk assessment is about working out what could possibly go wrong and finding ways to prevent it.

- Machines will have warning or caution signs.
- Floors will be non-slip.
- Machine areas will be marked out.
- Guards will be in place and be maintained.

Safe product design

Within a product potential hazards can be avoided by designing safe products. For example, if designing a toy:

- Avoid injury to the user by smooting any sharp edges or corners.
- Avoid toxic paint or varnish.

- Avoid small components that could cause choking hazards or ensure they are firmly attached.
- Use standard components that have undergone rigorous testing to meet safety standards.

Always think about the end user. There are safety laws and standards to help protect consumers.

Safety acts and certification

The Health & Safety at Work Act and COSHH (Control of Substances Hazardous to Health) are related to safety in the workplace. They are to protect you from hazardous or dangerous working practices that could pose a risk to your health.

Standards make the products we use safer and more reliable, so our lives are easier, healthier and safer. In the T&D workshop you are usually producing prototypes but if they were to be commercially produced they would have to be standardised by a company such as the British Standards Institute. This would guarantee that the product would be consistently reliable and safe to use.

The British Standards Institute is "a company who helps organisations improve their quality and performance, reduce their risk, manage and protect their reputations, and help them be more sustainable."* Products will be awarded the Kitemark if they meet BSI standards.

*Source: http://www.bsigroup.com/en/About-BSI/

CHECK YOUR LEARNING

1. What are the four categories that safety signs are divided into?
2. Identify the colours of each category of sign.
3. State examples for each category of sign.

KEY WORD CHECK

At the end of each section there is a list of key words. Explain what each word means.

You might also find it useful to put together a glossary of these key words. This will be an invaluable resource when you come to revise. Remember to add to your glossary as you work through the textbook.

- **Ferrous**
- **Non-ferrous**
- **Alloy**
- **Galvanising**
- **Plastic dip coating**
- **Permanent joints**
- **Semi-permanent joints**
- **Riveting**

- **Marking out tools**
- **Drilling**
- **Cutting tools**
- **Surface finishes**
- **Material efficiency**
- **Adhesive**
- **Wasting**
- **Fabrication**

- **Mould**
- **Jig**
- **Template**
- **CAM**
- **CAD**
- **Emerging technologies**
- **Nano technologies**

EXAM FOCUS

Past paper questions will appear at the end of each section to help you practice your exam skills.

1. Figure 1 shows six hand tools.

Make a copy of figure 1 and complete the table by inserting the correct name for each hand tool from the list in figure 2. The first one has been done for you. [5]

Figure 1

Tools	Name of tool
	**Flat File**

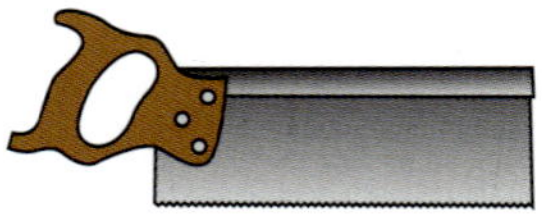	

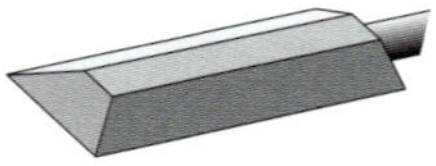	

Figure 2

Chisel	Tenon saw
Coping saw	Try square
Hacksaw	Flat file

CCEA GCSE Technology & Design Past Paper, Foundation Tier, Summer 2003, © CCEA

For copyright reasons the images in Figure 1 have replaced those from the CCEA past paper.

2. Many kitchen cupboards are made from MDF with a melamine surface.

(a) What is meant by MDF? [1]

(b) Is MDF a hardwood, softwood or a manufactured board? [1]

(c) Why are many kitchen cupboards normally covered with a melamine surface? [1]

CCEA GCSE Technology & Design Past Paper, Foundation Tier, Summer 2007, © CCEA

3. Aeroplane bodies (fuselage) are usually made from one specific metal.

(a) Write down the name of this metal. [1]

(b) Give a reason for the use of this metal. [1]

(c) Figure 3 shows two parts A and B of the aeroplane body to be joined.
Name component X that is used to join the parts together. [2]

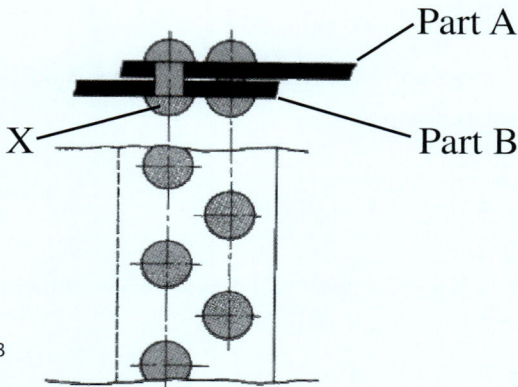

Part A

Part B

X

Figure 3

(d) Name the tool used to shape the end of component X. [2]

(e) Name another joining process (other than welding) that could be used to join the two metals together. [2]

(d) Name the tool used to shape the end of component X. [2]

(e) Name another joining process (other than welding) that could be used to join the two metals together. [2]

CCEA GCSE Technology & Design Past Paper, Foundation Tier, Summer 2007, © CCEA

4. Figure 4 shows a plastic holder for leaflets in a library. The holder is attached to a wooden board using screws which pass through the inserts.

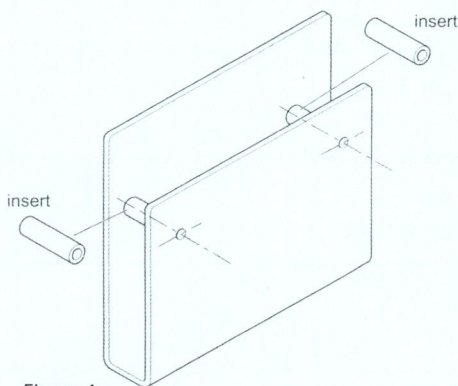

insert

insert

Figure 4

(a) State one specification point which should be considered in designing the leaflet holder. [1]

(b) Suggest a suitable plastic material for the holder and give one reason for your choice. [2]

(c) What equipment would be used to bend the material into the shape illustrated in Figure 4? [2]

(d) Give one reason for using inserts as shown in Figure 4. [2]

CCEA GCSE Technology & Design Past Paper, Unit 1, Technology and Design Core, Summer 2011, © CCEA

5. Figure 5 shows a drawing of a metal component for a school project. The component part is to be made from brass sheet 2 mm thick.

Figure 5

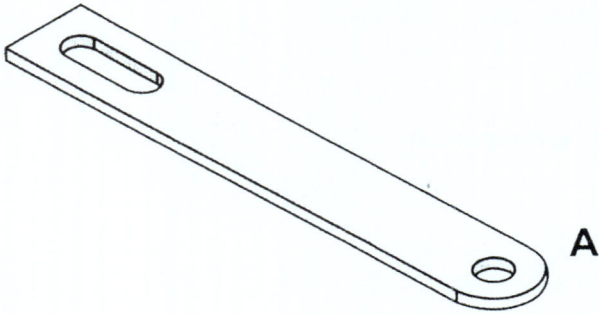

(a) Is brass a ferrous or a non-ferrous metal? [1]

(b) Why are alloys of metals formed? [2]

(c) Name the tool used to mark the centre of the hole in the metal component at end A to help drilling. [2]

(d) Suggest a suitable finish that could be applied to the metal component. [1]

CCEA GCSE Technology & Design Past Paper, Unit 1, Technology and Design Core, Summer 2011, © CCEA

6. Figure 6 lists a number of materials and their categories.

Make a copy of Figure 6 and complete the table by ticking (✓) the one correct category for each of the materials listed. The first one has been done for you. [5]

Figure 6

Category / Material	Hardwood	Plastic	Ferrous Metal	Manufactured Board	Softwood	Non-Ferrous Metal
MDF				✓		
Copper						
Cedar						
Melamine						
Beech						
Aluminium						

CCEA GCSE Technology & Design Past Paper, Foundation Tier, Summer 2005, © CCEA

7. (a) Figure 7 shows a bracket which is used to support a hanging basket.

Figure 7

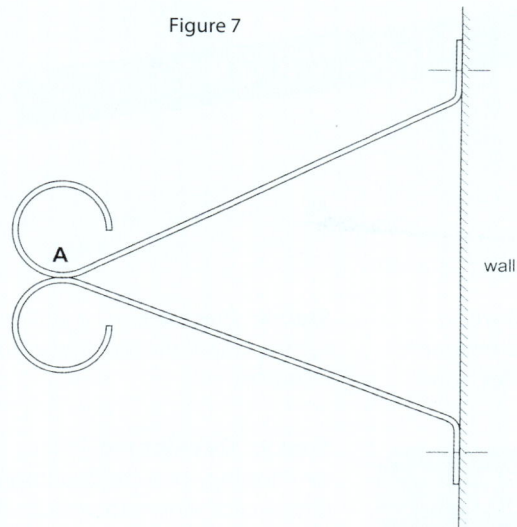

(i) Name a suitable material for the bracket. [1]

(ii) Suggest a suitable finish for the bracket. [1]

(iii) State a suitable permanent method for joining the two parts at A. [1]

(iv) Give one reason why a semi-permanent method may not be suitable for joining the parts at A. [2]

(b) Figure 8 shows a different design for the bracket.

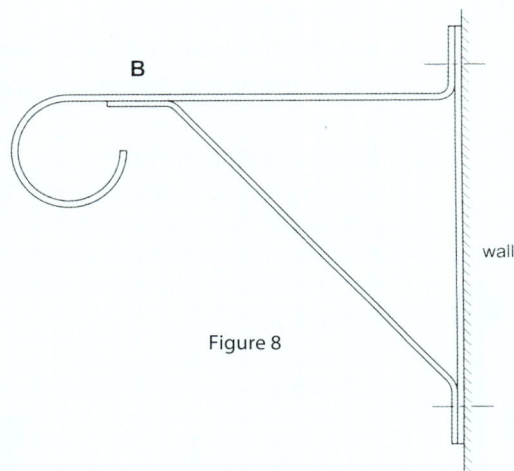

Figure 8

(i) State a semi-permanent method for joining the parts at B. [1]

(ii) Explain why a semi-permanent method may be suitable for joining parts at B. [1]

CCEA GCSE Technology & Design Past Paper, Unit 1, Technology and Design Core, Summer 2011, © CCEA

An understanding of basic electronics is essential when considering the design and manufacture of some products in T&D. This section will help you with the main electronic concepts in T&D.

CONSTRUCTION TECHNIQUES

To produce a reliable, functioning technological product you must be able to identify and select the correct tools and equipment to produce a PCB (printed circuit board), populate it with components and join them securely using the process known as **soldering.**

PCB (Printed Circuit Board)

A PCB is a plastic board with copper tracks on one side, which can be populated with electronic components to make a circuit for an electronic device.

How to produce PCB

To make a PCB you must remove most of the copper, to leave a strip that will become the conductor between the components on the board.

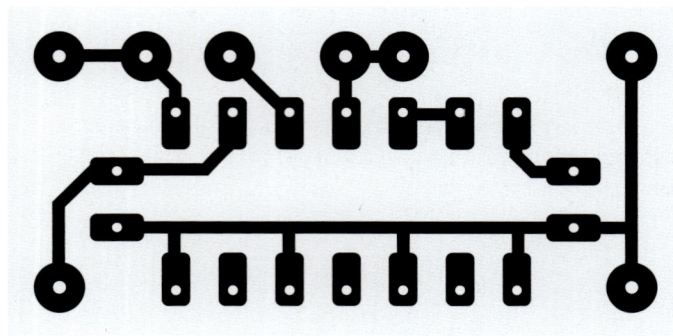

Step 1: Photocopy or trace a copy of the circuit on to an acetate sheet to make a mask. This is called the PCB art work.

Step 2: Place the mask into an ultra-violet light box and set the board on top. Close the box and expose for four minutes.

Step 3: Developing – Place the board carefully into the developing solution (Sodium Hydroxide) to remove all the film except where the tracks are. Rinse under water when you can see the copper tracks.

Step 4: Etching – The chemical (Ferric Chloride) is heated to about 50°C. It will dissolve any unprotected copper leaving a PCB with copper tracks on one side. Rinse with water.

The PCB is now ready for drilling, populating and soldering.

Safety
• Wear goggles and gloves.
• Use tongs to handle the circuit board.
• Wash the board with water and clean with wire wool.

Latest technology
Some schools are now using the latest technology to produce PCBs. They can be manufactured using CAD/CAM. A milling machine can be programmed to cut out and drill the PCB, which means the etching tank method is not necessary.

Making a PCB (Summary):

1. Make a mask
2. Expose under UV light
3. Develop
4. Etch
5. Drill
6. Populate (put in components)
7. Solder (join components with solder to the PCB)

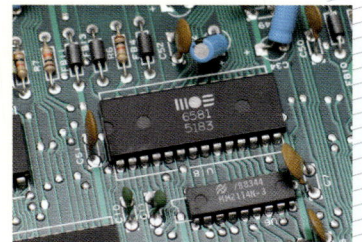

PCB drill

Before soldering, the PCB must be drilled using a special PCB drill to make holes for the legs of your components.

Soldering

Soldering is a method of joining components and wires together using a soldering iron and solder.

Solder is a type of metal, an alloy (mixture) of tin and lead. It melts at a relatively low temperature of 200°C and sets again when the heat is removed.

The following tools and equipment are needed for soldering:

Real life image	Name
	Soldering iron
	Soldering iron holder
	Roll of solder wire
	Desoldering pump
	Wire strippers
	'Helping hands' for soldering

The best solder to use is multi-core as it contains **flux**. Flux keeps the join clean and helps the solder flow. Successful soldering requires cleanliness, so avoid touching areas to be soldered, as dirt and oil from the skin can cause a poorly soldered joint. Use a pair of wire strippers to remove some of the plastic insulating sleeve before soldering.

Some components, such as LEDs, can be damaged by too much heat. Use a small pair of pliers to hold the component being soldered. The pilers will act as a *'heat sink'*, taking away some of the heat and protecting the component.

How to solder successfully

1. Clean the components with wire wool or emery paper.
2. Insert the component into the PCB.
3. Ensure the soldering iron is clean and tinned (tip coated with a thin layer of solder).
4. Solder the support work. Use the 'helping hands'.
5. Heat the component with the soldering iron.
6. Apply solder to the component and not to the iron. The solder will run when the heat is right.
7. Allow the work to cool without moving it about.
8. A good solder joint should look like the diagram below.

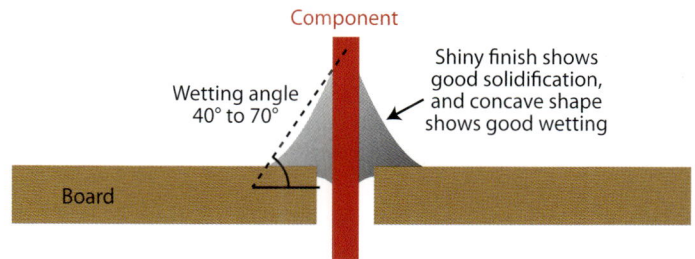

Component

Wetting angle 40° to 70°

Shiny finish shows good solidification, and concave shape shows good wetting

Board

Other construction techniques for circuits

Breadboards or protoboards

Breadboards or protoboards are used to build circuits without soldering, as a one off or prototype of a circuit before a PCB is made.

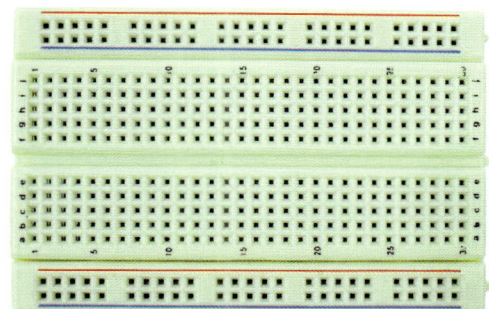

Stripboards

Stripboards are boards with parallel strips of copper on one side that can also be used for circuit prototypes. They work well for small, permanently soldered circuits but PCBs are a better choice if the circuit is larger and more complex.

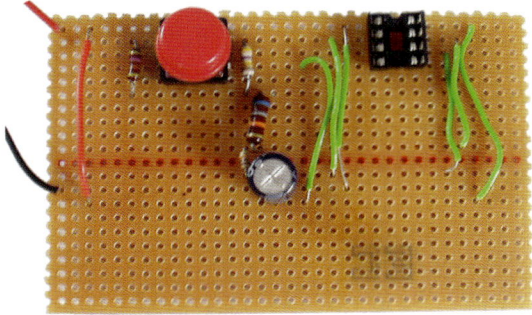

CHECK YOUR LEARNING

1. What is the name of the process used to join components together in a circuit?
2. Why is a 'heat sink' used when soldering?
3. What is solder?
4. What two metals is solder made of?
5. What could be the cause of a poorly soldered join?
6. At what temperature does solder melt at?
7. What does solder contain to keep the joints clean?

ACTIVITY

Sketch and label the following:
• a soldering iron and a roll of soldering wire.
• the tool used as a 'heat sink' when soldering.

INPUT — PROCESS — OUTPUT

All control systems require three things:

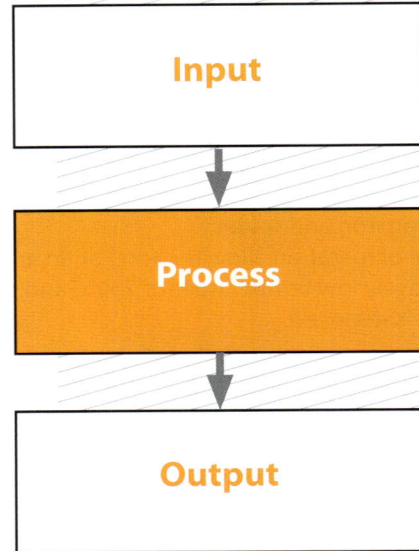

Input

Process

Output

An input to a system will cause the system to do something. For example, in an electronic control system:

• The input to a torch is the switch.

The **input** to a control system could be any of the following:

• A mechanical input
• An electronic input
• A pneumatic input
• Computer control

The **process** part of a system accepts the input and makes the output happen. For example, in an electronic control system:

• The processing part of a torch is the electrons flowing.

The **output** of a system will react to the process. For example, in an electronic control system:

• The output of a torch is the bulb lighting.

UNITS AND MEASUREMENTS

Current: is the flow of electric charge, the number of electrons passing a point in one second. It is measured in Amperes (A) or Amps.

Resistance: is when a material resists the flow of electrons. It is measured in Ohms (Ω).

Voltage: is the pressure causing the electrons in a circuit to move. It is measured in Volts (V).

Ohm's law

Ohm's law is the mathematical relationship between, voltage, current and resistance.

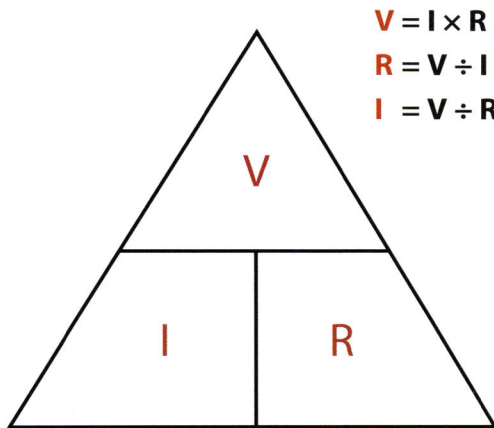

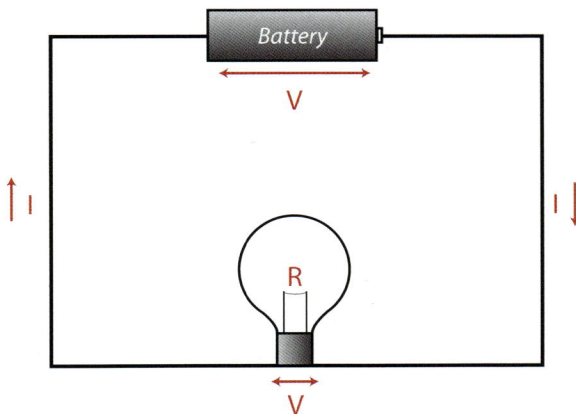

V = voltage

I = current

R = resistance

$$V = I \times R$$
$$R = V \div I$$
$$I = V \div R$$

RESISTORS

Resistors provide **resistance** to the flow of electrons, rather like a tap can do to the flow of water.

Resistors in series (one after another)

$$R_{total} = R_1 + R_2$$

For example:

$R_{total} = 100 + 200$
$R_{total} = 300\ \Omega$

The resistor code

The resistor code is used to easily work out the value of resistors worldwide. It allows large values of resistance to be identified without having to print a large number containing lots of zeros on a very small component. Each band is coloured:

Band 1: the colour represents a digit.
Write down the digit you see opposite the colour on the colour chart overleaf.

Band 2: the colour represents a digit.
Write down the digit you see opposite the colour on the colour chart.

Band 3: the number of zeros represented, or the multiplier.
Write down the number of zeros you see opposite the colour on the colour chart.

Band 4: (if present) is usually a tolerance band of +/− 5% or +/− 10%.

Using the Resistor Colour Code to calculate resistance

Band Colour	Band 1	Band 2	Band 3: No. of zeros	Band 4
Black	0	0	-	
Brown	1	1	0	
Red	2	2	00	
Orange	3	3	000	
Yellow	4	4	0000	If present, usually a tolerance of +/− 5% (**gold**) or +/− 10% (**silver**)
Green	5	5	00000	
Blue	6	6	000000	
Violet	7	7	0000000	
Grey	8	8	00000000	
White	9	9	000000000	

Example:
The following shows how to work out the value of various resistors using the resistor colour code.

Brown Black Red = 1000 Ω

Band 1	Band 2	Band 3
Brown	Black	Red
1	0	00

Red Red Red = 2200 Ω

Band 1	Band 2	Band 3
Red	Red	Red
2	2	00

Yellow Violet Brown = 470 Ω

Band 1	Band 2	Band 3
Yellow	Violet	Brown
4	7	0

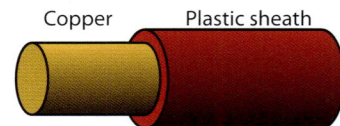

Copper   Plastic sheath

Insulators: is a material that does not allow the flow of electrons through it. Plastics and rubber are both insulators. The outer part of electrical wires is made of plastic or rubber to protect the user from electricity and heat. Handles of saucepans and kettles also use insulators.

Semi-conductor: is a material that allows the flow of some electrons through it. Resistors are semi-conductors. They reduce or limit the flow of electrons to protect other components in a circuit from being damaged by too much current. Diodes and LEDs are also semi-conductors. Most computerised products depend on semi-conductors as they make up microprocessors, which are usually made of silicon. The electronic components below all contain semi-conductors.

CONDUCTORS AND INSULATORS

Conductor: is a material that allows the flow of electrons through it. Metals are conductors. This is why copper is used for electrical wires where a good flow of electrons is necessary. Similarly, the prongs of a plug are made of metal, as they need to be conductors.

COMPONENTS

Component	Real life image	Symbol
Battery: is a cell that converts chemical energy into electrical energy. It is used as a source of power in an electrical circuit.		
Resistor: provides resistance to the flow of electrons. The resistance of a fixed resistor can be calculated using a resistor colour code chart (see table opposite).		
Variable resistor: is an adjustable resistor used to increase or decrease the amount of resistance to the flow of electrons. It is used to control the flow of electricity and the brightness of a bulb, for example.		
LDR (Light Dependent Resistor): is a piece of semi-conducting material that has low resistance in light conditions and high resistance when it is dark.		
Thermistor: is a temperature dependent resistor. As temperature rises the resistance of the thermistor increases and as temperature falls the resistance decreases.		
Diode: is a piece of semi-conducting material that only allows current to flow in one direction.		
LED (Light Emitting Diode): is a diode that emits light when electrons pass through it.		
Thyristor: When a small current is applied to the gate it causes a large current to flow between the anode and the cathode. A thyristor will continue passing anode/cathode current, even when the small gate current has ceased. This is called latching.		
Transistor NPN: can act as sensitive electronic switches in a circuit. It has three legs – the base, collector and emitter – that must be connected the correct way around for it to work.		
Buzzer: is an output device that gives off sound.		
Bulb: is an output device that gives off light.		
Motor: is an output device that produces rotary motion.		

SWITCHES AND SWITCHING

Switches are used to switch a circuit ON or OFF by making or breaking a connection.

Switch	Real life image	Symbol
Single Pole Single Throw (SPST) switch: is the simplest on/off switch. It has one moveable arm contact (single pole) and one switching position which conducts (single throw). Although the switch mechanism has two possible positions OFF (open) and ON (closed), it is known as 'single throw' because it conducts only in one position. Push switches and toggles switches are both SPST switches.		
Push switch: The switch is pushed to make or break the connection. *Push to make:* this switch will return to its OFF (normally open) position when the button is released. A door bell uses a push to make switch. *Push to break:* this switch will return to its ON (normally closed) position when the button is released. A circuit controlling a motor could use this switch to turn the motor off.		Push to make SPST Push to break SPST
Toggle switch: A lever is thrown or flipped to make or break the connection.		Single Pole Single Throw (SPST) switch
Single pole, double throw SPDT switch: can be ON in either position, to switch on separate devices. For example, a SPDT switch could be used to control two different coloured lights, both on and off. In one position it could switch on a green light and in another position switch on a red light. Another application for using a SPDT switch could be turning on a light at either the top or bottom of stairs. A micro-switch is a SPDT switch.		
Micro-switch: is designed for situations where the connection has to be broken by a moving object.		Single Pole Double Throw (SPDT) switch
Slide switch: is also known as a **Double Pole Double Throw (DPDT)** switch. It is used to switch on and off two or more circuits at the same time, and often used in motor reversing circuits. You can use a DPDT switch to reverse a motor's rotation by changing the polarity of the motor. When power comes from the positive side of the battery (+) and connects to the right hand side of the motor, it rotates **anti-clockwise.** When the switch is changed, the positive supply of the battery arrives at the left hand side of the motor, causing it to rotate **clockwise.**		Double Pole Double Throw (DPDT) switch
Reed switch: is a glass casing with switch inside. When a magnet passes over, the reed switch closes and completes the circuit. They are used in security circuits to check doors are closed. Standard reed switches are SPST but SPDT versions are available.		
Membrane switch: is an electrical switch used for turning circuits on and off. Two contacts that are conductors, such as copper tape, are Normally Open (NO) off, but when passed together they complete the circuit turning it on.		

KEY TERMS
Com = common contact. **NO** = normally open contact – means switch is in OFF position until turned on.
NC = normally closed contact – means switch is in ON position until turned off.

POTENTIAL DIVIDERS

The emf (electromotive force) of a battery creates a **potential difference (pd)** between its terminals. One terminal is positive and the other is negative. The pd makes current flow from the positive terminal to the negative terminal. The input part to a circuit is a **voltage divider**. The voltage in the circuit passes through the two resistors and back to the battery.

Potential dividers are used to split the voltage of a circuit. They are widely used to set and adjust voltages. They consist of two resistors connected as shown below. By adjusting the resistor value you can have any voltage between 0 and 9 V.

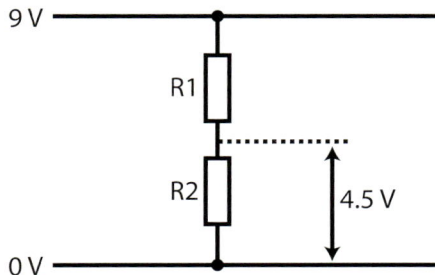

- When two resistors of equal value are connected across a supply, current will flow through them.

- If a meter is placed across a supply it will register 9 V. If the meter is then placed between the 0 V and the middle of the two resistors it will read 4.5 V. The battery voltage has been divided in half.

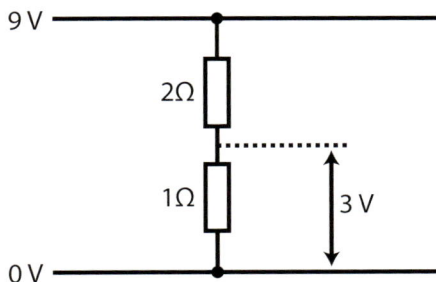

- If the resistor values are changed to 2 Ω and 1 Ω, the voltage will be **6 V**.

- The voltage at the centre is determined by the ratio of the two resistors.

- The bigger the resistance, the bigger the voltage over it.

$$V = \text{Supply Voltage} \times \frac{R2}{R1 + R2}$$

$$V = 9\,V \times \frac{2000}{1000 + 2000}$$

$$V = 9\,V \times (2000 \div 3000)$$

$$V = 9\,V \times 0.6666667$$

$$V = 6\,V$$

Sensing circuits: are circuits that sense changes in conditions such as light, temperature or moisture and cause an output such as an alarm to sound or a light to come on. Sensing circuits nearly always contain voltage divider circuits within them.

TRANSISTORS

A transistor (NPN type) is a component that can act as a sensitive electronic switch in a circuit.

It has three legs, the **base**, **collector** and **emitter**, that must be connected the correct way around for it to work.

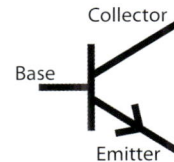

It connects with a protective resistor in a circuit to limit the flow of current and protect the transistor. When the input at the base of the transistor rises to 0.6 V, the transistor switches on the output side and allows current to flow in at the collector and out at the emitter. An output component such as a bulb or buzzer can be switched on. When the current at the base of the transistor drops below 0.6 V, the transistor switches off the output.

Example of a sensing circuit using a transistor as a switch:

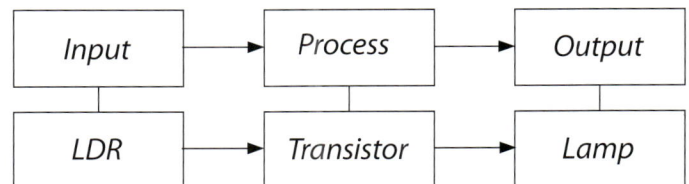

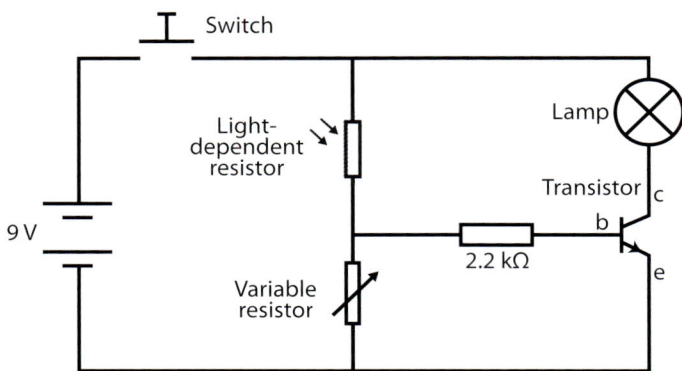

The circuit diagram above shows a sensing circuit that uses a transistor as a sensitive high-speed electronic switch. When there is a voltage of 0.6–1.6 V present at the base leg of the transistor, it will turn on.

The LDR (Light Dependent Resistor) is the sensor. The input and its resistance increases with darkness. The variable resistor allows you to set how dark it has to be before the light comes on.

LEDS (LIGHT EMITTING DIODES)

A LED is a diode that emits light when electrons pass through it. Electrons flow up the anode (+) through the semi-conducting material that glows and gives out light, back down the cathode (-) and around the circuit. A flat spot indicates the shorter negative leg.

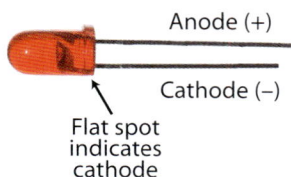

Anode (+)

Cathode (–)

Flat spot indicates cathode

Always use a resistor with a LED to limit the current and protect the LED from damage. This is shown below.

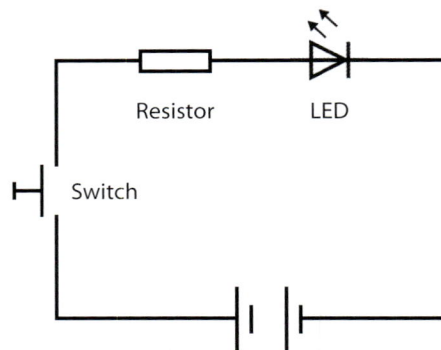

THYRISTORS

A thyristor has three legs, the **cathode**, **anode** and **gate**.

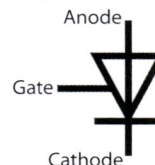

When a small current is applied to the gate it causes a large current to flow between anode and cathode. The important fact is that the thyristor will continue passing anode/cathode current even when the small gate current has ceased. This is called **latching**. In electronics, a circuit could be designed to turn on an alarm. The alarm can be made to stay on until it is reset. This is an example of latching the circuit.

Below is an example of a latching circuit used in a cheat proof electronic game. The thyristor causes the buzzer to latch on continuously until the game is reset.

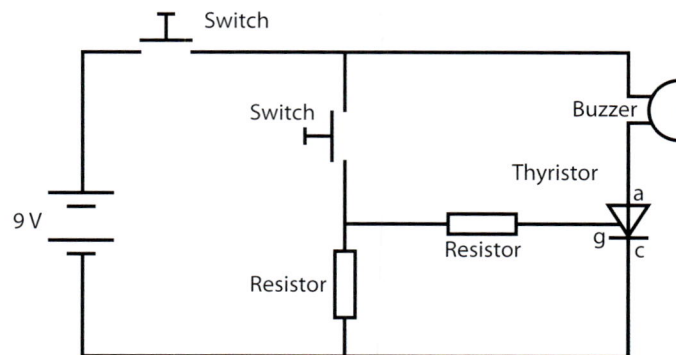

Below are some key words, explain what each means. Remember to add these words to your glossary.

- **Input**
- **Process**
- **Output**
- **Current**
- **Voltage**

- **Resistance**
- **Components**
- **Conductors**
- **Insulators**
- **Resistor**

- **Types of switches**
- **Potential divider**
- **LED**
- **Thyristor**
- **Transistor**

EXAM FOCUS

Complete the following past paper questions to help consolidate your learning and practice your exam skills.

1. Figures 1a and 1b show ways of connecting batteries and resistors in circuits.

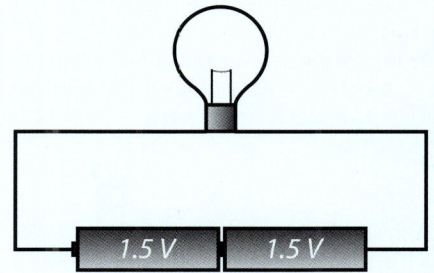

(a) (i) Name the kind of circuit that connects components in this way. [2]

(ii) What is the voltage?

(iii) If the three resistors shown in Figure 1b were to be replaced with one resistor calculate the value of the single replacement resistor. [2]

(iv) Use the colour code/values shown below to state the colours that would be shown on the first three bands on the replacement resistor.

- First colour band [1]

- Second colour band [1]

- Third colour band [1]

Figure 1a

0 = Black	1 = Brown	2 = Red	3 = Orange	4 = Yellow
5 = Green	6 = Blue	7 = Violet	8 = Grey	9 = White

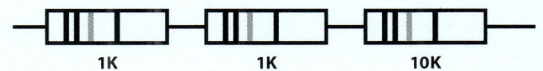

1K   1K   10K

Figure 1b

(b) Resistors are used with LEDs in electronic circuits.
State the reason for using a resistor with an LED in an electronic circuit. [2]

CCEA GCSE Technology & Design Past Paper, Higher Tier, Summer 2005, © CCEA
For copyright reasons the diagrams in Figures 1a and 1b have replaced those from the CCEA past paper.

2. (a) Figure 2 shows five electronic circuit symbols.
Make a copy of Figure 2 below and name the four remaining electronic circuit symbols. [4]

⊗				
Bulb				

Figure 2

(b) Make a copy of the circuit diagram in Figure 3. Insert all of the five symbols shown in Figure 2 into your copy of Figure 3. [5]

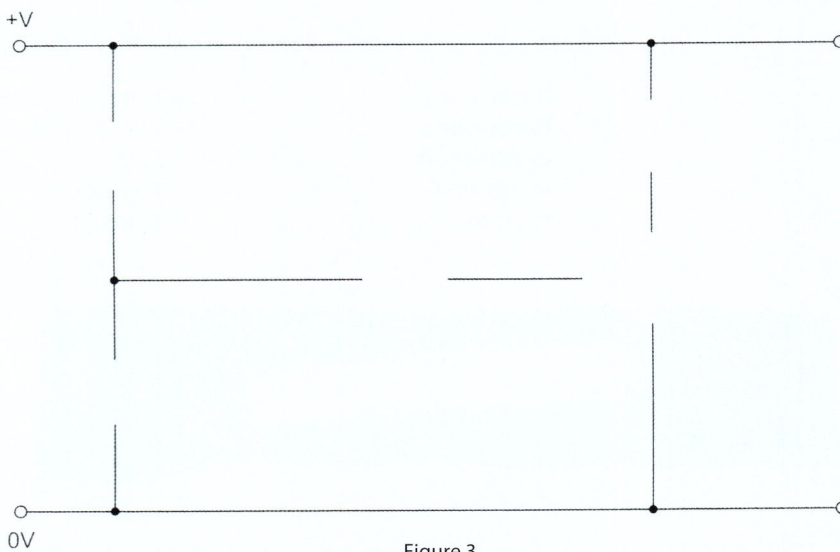

OV

Figure 3

3. **Figure 4 shows two electronic symbols and one electronic component.**
   A part completed circuit diagram is shown in Figure 5.

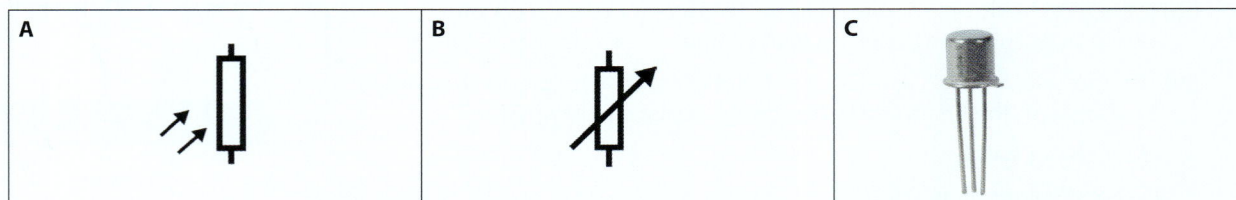

Figure 4

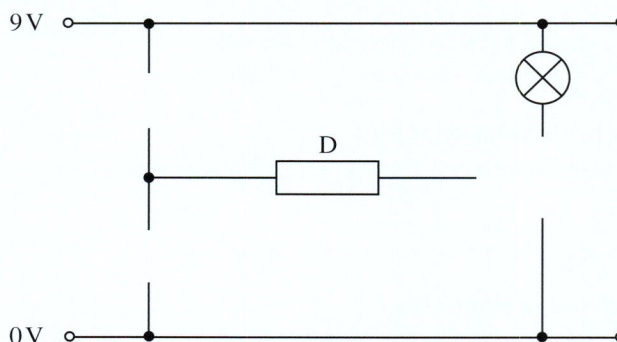

Figure 5

(a) Write down the names of each of the following as shown in Figure 4.
- Symbol A
- Symbol B
- Component C [4]

(b) Make a copy of the circuit diagram in Figure 5. Use the information from Figure 4 to complete your copy of Figure 5 by inserting the electronic symbols correctly to enable the bulb to switch on in dark conditions. [5]

(c) What is the purpose of component D in this circuit? [2]

1C MECHANICAL CONTROL SYSTEMS

Mechanical control systems are essential when considering the design and manufacture of some products in T&D. A system has different parts that perform a function when the parts all work together.

INPUT – PROCESS – OUTPUT

All systems can be broken down into input, process and output. Mechanical control systems use mechanisms to control the input and output movement, and are designed so you get some advantage from using them, meaning they make work easier. This is known as '*mechanical advantage*'. For example, you could not lift a car without a mechanism, so a car jack is used to give you an advantage.

All systems can be broken down into a number of small systems known as subsystems. To understand this better think of a bicycle as a system. The input is the movement of your legs, the process is the pedals turning, which are linked to the wheels, and the output is the bicycle moving forward.

As part of this section you should be able to analyse and describe mechanisms in terms of input–process–output.

ACTIVITY

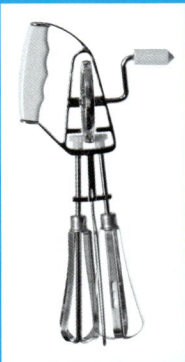

Look at the photograph of this mechanical whisk. Can you identify the mechanism that has been used and describe how it works in terms of input–process–output?

After you have learned the theory on different mechanisms, and feel confident that you understand it, this type of task will be much easier.

CONSTRUCTION TECHNIQUES

In the workshop you should be able to construct a simple model of a mechanism that works. Models could be made of many things, for example, mechanical children's toys, crane systems, advertising units or even futuristic vehicles. These could be easily constructed using standard components such as gear wheels, pulleys and cams, which are readily available in the school workshop, as well as small 9 V motors connected to batteries and switches for power and control. You will have a good knowledge of the range of resistant materials available to you from Unit 1A Technology and Design Core and from working with a variety of different materials at KS3. This should allow you to select the most appropriate material for building a model.

During Key Stage 3 T&D you may have completed a number of projects that used mechanisms. The activity on the next page will help you recall any information you already know about mechanisms before you begin studying this section.

Think of the projects you completed at KS3 and identify which projects used a mechanism in them. Select one of these projects and in a copy of the table below state the name of the project, the mechanism used, the function of the mechanism, the resistant materials used and the reasons or advantages of this choice.

Project Name	Mechanism used	Function of the mechanism	Resistant materials used	Reasons or advantages of choice

Some schools may have mechanism kits that you could use to gain some hands on experience building models of simple mechanism control systems in the classroom to help consolidate your learning and understanding of this unit.

TYPES OF MOTION
Note: motion = movement

1. Linear Motion
Movement in a straight line.
Example: train

2. Reciprocating Motion
Repeated backwards and forward motion in a straight line.
Example: sewing machine needle

3. Rotary Motion
Movement in a circle.
Example: helicopter rotors

4. Oscillating Motion
Movement backwards and forwards in a circular movement.
Example: pendulum

CHECK YOUR LEARNING

1. What are mechanisms used for?
2. What does motion mean?
3. Name four types of motion and state an example for each.

COMPONENTS

To understand mechanical control systems you must be able to identify the following mechanical components by both their physical appearance and symbols:

- Wheel and axle
- Gears
- Cams and followers
- Levers
- Belts and pulleys
- Shafts

WHEEL AND AXLE

Lots of different products use a wheel and axle as part of their mechanism system. The axle is the rigid bar that must be attached to the centre of the wheel.

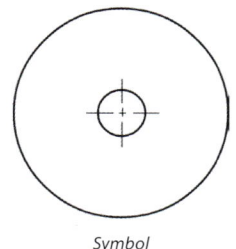

Real life image

Symbol

Examples include·

- taps
- windmills
- ferris wheels
- door knobs
- cars
- steering wheels

- gears
- bicycles – both the front and back wheels of a bicycle spin on axles, and an axle is used to connect the front pedal sprocket to both pedals.

GEARS

Gears are wheels with teeth on the outer edge. The teeth are designed to fit into the teeth of other gears, so that they mesh or interlock together. Gears are fixed on to shafts and their function is to transfer motion from one shaft to another. The shafts must be parallel to ensure that the gears mesh together properly. Gears produce very precise and efficient movement. Small gears are called **pinion gears** and large gears are called gear **wheels**.

Gear Type	Real life image	Symbol
Spur gears: are used to transmit rotary motion in the driver wheel to rotary motion in the driver pinion. They are mounted on parallel shafts.		Side view · Top view
Bevel gears: are useful when the direction of a shaft's rotation needs to be changed. They are usually mounted on shafts that are 90° apart. The teeth are cut on a cone instead of on a disc or wheel.		Bevel Gear · Meshed Bevel Gear
Worm wheel and worm gears: are used to give large speed reduction. The worm drives the wheel, the wheel cannot drive the worm. The worm is like a threaded screw that will move the gear by one tooth for every full revolution it makes.		Worm and worm wheel
Rack and pinion gears: change the rotary motion of the pinion to the linear motion of the rack.		Rack and Pinion
Sprockets and chains: are used to transmit rotary motion from one gear to another. A traditional gear train requires many gears arranged to mesh with each other in order to transmit motion. However, the advantage of a chain drive is that it only needs two gear wheels and a chain to transmit rotary motion over a distance. The chain is made up of a series of links joined with steel pins. The sprockets are profiled wheels with teeth that mesh with the chain.		

Sketch a rack and pinion gear.

Draw symbols for each of the following:
- Spur gear
- Simple gear train
- Meshed bevel gear
- Meshed gears
- Compound gear train

Power Transmission

Power transmission is when energy is moved from where it has been generated, for example, from a motor, to the place it is needed to do useful work. Mechanism systems need energy to work. A motor can be used to turn a gear train, cam, lever or any mechanism system it is attached to. A motor could be used as the input of the system.

Gear train

A gear train is two or more gears formed in a way that ensures the teeth can mesh.

A simple gear train: has one gear per shaft.

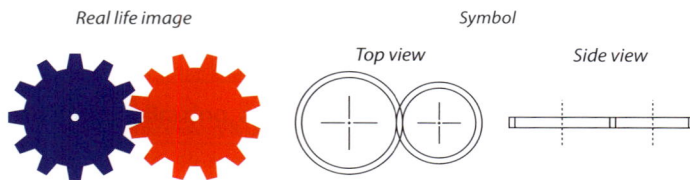

Real life image	Symbol	
	Top view	Side view

A compound gear train: has more than one gear on a shaft.

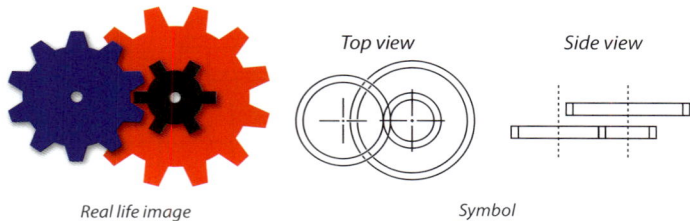

	Top view	Side view
Real life image	Symbol	

1. What is a gear?
2. What is the function of a gear?
3. What does it mean when gears mesh?
4. Small gears are called _____ gears and large gears are called _____.
5. List 4 common types of gears.
6. In what type of gear does a shaft turn at 90° to the driving wheel?
7. What type of shaft is needed to ensure the gears mesh together properly?

Calculating gear ratios

To demonstrate an understanding of how gear systems can be used to change speed you need to be able to calculate gear ratios. If two gears of different sizes are meshed together, the smaller gear will turn faster than the larger gear. The difference in the speed of the two gears is known as the gear ratio. To ensure the shaft is turning at the speed you want, you need to know the speed of the driven gear in relation to the driver.

$$\text{Gear Ratio} = \frac{\text{Number of teeth on the \textbf{driven}}}{\text{Number of teeth on the \textbf{driver}}}$$

Gears need a power source and often this is provided by an electric motor. The gear fixed to the motor is called the **driver** gear. The gear driven by the driver is called the **driven** gear.

An **idler gear** is the small gear, or pinion as it is known, that is used between the driver and the driven to make the driven move in the same direction as the driver gear. The size of the idler gear will not change the speed of the other two gears.

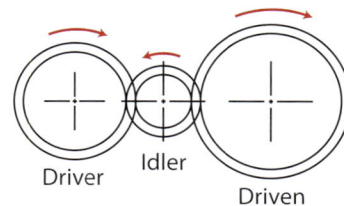

Driver   Idler   Driven

Examples:

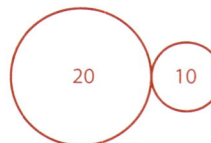

$$\frac{20}{10} = \frac{2}{1} = 2:1$$

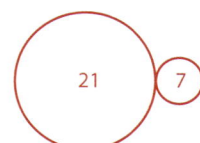

$$\frac{21}{7} = \frac{3}{1} = 3:1$$

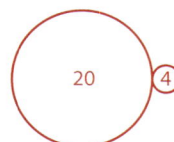

$$\frac{20}{4} = \frac{5}{1} = 5:1$$

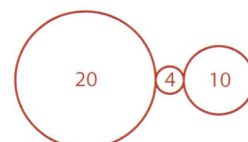

Ignore idler gear in calculation

$$\frac{20}{10} = \frac{2}{1} = 2:1$$

ACTIVITY

Name the gear types used in the products below:

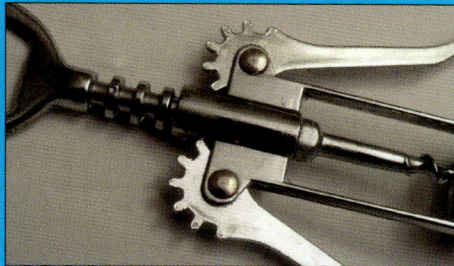

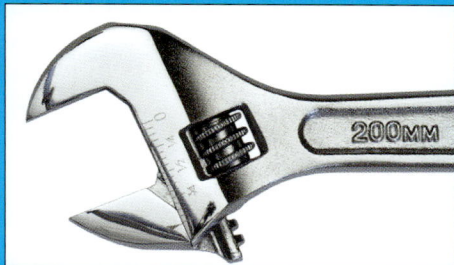

At this stage of your learning on gears you should have a good understanding of how gear systems can:

be used to change speed: By selecting different sizes of gear wheels and pinions with different numbers of teeth, the gear ratios can be changed, which changes the speed of the gear trains.

be used to change the direction of rotation: By using an idler gear between the driver and the driven, the direction of rotation can be changed.

CAMS AND FOLLOWERS

Cams are mechanisms that change one type of motion into another type of motion. A cam is made up of two parts, the shaped part (or the profile) and the cam follower, which is moved when the shaped cam part itself rotates. The follower is defined as the part of the cam that moves as it slides or rolls on the edge of the cam shape.

Types of cams

Cams are available in a number of different shapes that will determine the way the follower moves. The shape of the cam is called the profile. Below are the different profiles that you need to know.

Circular (eccentric)

Circular or eccentric cams produce a smooth, symmetrical rise and fall motion of the follower. These cams are used in steam engines.

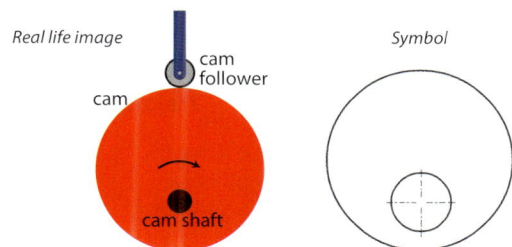

Real life image *Symbol*

cam follower

cam

cam shaft

Pear shaped

With pear shaped cams, the follower does not move for about half of the cycle of the cam rotating, then during the second half of the cam's rotation the follower rises and falls. They are used on the shafts of cars.

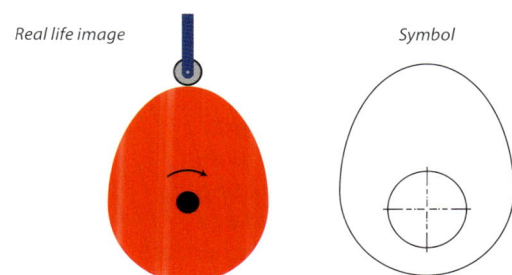

Real life image *Symbol*

51

Heart shaped

Heart shaped cams allow the follower to rise and fall at a constant speed.

Real life image   *Symbol*

The **cam shaft** is not in the centre of the cam but off centre. This causes the cam to turn in a **rotary motion** and the cam follower to move in a **linear motion**. If the cam shaft was in the centre of the cam it would not rise to make the cam follower move.

Remember – A cam changes one type of motion into another type of motion.

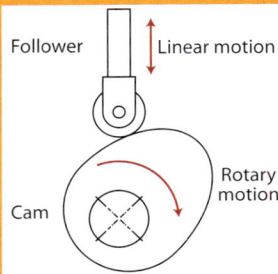

Types of followers

As well as different shaped cam profiles, different shapes of followers exist. As defined previously, the follower is the part of the cam system that moves as it slides or rolls on the edge of the cam shape. You need to be aware of flat, knife and roller followers that have these symbols:

Knife follower

The knife follower has a sharp knife edge but is rarely used because it wears away quickly because of its small area of contact. These followers give a lot of push.

Flat follower

The end of the flat follower is perfectly flat faced. The push exerted on the follower is less than that by other follower types. It is used in cars, to open and close inlet and exhaust valves in an engine.

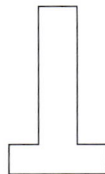

Roller follower

A follower with a roller end gives a reduced rate of wear because of the rolling motion between contacting surfaces. They are common in large stationary gas or oil engines and aircraft engines.

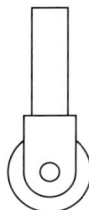

In this image of a pear shaped cam and follower, the motion of the follower is reciprocating as it will move backward and forward in a straight line as the cam rotates. The follower produces the output motion. If the cam turns until the point X is in contact with the follower, the direction of the follower will be downwards and it will have moved a distance of 10 mm.

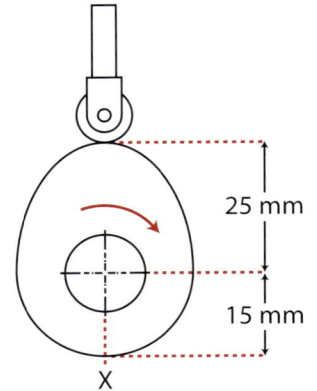

25 mm – 15 mm = 10 mm

CHECK YOUR LEARNING

1. What is a cam?
2. What would happen if the cam shaft was in the centre of the shaft?

ACTIVITY

• Sketch and label three types of rotary cams.
• Sketch and label a diagram of a cam, cam follower and cam shaft.
• Sketch a child's toy that uses a cam mechanism. Explain how it works.

LEVERS

Levers are used for a mechanical advantage in lifting heavy loads, moving things greater distances or increasing the speed of an object.

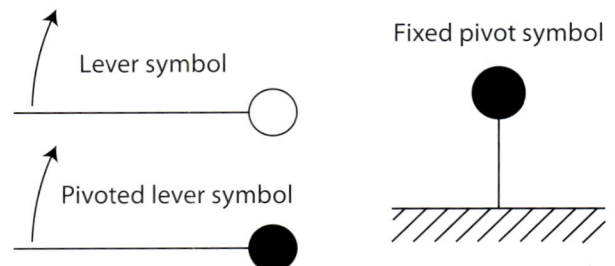

Lever symbol

Pivoted lever symbol

Fixed pivot symbol

There are three classes of lever, depending on the position of the **effort, fulcrum (pivot)** and **load.**

Class 1 lever

The fulcrum is placed between the effort and the load.

Example:

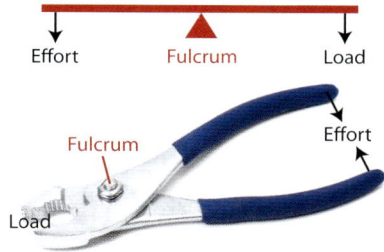

Class 2 lever

The load is in between the effort and the fulcrum.

Example:

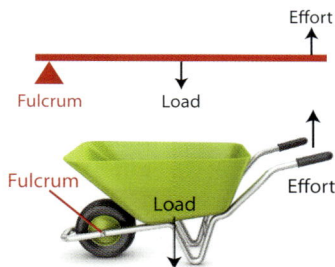

Class 3 lever

The effort is in between the load and the fulcrum.

Example:

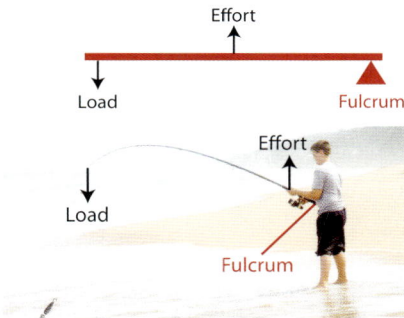

If you learn the table below it should help you identify the different classes of levers. It states which part of the lever is in the middle position and identifies the class. For example, if you remember F1, you will be able to work out that the Fulcrum (F) is in the middle of a Class 1 lever.

F	1	When the fulcrum is in the middle it is a class 1 lever.
L	2	When the load is in the middle it is a class 2 lever.
E	3	When the effort is in the middle it is a class 3 lever.

CHECK YOUR LEARNING

1. What is a lever used for?
2. State an example of where each class of lever could be found in everyday products.

ACTIVITY

• Sketch a diagram for each class of lever.
• Mark the fulcrum, effort and load on each.

BELTS AND PULLEYS

Real life image

Symbol

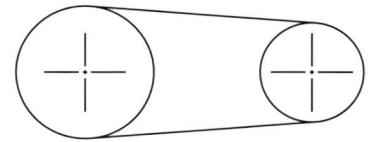

A pulley is a wheel with a belt or rope that goes around it. The wheel has a groove in it to prevent the belt or rope from slipping off.

Belts and pulleys transfer motion from one part of a machine to another. They can be used to increase or decrease the relative speeds of two shafts.

The main advantages: of belts and pulley transmission systems are:

• they are quiet in operation.
• they require no lubrication and are relatively cheap to produce.

This is why they are used in domestic appliances.

The main disadvantage: is that slip can occur, so they should only be used where slip will not affect the operation of the machine. At times slip is useful, for example, if a machine like a pillar drill jams, the drive belt can slip. This could protect the user from injury and protect the drive motor from damage.

CHECK YOUR LEARNING

1. What is a pulley?
2. What is the function of belts and pulleys?
3. What are the advantages of belts and pulleys?
4. What is the main disadvantage of belts and pulleys?
5. Name two household products that use pulley systems in them?

Power transmission

When a small pulley is used to drive a large pulley, the large pulley rotates more slowly than the small pulley. The circumferences of the pulleys are used to calculate the speed ratio (or velocity ratio) between the output shaft and the motor shaft. The driver pulley is connected to the motor.

$$\text{Speed ratio} = \frac{\text{circumference of } \textbf{driven} \text{ pulley}}{\text{circumference of } \textbf{driver} \text{ pulley}}$$

Examples:

If the driver pulley has a circumference of 8 cm and the driven pulley has a circumference of 24 cm, the ratio speed is 3:1.

$$\text{Speed ratio} = \frac{24}{8} = \frac{3}{1} = 3{:}1$$

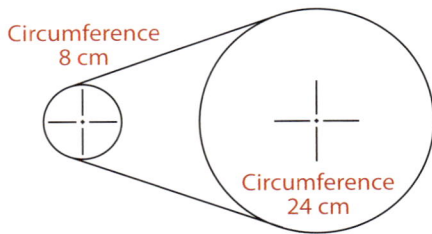

Circumference
8 cm

Circumference
24 cm

A quiet, no slip drive is essential in a car engine, as slip would cause serious damage to the engine.

To prevent this, a special toothed belt and pulley can be used.

Round belts

The cross-section of a round belt is round, as seen in the diagram opposite. They are used on light machines, where the belt has to turn through 90° or only a small drive force is required, for example, CD players, light-duty milling machines, drills, power tools and vacuum cleaners.

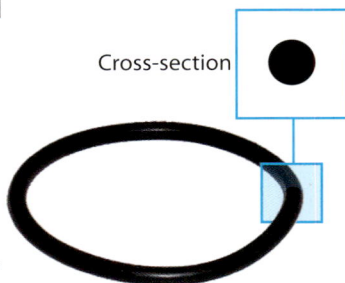

Cross-section

Vee belts

With vee belts, a larger area of the belt is in contact with the pulley. This gives a greater drive force before the belt starts to slip because of the increased friction, for example, pillar drills. The shaft speed can be controlled by placing pulleys of different diameters on the same shaft. A pillar drill uses a stepped cone pulley. The output, which is the chuck and drill bit turning, can be slowed down if the vee belt is moved downward on the pulleys.

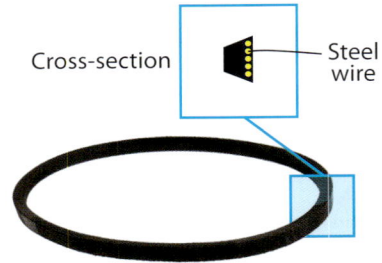

Cross-section

Steel wire

CHECK YOUR LEARNING

1. What is used in a car engine to give a quiet, no slip drive?
2. When would a round belt be used? Give examples.
3. Why is a vee belt used in a pillar drill?
4. What type of pulley is used in a pillar drill and why?
5. What is the driver pulley connected to?
6. What are the two formulae that can be used to calculate the speed ratio of pulleys?

ACTIVITY

Calculate the following:

- If the driver pulley has a circumference of 6 cm and the driven pulley has a circumference of 24 cm, what is the ratio speed?
- If the driver pulley has a diameter of 50 mm and the driven pulley has a diameter of 150 cm, what is the ratio speed?

SAFETY

Safety is important when dealing with moving parts so you must be aware of the following precautions:

- Keep fingers clear of moving parts.
- Never attempt to remove an obstruction from a machine in motion.
- Keep moving parts clean to avoid obstructions occurring.
- Never try to slow a moving part with your hands.
- Ensure guards are in place before starting.
- Dress properly, avoiding clothing that could get stuck in moving parts and wear eye protection.

KEY WORD CHECK

Below are some key words, explain what each means. Remember to add these words to your glossary.

- Rotary motion
- Linear motion
- Oscillating motion
- Reciprocating motion
- Gears
- Simple gear trains
- Gear ratios
- Cam types
- Cam followers
- Shafts
- Belts and pulleys
- Classes of levers
- Uses of levers

EXAM FOCUS

Complete the following past paper questions to help consolidate your learning and practice your exam skills.

1. Figure 1 shows a cam and follower.

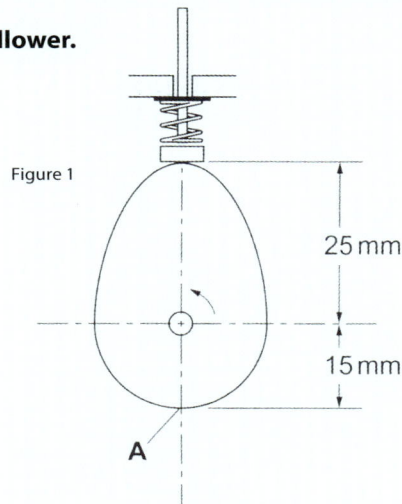

Figure 1

25 mm

15 mm

A

(a) Select a word from the list below to describe the motion of the follower. [1]

Reciprocating   Linear   Rotary   Oscillating

(b) Which component produces the output motion? [1]

(c) Select the correct name for the cam from the following. [1]

Eccentric   Heart shaped   Pear shaped

(d) The cam turns until the point A is in contact with the follower. Determine the direction and distance moved by the follower. [2]

CCEA GCSE Technology & Design Past Paper, Unit 1, Technology and Design Core, Summer 2011, © CCEA

2. **Figure 2 shows a number of mechanical components. Make a copy of the table in Figure 2. You do not have to draw the diagrams in the mechanical component column but can identify them by A, B, C, D and E instead. Complete the table by inserting the correct name for each component from the following list.** [5]

| wheel and axle | eccentric cam | lever |
| belt drive | roller follower | |

Figure 2

	Mechanical component	Name
A 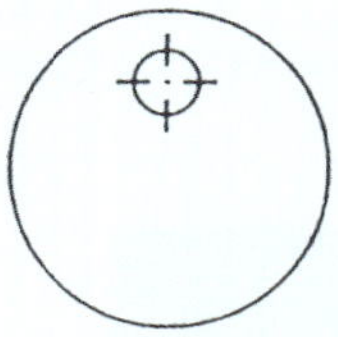		
B 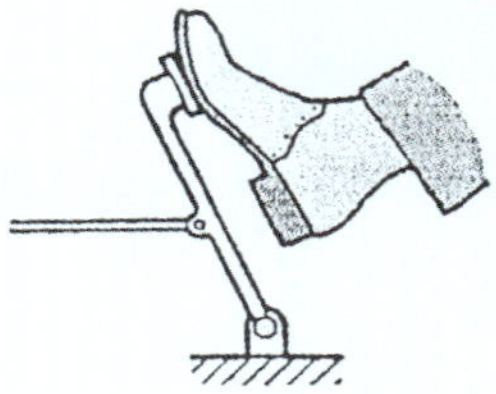		
C 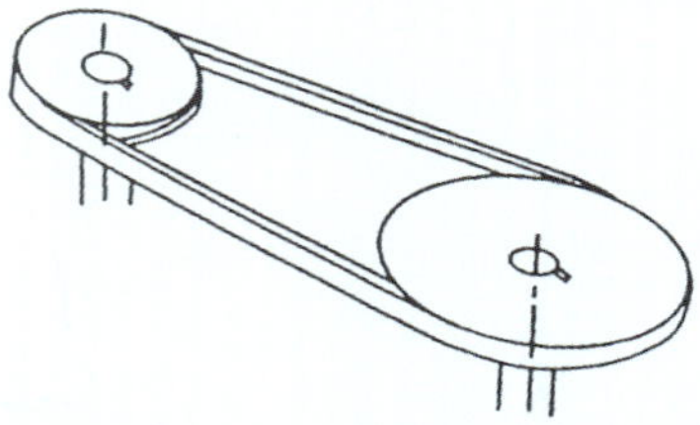		
D 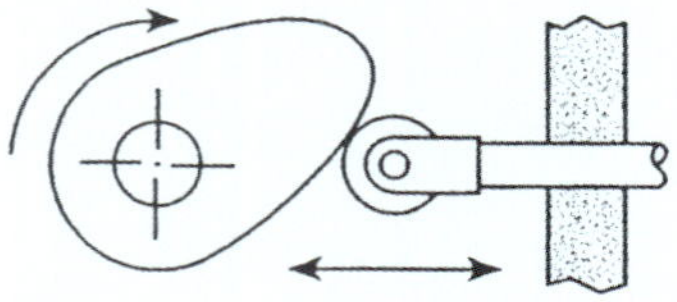		
E 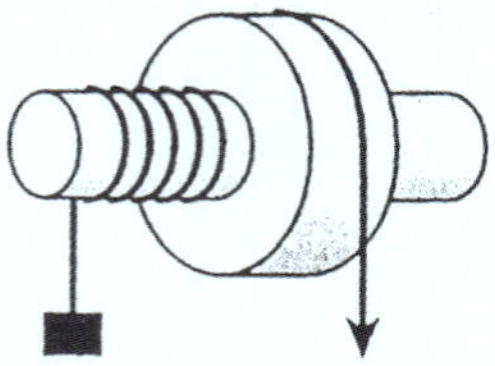		

CCEA GCSE Technology & Design Past Paper, Higher Tier, Summer 2005, © CCEA

3. Sketch a copy of Figure 3, which shows a wheelbarrow in use. The wheelbarrow is a practical example of a lever.

Figure 3

(a) Clearly mark and label on your copy of Figure 3 the fulcrum point of the wheelbarrow. [2]

(b) State the class of lever represented by the wheelbarrow. [2]

(c) The body of the wheelbarrow in Figure 3 is made from aluminum. State two reasons for using aluminum for the body of the wheelbarrow. [2]

Question taken from CCEA's GCSE Technology and Design Foundation Tier Paper (Summer 2005)
For copyright reasons the image in Figure 3 has replaced the one from the CCEA past paper.

4. The bottle opener, shovel and see-saw shown in Figure 4 can all be classified as types of levers.

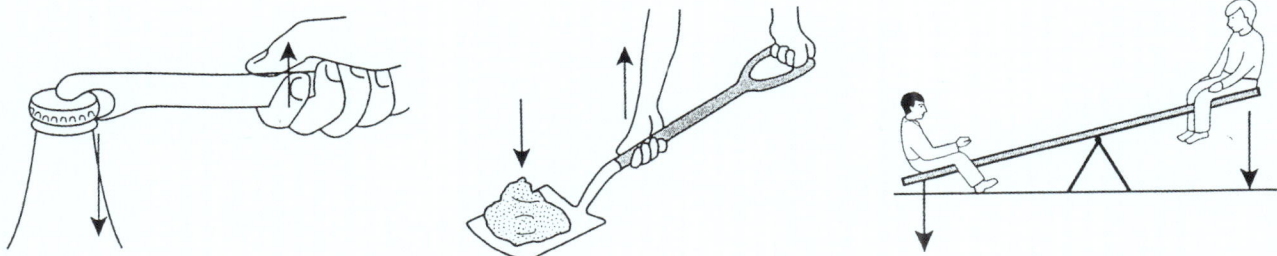

Figure 4

(a) Sketch a copy of Figure 4 and clearly mark and label the fulcrum point on each drawing. [3]

(b) Identify the class of lever shown in each case. [3]

      (i) Bottle opener

      (ii) Shovel

      (iii) See-saw

CCEA GCSE Technology & Design Past Paper, Higher Tier, Summer 2004, © CCEA

5. Figure 5 shows gear wheels used in a child's activity centre. Wheel A can be turned by a handle. Draw four circles to represent the gear wheels in Figure 5.

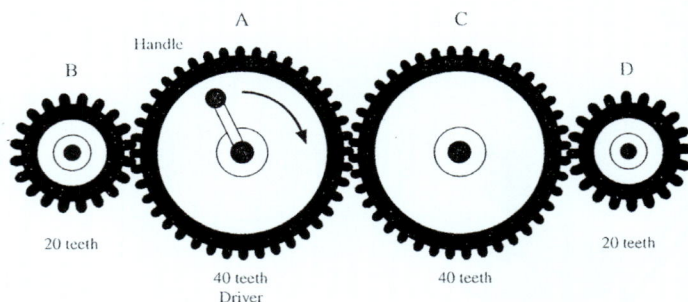

Figure 5

(a) When the driver wheel A is rotated as shown, mark on your copy of Figure 5:
- The direction of rotation of wheel B. [1]
- The direction of rotation of wheel D. [1]

(b) When the driver wheel A is rotated at 60 rev/min calculate the speed of:
- Wheel B [1]
- Wheel D [1]

(c) Write down which of the gears wheels A, B, C or D is called an idler gear. [1]

CCEA GCSE Technology & Design Past Paper, Foundation Tier, Summer 2007, © CCEA

1D COMPUTER CONTROL SYSTEMS

It is important that you have knowledge and understanding of how computer control systems work as you may design a product in T&D that requires computer control. You are now aware from previous sections in the book that a system requires an input, process and output.

Input	→	Process	→	Output

Remember – An *input* to a system will cause the system to do something.

The *process* part of a system accepts the input and makes the output happen.

The *output* of a system will react to the process.

CHECK YOUR LEARNING

Can you recall any examples of devices used for inputs, processing and outputs?

COMPUTER CONTROL SYSTEMS

A computer control system enables you to control external devices such as motors, buzzers, solenoids and lamps to perform very precise output functions.

Again all computer control systems are broken down into:

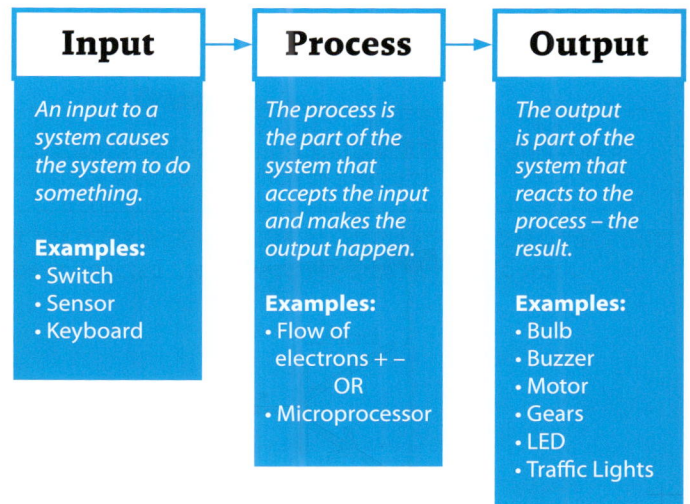

Input	→	Process	→	Output

Input
An input to a system causes the system to do something.

Examples:
• Switch
• Sensor
• Keyboard

Process
The process is the part of the system that accepts the input and makes the output happen.

Examples:
• Flow of electrons + – OR
• Microprocessor

Output
The output is part of the system that reacts to the process – the result.

Examples:
• Bulb
• Buzzer
• Motor
• Gears
• LED
• Traffic Lights

Example:

Input
Keyboard

Process
Microprocessor

Output
Traffic Lights

The following products contain microprocessors:

• Computers
• Washing Machines
• Televisions
• Calculators
• Mobile phones
• Remote control

As with all systems, there are some advantages and disadvantages to be aware of with computer control systems:

Advantages
- They respond faster than humans.
- Rarely fail and can be replaced easily.
- Computer does the processing, the hard work.

Disadvantages
- High initial investment in computers.
- Job losses as computers replace humans.

QUESTIONS & ANSWERS

Q. What is the main advantage of computer control?

A. The main advantage of computer control is that the computer does the hard work, the processing, if you provide the input and the output.

CHECK YOUR LEARNING

1. What three things do all computer control systems need?
2. What does each of these things do within the control system?
3. List four possible inputs to a control system.
4. What part of a computer system does the processing?
5. List four possible outputs of a control system.
6. What is a computer control system?
7. List some products that use a microprocessor.

To make your computer process the input and perform the output you will need to use a piece of software.

Hardware

Hardware is the computer equipment such as the physical machine, including the keyboard, mouse, processing unit, printer and cables.

Software

Software is the computer programs that run on the computer such as Microsoft Word, Excel, Powerpoint, Logicator or games.

QUESTIONS & ANSWERS

Q. What is computer control used for?

A. Computer control is used for controlling and monitoring.

Examples:
- Burglar alarm systems
- Temperature control in green houses

Using an interface

You must know the importance of using an interface as a protection and connection device. An interface has two functions in a computer control system:

1. To connect your input and output devices to your computer you must plug them into an *interface* (control box) first so they can be controlled by the computer software you write your control program on.

2. It is also essential to use an interface to protect you and the computer from damage should you make a wrong connection.

CHECK YOUR LEARNING

1. What is an interface?
2. Why is an interface needed?

BUILDING A FLOWCHART ON LOGICATOR

LOGICATOR is the software used in school to design flowcharts to control external devices (outputs).

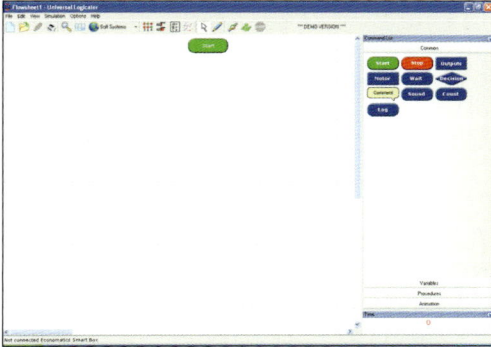

If you were writing a program on Logicator, this is what the screen would look like. The command cells are listed on the right and easily dragged onto the centre of the sheet to begin designing the control program.

To design flow charts you must use the function cells below:

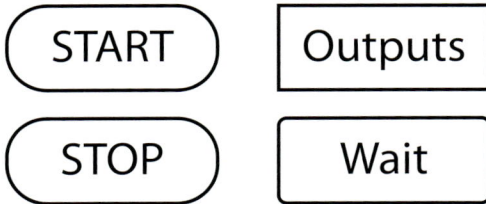

START   Outputs

STOP   Wait

Example: This flow chart will enable a red bulb to turn on then wait five seconds before turning off.

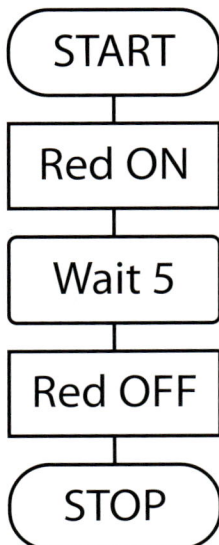

START

Red ON

Wait 5

Red OFF

STOP

Output Bit Patterns

As you draw the flowchart using the function cells, they have to be programmed by you. A control panel will appear for each input and output function cell drawn. This allows you to switch inputs and outputs ON and OFF. The numbers 0–7 represent the 8 possible input and output ports on an interface box that could be controlled by the computer software. 0 = OFF and 1 = ON. For example, if three lights were to be computer controlled they could be plugged into the output ports of the interface like this:

- A green light is plugged into Port 0 and is OFF as the corresponding digit is 0.
- A red light is plugged into Port 1 and is OFF as the corresponding digit is 0.
- A yellow light is plugged into Port 2 and is programmed to come ON as the corresponding digit is 1.

This is simple computer programming and the Output Bit Pattern would look like this:

Output ports for RED ON

		R	Y	G			
0	1	2	3	4	5	6	7
0	0	0	0	0	1	0	0

Output ports for RED OFF

		R	Y	G			
0	1	2	3	4	5	6	7
0	0	0	0	0	0	0	0

A **sequence** is the simplest kind of control system. It switches output devices on and off in any order, and for any length of time.

CHECK YOUR LEARNING

1. What is software?
2. What is hardware?
3. Name the software often used for computer control in schools.

ACTIVITY

Using the software package Logicator, complete the following designs of flowcharts on screen:

- Design a flowchart to enable a buzzer to come on for six seconds before turning off.
- Design a flowchart to enable a green bulb to come on for ten seconds before turning off.
- Design a flowchart to enable a red and yellow bulb to come on for ten seconds before turning off.

61

Programmable control

It is important that you can apply your new knowledge and understanding of computer control systems and software to construct programs. These programs will control input and output devices through an interface, which contain the following:

- decisions
- loop
- time delay
- increment/decrement

Decisions

A decision cell can be used to make decisions within a control flowchart by:

- Using inputs such as switches or sensors
- Counting
- Timing

Example:

This flowchart will make the 'NEXT PLAYER' sign flash red and green until somebody comes along and presses the 'GO' switch to play the game.

Loop

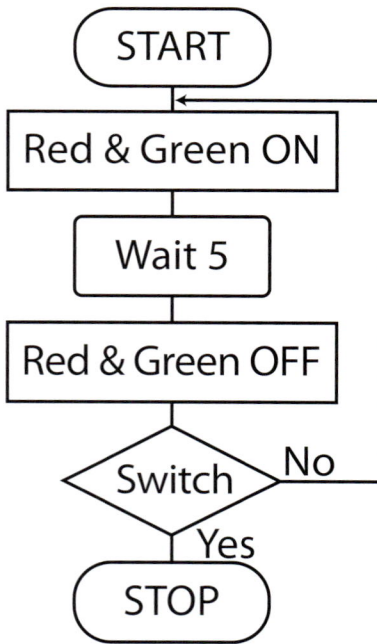

This flowchart is using a switch. A switch has to be programmed into a decision cell because otherwise the programme will run continuously. This is an example of a loop. The programme is deciding whether a switch has been pressed or not pressed. If the switch is pressed, the programme makes the decision to stop running the flowchart programme. A sensor could also be used as an input device.

Timing

A timer can be used to program *time delays* into a flowchart, to make something happen precisely for a number of seconds. If a timer is being used the computer must be told each time to reset at 0 seconds.

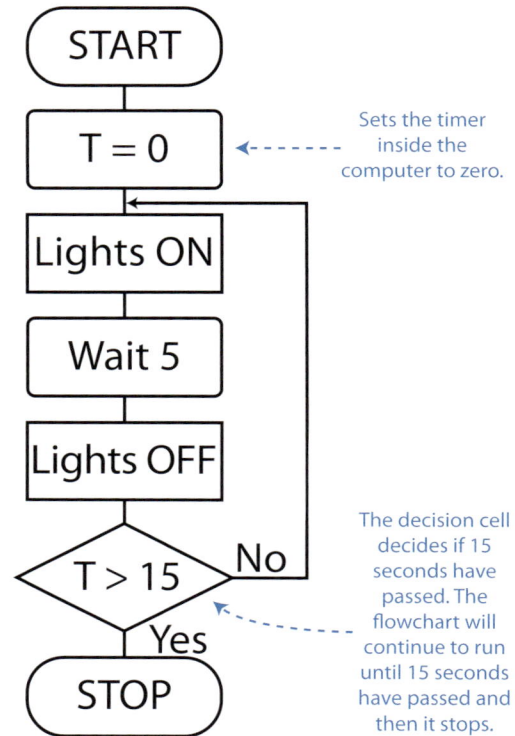

Sets the timer inside the computer to zero.

The decision cell decides if 15 seconds have passed. The flowchart will continue to run until 15 seconds have passed and then it stops.

Counting

A counter can be used to program increments and decrements into a flowchart. This allows you to program the flowchart to make something happen precisely and repeat it a set number of times.

Increment is the term recognised by the program to count up in 1s. INC is short for increment. *Decrement* is a term recognised by the program to count down in 1s. DEC is short for decrement. Each complete flow of the program will be counted by the program as 1. When the flowchart has repeated the desired number of times the program continues to the STOP cell. If a counter is being used the computer must be programmed each time to start the counter 0.

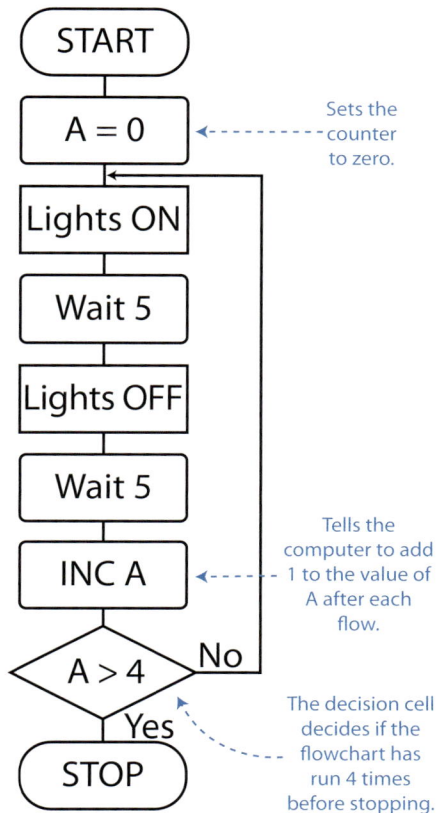

Flowchart

```
        START
          |
        A = 0   <---- Sets the counter to zero.
          |
      Lights ON
          |
       Wait 5
          |
      Lights OFF
          |
       Wait 5
          |
        INC A   <---- Tells the computer to add 1 to the value of A after each flow.
          |
       A > 4  --No-->
        Yes          The decision cell decides if the flowchart has run 4 times before stopping.
          |
        STOP
```

ACTIVITY

Design the following flowcharts to consolidate your understanding of how to use decision cells as inputs, timers and counters:

1. Make a yellow light flash on for 0.5 seconds and off for 0.5 seconds until a switch is pressed.
2. Make a yellow light flash on and off for 0.5 seconds and then a green light flash on and off for 0.5 seconds for a total of 20 seconds.
3. Make a yellow light flash on and off for 0.5 seconds and then a green light flash on and off for 0.5 seconds for a total of 15 times.

RECAP

- **Loops** are used for making parts of a program **repeat**.
- **Decision cells** are used for making **decisions** within a program.
- **Timers** are used for making something happen for a number of **seconds**.
- **Counters** are used for making something happen for a number of **times**.
- Switches, sensors, timers and counters are all programmed into decision cells.

KEY WORD CHECK

Below are some key words. You need to be able to explain each term or key word, identify the physical appearance of components, identify and sketch symbols, and use them were appropriate for computer control. Remember to add these words to your glossary.

- **Input – Process – Output**
- **Interface**
- **Use of flowcharts**
- **Symbols of flowchart**
- **Loop**
- **Decision cell**
- **Timer**
- **Counter**

EXAM FOCUS

Complete the following past paper questions to help consolidate your learning and practice your exam skills.

1. (a) Write down the name of **one** application that uses computer control. [2]

   (b) Write down the names of **two** household products that use microprocessors in their control system. [4]

   (c) Modern computer programs often use the binary digit system. State the two digits used. [2]

   (d) Flow charts or diagrams are sometimes used to give clear step by step procedures in computer control.

Make a copy of Figure 1. Fill in the table by writing down the name and application for each of the symbols. The first one has been done for you. [8]

Figure 1

Symbol	Name	Application
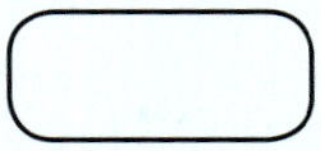 (rounded rectangle)	Terminal	A point for a sequence, eg start, stop, etc.
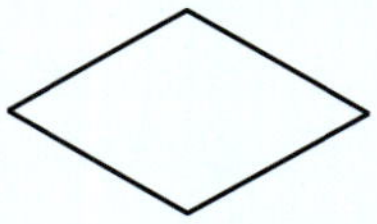 (diamond)		
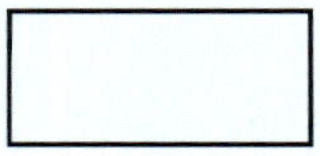 (rectangle)		

CCEA GCSE Technology & Design Past Paper, Higher Tier, Summer 2001, © CCEA

2. **(a) Figure 2 shows the head of a robot. The eyes of the robot are to be controlled by two electric motors A and B.**

When the sensor in the nose of the robot is covered, both eyes rotate in a clockwise direction for four seconds. The program then stops.

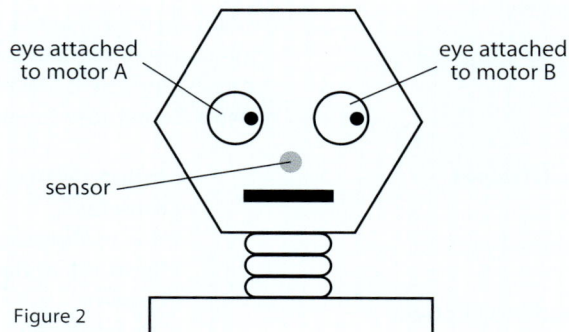

eye attached to motor A

eye attached to motor B

sensor

Figure 2

Make a copy of the flowchart in Figure 3 and complete it to show the process. [4]

(b) The program in 2 (a) is to be changed so that when the sensor is covered motor A comes on for three seconds.

Then motor B comes on to rotate the other eye for three seconds. The program then stops.

Make a copy of the flowchart in Figure 4 and complete it to show this process. [7]

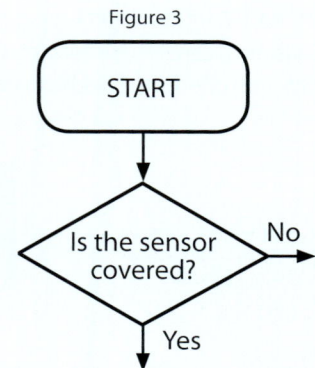

Figure 3

START

Is the sensor covered?   No

Yes

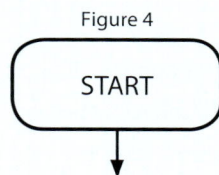

Figure 4

START

CCEA GCSE Technology & Design Past Paper, Unit 1, Technology and Design Core, Summer 2011, © CCEA
For copyright reasons the drawing in Figure 2 has replaced the one from the CCEA past paper.

PNEUMATIC SYSTEMS AND CONTROL

It is important to have an understanding of how a pneumatic control system works in case you design a product in T&D that requires one. Pneumatic systems use the stored (potential) energy in **compressed air** to do useful work. Air is compressed (pressurised) by a compressor, which is driven by an electric motor or an internal combustion engine. These pneumatic systems are commonly found in industry, where they are used to automate production. Factories are plumbed with compressed air from a central compressor.

From studying other types of control systems earlier in the book you know that a system requires an input, process and output. The following is an example of a pneumatic system:

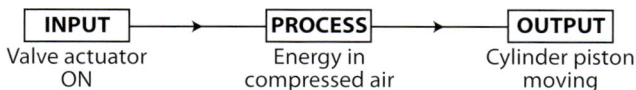

INPUT	PROCESS	OUTPUT
Valve actuator ON	Energy in compressed air	Cylinder piston moving

In this example, valves are used to control the routing of the compressed air through pipes in a pneumatic system. Think of a valve as a switch that can be turned on and off by the **actuator** on it. When the actuator of a valve is pressed (input) the air is routed into cylinders. The cylinders convert the energy in the compressed air (process) into linear motion (output), which is movement in a straight line. The used compressed air is released as exhausted air into the atmosphere.

VALVES

Valves are pneumatic components used in pneumatic systems to control the switching and routing of air. Valves are used to control both the flow of compressed air in and out of cylinders and the flow of exhaust air out into the atmosphere. The two main types of valves used in pneumatic circuits are the 3/2 valve and the 5/2 valve. *Note: You are only required to know about a 3/2 valve at this point.*

3/2 valves

3/2 valves are used to control single acting cylinders. Single acting cylinders only have one connection or input for air. The '3' represents the valve's three ports and the '2' represents its two states. The two states are actuated or not actuated, which is basically on and off. The three ports have different functions.

- **Port 1:** the main air supply is connected here.
- **Port 2:** is used for connecting the input air from the valve to the next component in a circuit or for directing the flow of exhausted air towards Port 3.
- **Port 3:** is used for exhausted air to escape into the atmosphere.

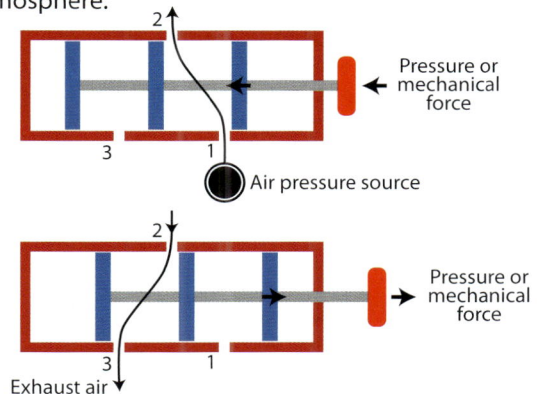

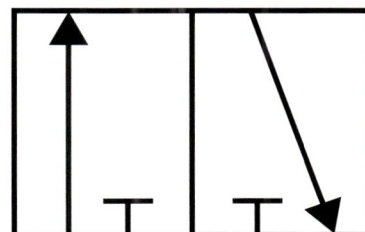

This side of the symbol is the valve **actuated**.

Main air is flowing in at Port 1 to Port 2 and no air is being exhausted at Port 3.

This side of the symbol is the valve **not actuated**.

Main air is not flowing in at Port 1 and used air is flowing from Port 2 to be exhausted at Port 3.

Actuators

Think of a valve as a switch that can be turned on and off by the actuator on it. This is known as actuating, which means to switch it on or off. Valves can be actuated by different methods:

Push

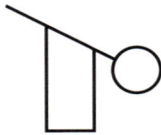
Lever

Roller

Plunger

A real life roller actuator on a 3/2 valve.

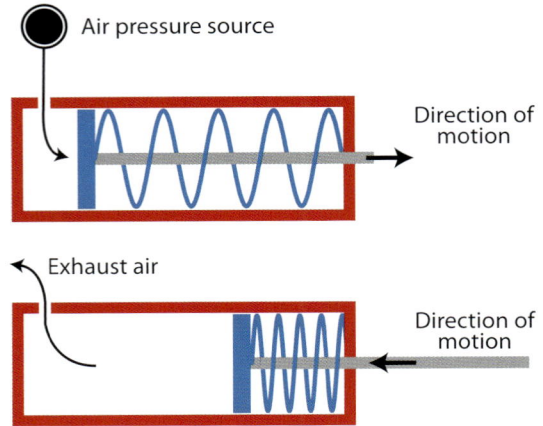
Air pressure source

Direction of motion

Exhaust air

Direction of motion

CYLINDERS

Linear motion

Linear motion is movement in a straight line. The energy in compressed air is converted into linear motion by cylinders. The air enters the cylinder and pushes a piston from one end of the cylinder to the other. There are two main types of cylinder: **single acting** and **double acting** (SAC and DAC).

A single acting cylinder only has one connection for air, whilst a double acting has two. *Note: you are only required to know about a single acting cylinder at this point.*

Single acting cylinders

In a single acting cylinder compressed air enters through the one air connection. The piston is forced out of the cylinder by the pressure of the compressed air. When the compressed air supply is removed, the force of the spring inside the single acting cylinder drives the piston back inside the cylinder and the used air escapes.

Real life

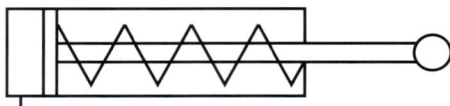
Symbol

Speed control

Controlling speed in a circuit can be achieved by introducing further components:

Unidirectional flow regulator

Reservoir

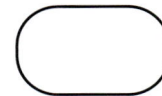
Spring return

Time delays can be built into pneumatic circuits by using a reservoir along a section of pipe, as shown in the example. If the valve is actuated, compressed air flows through a **unidirectional flow regulator** and builds up in the **reservoir**. This increases the time needed to build up enough pressure to allow the circuit to continue functioning.

Once the pressure has built up it will send the pilot signal, which is air under pressure, into the second valve, causing the cylinder to activate. The stored air in the reservoir can exhaust quickly once the first valve is switched off, as the unidirectional flow regulator has been used. This causes the piston to return to its original position almost immediately.

Example:

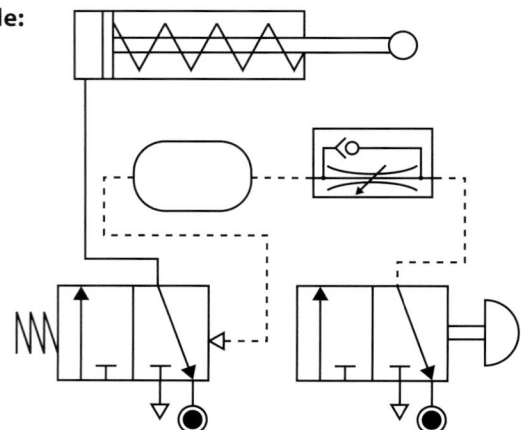

Logic circuits

Combining valves together allows us to produce *logic circuits*. The simplest of these is an AND circuit.

AND circuit

If valves are connected in series, as shown in the example below, the cylinder can only be operated if the first valve and the second valve are **both** actuated.

Example:

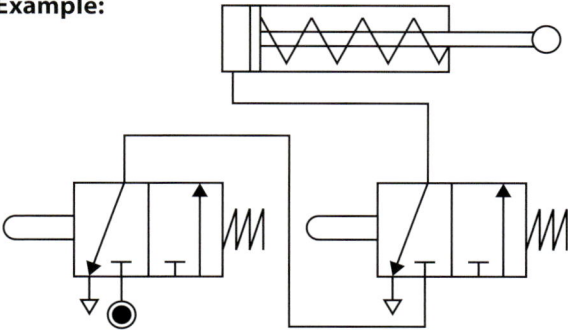

OR circuit

To build an **OR** circuit the outputs of two valves are combined with a **shuttle valve**.

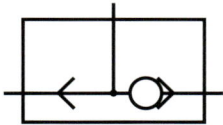

The shuttle valve allows compressed air to be routed from either the first *or* second valve, depending on which one has been actuated. If the pipes were connected without a shuttle valve and one 3/2 valve was actuated but the other was not, the compressed air would escape as exhaust air through the valve that was not actuated. The cylinder in an OR circuit is activated when either the first valve *or* the second valve is actuated.

Example:

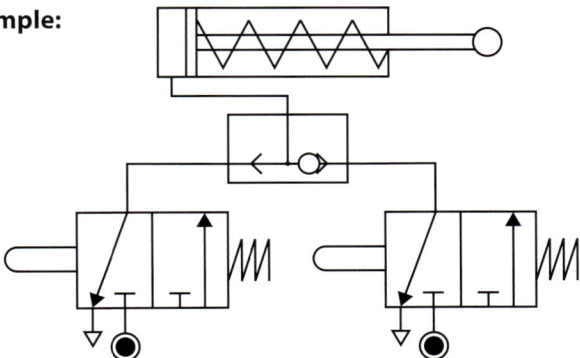

In school you may have an opportunity to build pneumatic circuits on a platform using different real life pneumatic components that are available in a kit. The components are bolted with plastic bolts to the platform for safety. Red and blue plastic tubing is inserted into the components for air to flow through the circuit. The main air supply comes from the compressor and travels through a manifold bolted to the platform. The manifold is used to safely route the compressed air to the pneumatic components of the circuit. Red tubing pipes are used to represent where the main air is flowing and blue pipes are used for air exhausted from a component. You must check that all the piping is securely fixed into the components before turning on the compressed air.

SAFETY

Compressed air can be very dangerous. If it enters the body it can kill, so keep it away from your eyes, nose, mouth, etc, and never use your fingers to see if compressed air is present. Also keep your fingers away from live pneumatic systems, as pneumatic pistons can move with great force and speed. Finally, always wear safety goggles when working with pneumatic circuits and check that all the connections are secure before connecting your circuit to the compressed air supply.

KEY WORD CHECK

Below are some key words. You need to be able to explain each term or key word, identify the physical appearance of components, identify and sketch symbols, and use them were appropriate for pneumatic control. Remember to add these words to your glossary.

- **Compressed air**
- **Single acting cylinder**
- **3/2 valve**
- **Valve actuators**
- **Shuttle valve**
- **OR circuit**
- **AND circuit**
- **Flow regulator**
- **Safety**

Complete the following past paper questions to help consolidate your learning and practice your exam skills.

1. **(a) Make a copy of Figure 1, which shows the symbols for methods of operation of valves.**

   Complete the table by inserting the correct name for each symbol from Figure 2. [4]

Figure 1

Symbol	Name of symbol

Figure 2

Plunger
Roller trip
Lever
Push button

(b) Make a copy of Figure 3, which shows part of a pneumatic circuit that is used to apply brakes to a wheel.

   Complete Figure 3 to show how the brakes could be applied. [3]

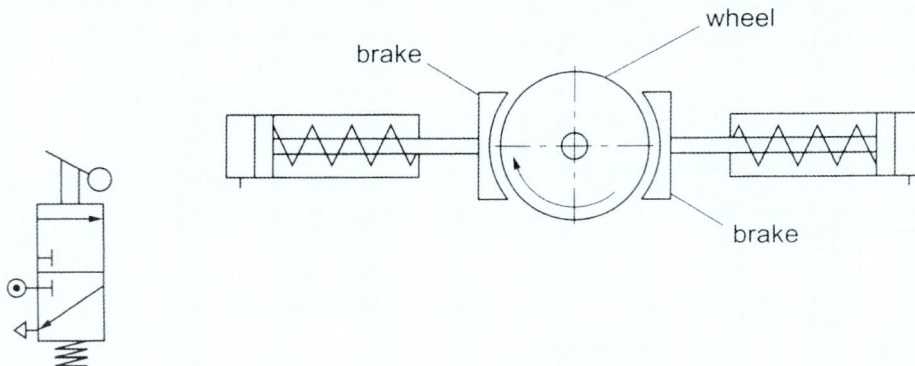

CCEA GCSE Technology & Design Past Paper, Unit 1, Technology and Design Core, Summer 2011, © CCEA
For copyright reasons the symbols in Figure 1 have replaced those from the CCEA past paper.

2. Figure 4 shows a pneumatic circuit.

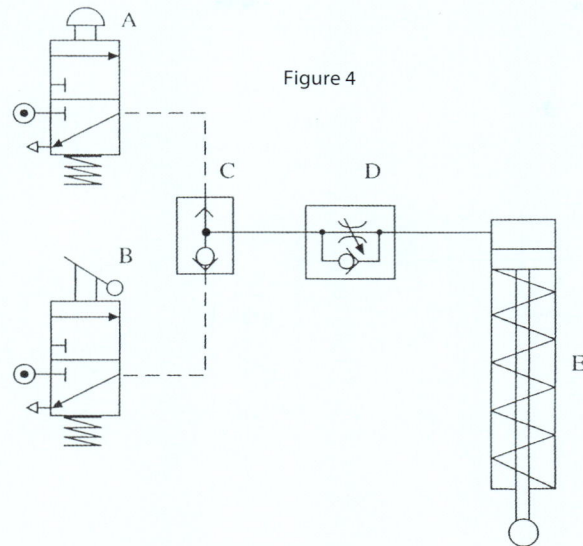

Figure 4

Make a copy of Figure 5 and complete the table by inserting the correct letter from Figure 4 for each pneumatic component. [5]

Figure 5

Pneumatic Component	Reference Letter
Shuttle valve	
3/2 Valve button operated	
Single acting cylinder	
3/2 valve lever operated	
Flow regulator	

CCEA GCSE Technology & Design Past Paper, Foundation Tier, Summer 2003, © CCEA

3. **Look at Figure 6. It shows a pneumatic cylinder which is used to stamp parcels.**

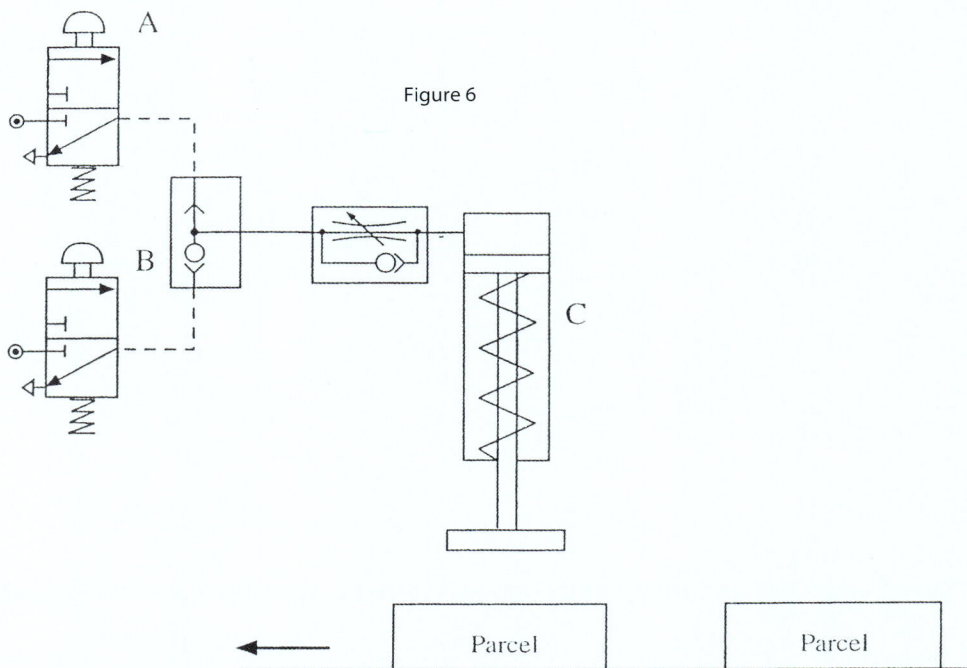

Figure 6

For each of the following statements, choose either A or B to complete the sentence correctly. [4]

(i)   Valve A is:

   A. Operated by a button and reset by a spring.
   B. Operated by a roller and reset by a spring.

(ii) In cylinder C the return stroke is caused by:

   A. Compressed air.
   B. A spring.

(iii) To stamp a parcel:

   A. Valve A and valve B must be operated.
   B. Valve A or valve B must be operated.

(iv) The type of cylinder shown at C is:

   A. A single acting cylinder.
   B. A double acting cylinder.

CCEA GCSE Technology & Design Past Paper, Higher Tier, Summer 2006, © CCEA

4. **Pneumatic systems use the energy stored in compressed air to do the work.**
   By controlling the supply of the air to pneumatic cylinders, movement can be produced. Describe how you would construct a pneumatic circuit using a platform and discrete components. In your answer make reference to the attachment of the components to the platform, the connection of the piping and the testing of the circuit. Include any specific safety precautions for this process. [10]

CCEA GCSE Technology & Design Past Paper, Unit 1, Technology and Design Core, Summer 2011, © CCEA

UNIT 2

CONTROL

This unit is a choice for students. In this chapter you will be studying ONE of the following:

○ **Electronic and Microelectronic Control Systems**

○ **Mechanical and Pneumatic Control Systems**

Your school will advise you on your chosen element of study.

2A ELECTRONIC AND MICROELECTRONIC CONTROL SYSTEMS

BASIC ELECTRONIC CONCEPTS

Electric currents flow through wires very easily as they are metal (usually copper). There are lots of electrons within the metal. These come from the metal's atoms but are able to move around in the spaces between the atoms. The electrons are charge carriers and when they flow in the wire there is an electric current. The atoms of conducting materials let their electrons go free very easily. These free electrons can then carry electric charge. Non-conducting materials do not let their electrons go free so there are no free electrons to carry charge.

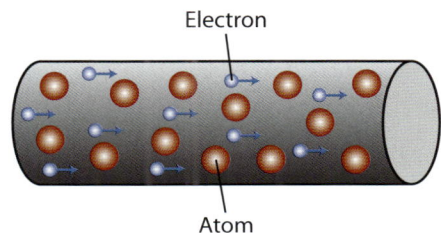

Electron

Atom

Current will flow as long as there is **positive charge** at one end of the material and **negative charge** at the other. The rate at which the charge is transferred from positive to negative is called the current. Therefore current can be defined as the number of electrons passing a given point in one second. An electron only moves if given energy and it gets its energy from a battery or power pack. A battery is made of cells that contain chemicals. Energy is stored in the cell as chemical energy.

In an electric circuit the chemical energy is gradually turned into electrical energy, which creates a force that moves the electrons. This force is referred to as **EMF (electromotive force)**. The EMF of a battery creates a potential difference between its positive and negative terminals, making the current flow.

OHMS LAW

$$I = \frac{V}{R} \qquad R = \frac{V}{I} \qquad V = I \times R$$

Current

Current is the flow of electric charge, the number of electrons passing a point in one second. Current is measured in **Amperes** (A) amps. Milliamps is used to measure small currents.

Resistance

Resistance is when a material resists the flow of electrons. Resistance is measured in **Ohms** (Ω).

1,000 Ohms (Ω) = 1 Kilohm (kΩ)
1,000 Kilohms = 1 Megohm (MΩ)

Resistors are given multipliers of:
R = times one   820 Ω = 820 R
K = times a thousand   1,000 Ω = 1 K
M = times a million   1,500,000 Ω = 1.5 M

Voltage

Voltage is the pressure causing the electrons in a circuit to move. Voltage is measured in **Volts** (V).

Capacitance

Capacitors are used in electronic circuits to store an electrical charge. Capacitance is the ability of a device to store an electrical charge. The unit of capacitance is **Farad** (F). The capacitance value and the working voltage are printed on the capacitor.

1 microfarad (1 µF) =	millionth of a Farad 10-6 F (0.000001 F)
1 nanofarad (1 nF) =	thousand-millionth of a Farad (0.000000001 F)
1 picofarad (1 pF) =	million-millionth of a Farad (0.000000000001 F)

Connection of capacitors in series

They work the opposite to resistors and the overall value of the capacitance will reduce. The formula to calculate total capacitance in a series circuit is:

$$\frac{1}{C_T} = \frac{1}{C_1} + \frac{1}{C_2} + \frac{1}{C_3}$$

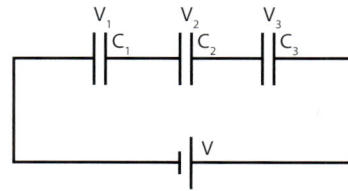

Connection of capacitors in parallel

When capacitors are connected in parallel, the result is the sum of all the capacitors. The formula to calculate total capacitance in a parallel circuit is:

$$C_T = C_1 + C_2 + C_3$$

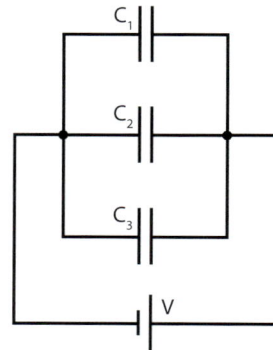

CHECK YOUR LEARNING

1. Write a definition for each of the following terms and state the units they are measured in:

   - current
   - resistance
   - voltage
   - capacitance

2. State the formulas derived from Ohms law for current, resistance and voltage.

3. State the formulas to calculate total capacitance in a series circuit and a parallel circuit.

RESISTORS IN PARALLEL

When two or more resistors are connected in parallel, the voltage across each resistor is the same and the current flowing through each separate resistor is dependent upon the resistance. The total resistance is always smaller than smallest individual resistance.

The circuit below shows two resistors connected in parallel to a 6 V battery.

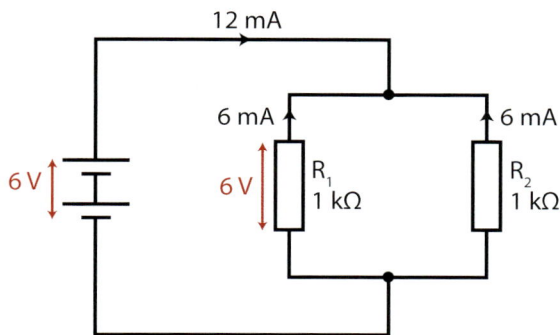

Parallel circuits always provide alternative pathways for current flow.

The total resistance is calculated from:

$$R_{total} = \frac{R_1 \times R_2}{R_1 + R_2} \quad \text{or} \quad \frac{1}{R_{total}} = \frac{1}{R_1} + \frac{1}{R_2}$$

The current is calculated from:

$$I = \frac{V}{R} = \frac{6}{0.5 \text{ k}\Omega} = 12 \text{ mA}$$

QUESTIONS & ANSWERS

Q. What is the total resistance in the circuit above?
A.
$$R_{total} = \frac{1 \times 1}{1 + 1} = \frac{1}{2} = 0.5 \text{ k}\Omega$$

Q. How does this current compare with the current for the series circuit?
A. It is more. This is sensible. Connecting resistors in parallel provides alternative pathways and makes it easier for current to flow.

Q. How much current flows through each resistor?
A. Because they have equal values, the current divides, with 6 mA flowing through R_1, and 6 mA through R_2.

Q. What is the voltage across R_1?
A. $V = IR = 6 \text{ mA} \times 1 \text{ k}\Omega = 6 \text{ V}$

This is the same as the power supply voltage. The top end of R_1 is connected to the positive terminal of the battery, while the bottom end of R_1 is connected to the negative terminal of the battery. With no other components in the way, it follows that the voltage across R_1 must be 6 V.

Q. What is the voltage across R_2?
A. It is also 6 V.

KEY POINT: When components are connected in parallel, the voltage across them is the same.

Q. If two resistors are combined in parallel and they have values of 2 KΩ and 2 KΩ, determine the value of their combined resistances.
A. Use either of the formulas opposite to calculate Total Resistance of resistors in parallel:

$R_1 = 2 \text{ k}\Omega$
$R_2 = 2 \text{ k}\Omega$

$$R_{total} = \frac{R_1 \times R_2}{R_1 + R_2} \qquad R_{total} = \frac{2 \text{ k}\Omega \times 2 \text{ k}\Omega}{2 \text{ k}\Omega + 2 \text{ k}\Omega} = \frac{4 \text{ k}\Omega}{4 \text{ k}\Omega} = 1 \text{ k}\Omega$$

Now use the other formula to calculate the total resistance to check if the answer is the same.

Voltage is also known as potential difference (pd). With two resistors in parallel, the potential difference across each resistor is the same as the potential difference across the battery. Ohms law still applies: $I = V \div R$

PULL-UP AND PULL-DOWN RESISTORS

Pull-up resistors are typically used in electronic circuits. Their function in a logic circuit is to make sure that logic system inputs remain stable (at the correct level) should some devices be removed from the circuit. These resistors 'pull' or 'raise' the voltage of the wire to a default or pre-determined voltage level. If the removal of a device from the system changes the voltage of the wire to another voltage, the pull-up resistor, which is left deliberately weak, will not oppose it and therefore prevent excessive current from passing through the circuit. Pull-down resistors are used to pull the voltage down to a pre-determined level. If nothing is connected to Pin 1 the input value fluctuates, meaning it varies up and down but most gates will tend to move towards a high state. This is a very weak state and the input can be caused to go low by any electrical noise.

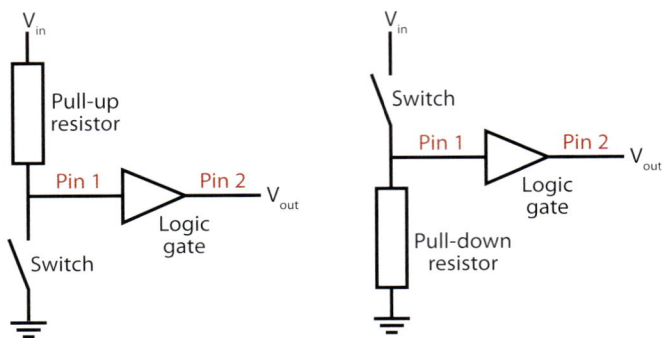

The input state at Pin 1 is low when switch is ON (closed). It is also stable as it is connected to an electrical potential, which is the ground in this case.

The input at Pin 1 is susceptible to electrical problems when switch is OFF (open). The wires connected to Pin 1 act like small antennas, allowing electrical noise in and causing confusion, which can cause the Pin to switch to the wrong state. To rectify this problem and keep Pin 1 in a steady state, Pin 1 needs to be connected to an electrical potential V_{in} that can be removed when the switch is closed.

NEAREST PREFERRED VALUES

E12 series is the name given to resistors with a tolerance of ± 10%
E24 series is the name given to resistors with a tolerance of ± 5%

Over 100 years ago, the Electronic Industries Association in co-operation with other electronic organisations first established the nearest *'preferred value system'* of standard values for resistors. At this time tolerances within manufacturing processes were poor (50%, 20%, 10% …) and the industry decided that the value for components should be selected on the basis of the tolerances with which they could be manufactured. For example, if a 100 Ω resistor was required, the industry knew they could manufacture it with 10% tolerance. If a 108 Ω resistor was required, there was no point in trying to manufacture such a resistor, since 108 Ω falls within the tolerance limit of the 100 Ω resistor. Extending this approach, the manufacturers decided upon the preferred values (at 10% tolerance level, E12 series) for resistors between 100 and 1000 Ω. Thus 10% tolerance resistors were generally used. Today, however, 5% tolerance high precision resistors (E24) are affordable to manufacture and used as the standard resistor in modern electronic circuits.

Using the Resistor Colour Code to calculate resistance

The 4-band code is used for marking low precision resistors with 5% and 10% tolerances. Resistors with 20% tolerance only have 3 colour bands.

Band Colour	Band 1	Band 2	Band 3 No of zeros or multiplier		Band 4 Tolerance
Black	0	0	-	$\times 10^0$	
Brown	1	1	0	$\times 10^1$	
Red	2	2	00	$\times 10^2$	
Orange	3	3	000	$\times 10^3$	
Yellow	4	4	0000	$\times 10^4$	
Green	5	5	00000	$\times 10^5$	
Blue	6	6	000000	$\times 10^6$	
Violet	7	7	0000000	$\times 10^7$	
Grey	8	8	00000000	$\times 10^8$	
White	9	9	000000000	$\times 10^9$	
Gold					± 5%
Silver					± 10%

Identifying the value will become easy with a little practice, as there are only a few simple rules to remember:

- The **first band** gives the **first digit**.
- The **second band** gives the **second digit**.
- The **third band** indicates the **number of zeros** or **multiplier**.
- The fourth band is used to shows the tolerance (precision) of the resistor.

This resistor has **red** (2), **green** (5), **orange** (3 zeros) and a **gold** band.

So its value is: 25,000 = 25 K ± 5%

On circuit diagrams the tolerance is usually omitted and the value is written 25 K.

The **tolerance** band (the deviation from the specified value) is usually spaced away from the others, or it is a little bit wider. A color is assigned to each tolerance: **gold** is 5% and **silver** is 10%. 20% resistors have only three colour bands – the tolerance band is missing.

ACTIVITY

In the questions below, the letters denote the following:

V = Voltmeter, for measuring the potential difference in volts, V

A = Ammeter, for measuring current in amps, A

R = Resistor, measured in ohms, Ω

This is a digital voltmeter for giving readings of potential difference in volts. It can be connected to a circuit to give digital readings.

1. (a) What is the resistance of R?

   (b) If the resistance of R was doubled, calculate how much current would flow?

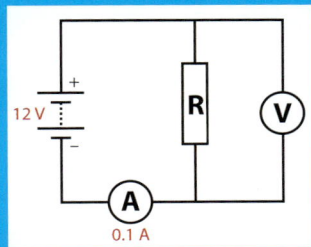

2. (a) In this circuit, how much current would flow?

   (b) If the resistance was reduced to 50 Ω, what reading would be shown on the ammeter?

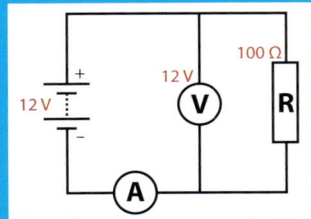

3. (a) What is the voltage across the 1000 Ω resistor in this circuit?

   (b) If the voltage across the 1000 Ω resistor was doubled, what amount of current would flow?

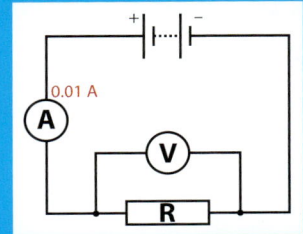

4. (a) Work out the current flowing through each of the resistors in the circuit.

   (b) What will the ammeter read?

   (c) Are the resistors in series or parallel in this circuit?

   (d) Calculate the total resistance R_{total} for this circuit.

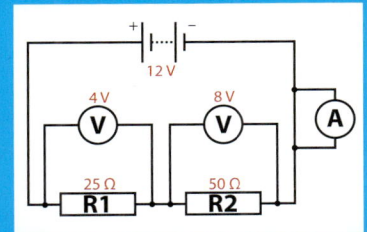

5. A current of 1.2 A flows when 12 V are passed across a 10 Ω resistor (diagram A).

   The current flow will double to 2.4 A when two 10 Ω resistors are connected in parallel. The total resistance provided by R_1 and R_2 when in parallel must be less than 10 Ω. Calculate the total resistance R_{total} (diagram B).

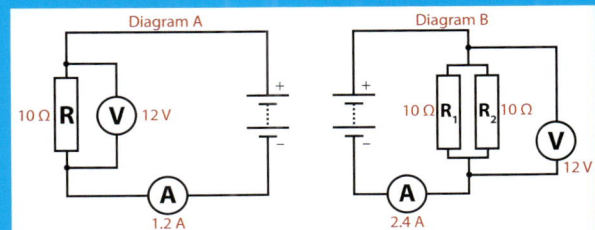

TRANSISTORS (NPN TYPE)

NPN type transistors are components that can act as sensitive electronic switches in a circuit. A NPN transistor is made from a piece of semi-conducting material, usually silicon. It has three areas, a thin area of p-type silicon in between two layers of n-type silicon. The two n-type regions are called the collector (C) and the emitter (E). The p-type area is called the base (B). The three legs of an NPN transistor attach into these areas so are also called the base, collector and emitter. They must be connected in the correct order. Each manufacturer makes its transistors differently, so this order varies depending on who has made it. Every transistor purchased is supplied with information that can be used to identify each leg. When the input at the base of the transistor rises to 0.7 V the transistor switches on the output side and allows current to flow in at the collector and out at the emitter. An output component such as a bulb or buzzer can be switched on.

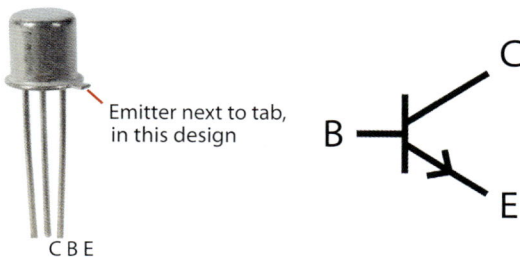

Emitter next to tab, in this design

C B E

NPN type transistors need to be connected with a protective resistor in a circuit to limit the flow of current and protect the transistor from being damaged.

The diagram below shows the two current paths through a transistor. This circuit can be built with two standard red LEDs and any general purpose, low power NPN transistor.

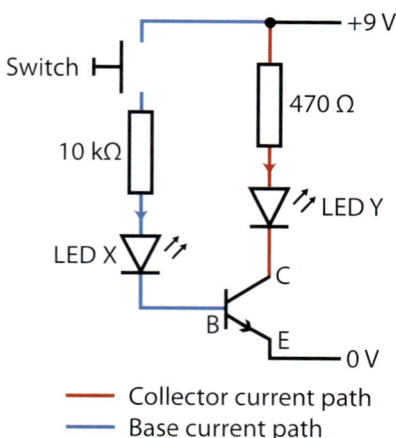

Switch

470 Ω

10 kΩ

LED Y

LED X

C

B

E

+9 V

0 V

—— Collector current path
—— Base current path

When the switch is closed, a small current flows into the base (B) of the transistor. The input at the base of the transistor must rise to 0.7 V for the transistor to switch on the output, which is just sufficient to make LED X glow dimly. This small current is amplified by the transistor to allow a larger current to flow from its collector (C) to its emitter (E). This collector current is large enough to make LED Y glow brightly.

When the switch is open no base current flows, so the transistor switches off the collector current and both LEDs are off.

Transistor off = resistance between collector and emitter is high.

Transistor on = resistance between collector and emitter is low.

In Unit 1B Electronics, you designed circuits that used transistors in sensing circuits for the following situations:

  (i)   A circuit that senses a change in temperature for a blind person.

  (ii) A circuit that will indicate if your house plant dries up.

  (iii) A circuit that will act as a child's night light.

  (iv) A circuit that will automatically activate a fan when the temperature gets too high.

Now you should be able to demonstrate knowledge and understanding of the use of the transistor in switching circuits as well as sensing circuits.

INPUTS

Digital

Analogue

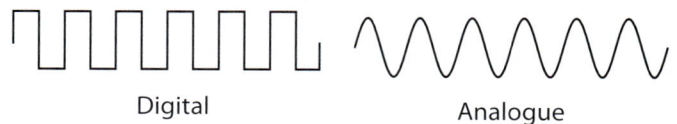

Analogue signals are continuous, whereas digital signals are discrete. Analogue signals are continuously varying. To help you remember the difference between analogue and digital signals here are a few examples:

Light switches

  (a) a light switch that is either on or off is an example of a digital signal .

  (b) a dimmer switch that allows you to vary the light in different degrees of brightness is an example of an analogue signal.

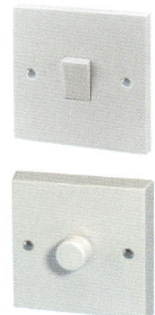

Clocks

a) a clock where the second hand smoothly circles the clock face uses an analogue signal.

b) a clock in which the seconds digits jump as each second passes uses a digital signal.

OUTPUTS

You have covered a lot of information about outputs and output devices in the different control sections you studied throughout Unit 1, Technology and Design Core. To recap, remember the following definition: ***The output of a system will react to the process.*** Output devices you should be familiar with include bulbs, relays, LEDs, motors and buzzers. A seven segment LED is a special type of LED display used for counting and timing. Seven segment displays are used in digital clocks, video recorders and microwave ovens.

ACTIVITY

In the table below there is a list of input devices.

From memory, sketch the symbols and write an explanation of each of these devices.

When you have finished, refer back to 1B, Electronics, pages 41–42 to see how many you got right.

Inputs	Sketch the Symbol
LDR	
Thermistor	
Variable resistor	
Toggle switch*	

* **Note:** All types of switches are input devices.

ACTIVITY

In the table below there is a list of output devices.

From memory, sketch the symbols and write an explanation of each of these devices.

When you have finished, refer back to 1B Electronics, page 41 to see how many you got right.

Finally, read over the electronics theory in Unit 1B to refresh your memory.

Outputs	Sketch the Symbol
Motor	
Bulb	
Buzzer	
LED	

PROTECTIVE RESISTORS

Current-limiting resistors are used to protect LEDs and transistors. They limit the current and prevent components from being damaged.

The formula derived from Ohms law R = V ÷ I is used to calculate the protective resistance needed from the resistor.

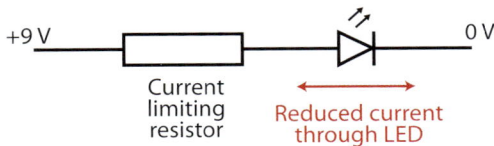

+9 V ── Current limiting resistor ──▷◁── 0 V

Reduced current through LED

POTENTIAL DIVIDERS

Potential dividers are used to split the voltage of a circuit. They are used for setting and adjusting voltages in electronic circuits such as those in games, toys and radios. For example, if you have a 9 V battery but need a supply of 6 V you can solve the problem by making a potential divider.

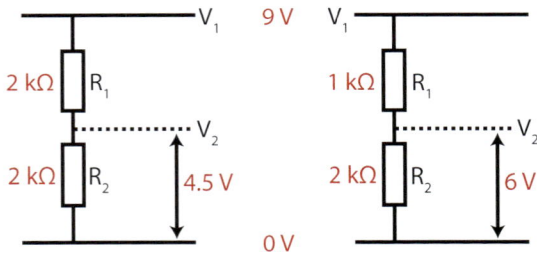

V_1 9 V — 2 kΩ R_1 — V_2 4.5 V — 2 kΩ R_2

V_1 — 1 kΩ R_1 — V_2 6 V — 2 kΩ R_2 — 0 V

When two resistors of equal value are connected across a supply, current will flow through them. If a meter is placed across the supply it will register 9 V. However, if the meter is then placed between the 0 V and the middle of the two resistors, it will read 4.5 V, as the battery voltage has been divided in half.

If the resistor values are changed to 2 K and 1 K, the voltage will be 6 V. The voltage at the centre is determined by the ratio of the resistor values and is given by the formula:

$$V_2 = V_1 \times \frac{R_2}{R_1 + R_2}$$

Potentiometer/variable resistor

A **potentiometer/variable resistor** is a three-terminal resistor with a sliding contact that forms an adjustable voltage divider. If only two terminals are used (one side and the wiper), it acts as a variable resistor. Potentiometers are commonly used to control electrical devices such as volume controls on audio equipment.

Instead of using a fixed resistor, a variable resistor allows the sensitivity of a potential divider and the output voltage to be adjusted. **Sensitivity** means how soon the potential divider will respond to the variable resistor being adjusted. Thus the amount of resistance can be controlled to a very precise, desired level within a potential dividing circuit. A low-value fixed resistor should be placed in series with the variable resistor to prevent the full power of the circuit from being routed down the output voltage path if the variable resistor is accidentally moved to a low resistance.

Real life image

Symbol

RELAYS

A relay is an electrically operated switch that uses electromagnetism to enable one electrical circuit to switch on a second without an electrical connection between the circuits. It consists of a coil wrapped around a soft iron core and an armature that moves a pair of switch contacts when current flows through it.

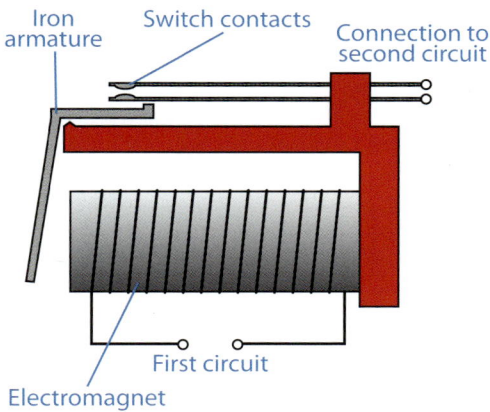

Iron armature · Switch contacts · Connection to second circuit · First circuit · Electromagnet

Coil · Contact

Disadvantages:
- For switching small currents, relays are **bulkier** components than transistors.
- They **cannot switch quickly**, unlike transistors, which can switch numerous times per second.
- They **use more power** than transistors because of the current flowing through the coil.
- They **need more current than many integrated circuits can provide**, this means a low power transistor is required with a relay to switch the current for the relay's coil.

For the section on relays in your exam you must be able to draw circuits which use a relay for switching, for example, to use with motors and solenoids.

When the relay is switched off, the magnetic field around the coil collapses. This causes a large voltage spike to be created in the relay coil. This is **back EMF** which can damage **integrated circuits** (see next section) and transistors, so a diode is used to prevent this from occurring.

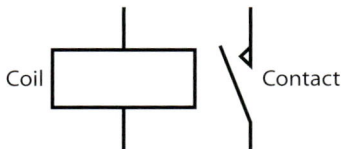

Diode · Relay · +9 V · 0 V

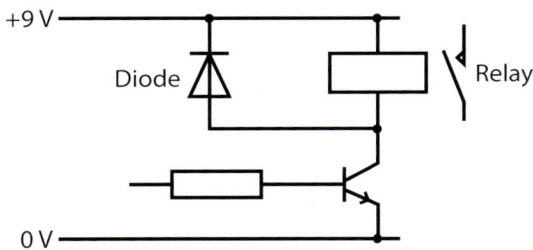

ACTIVITY

Circuit for relay used with motor

+9 V · 0 V

Identify and explain the function of each component in this circuit

A relay should be used in situations that require AC; high voltages such as mains electricity; or where large currents more than 5 A need to be switched. A transistor alone cannot perform these types of switching (but remember a low power transistor might still be needed with the relay to switch the current for the relay's coil). Relays are used in many products, such as cars and household appliances, to control the lights in theatres and the motors in lifts. They can also be used to latch a switching circuit.

Advantages:
Good for switching as they can switch:
- **both AC and DC**, whereas transistors can only switch DC.
- **high voltages**, whereas transistors cannot.
- **large currents** more than 5 A.
- **numerous contacts** at once.

A **solenoid** is represented in an electronic circuit with this symbol:

Symbol · *Real life image*

A solenoid has a coil wire with a moveable iron core. This moveable core will do some work, such as opening a valve or moving a starter drive. This is achieved when current passes through the wire coil producing a strong magnetic field. It is the strong magnetic field that creates a pull on the moveable core, enabling it to do the work the circuit has been designed to do, for example, opening a valve.

1. Complete the circuit diagram by including the symbol for a solenoid.

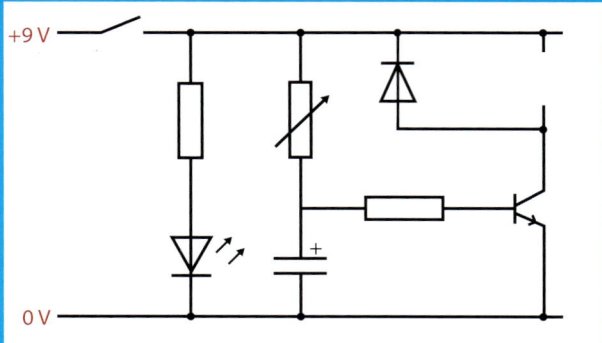

2. (a) Explain what is happening in this circuit.
   (b) Suggest an application for this circuit.

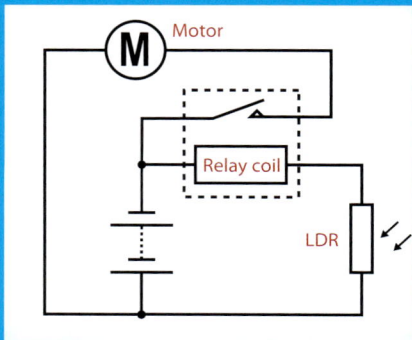

3. (a) Explain what is happening in this circuit.
   (b) Suggest an application for this circuit.

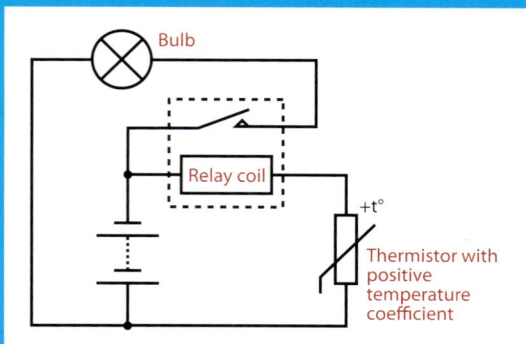

4. (a) Explain what is happening in this circuit.
   (b) Suggest an application for this circuit.

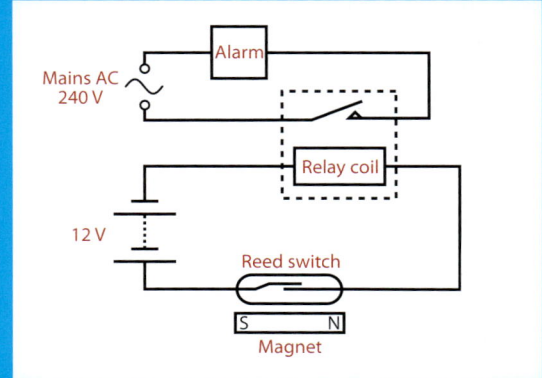

An integrated circuit (IC) is a complete electronic circuit on a chip, packaged in a plastic case. Most ICs are produced in plastic packages with two rows of metal connecting pins. These are known as **Dual in Line (DIL)**.

A DIL with 8 pins

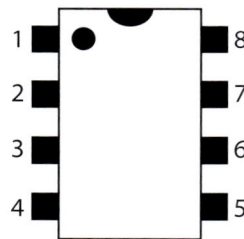

Pin 1 can be identified as the pin left of the notch on the top of the IC. The highest numbered pin is directly opposite. Some ICs also have a small dot to indicate pin 1. ICs are always numbered in an anti-clockwise direction and can have between 4 and 64 pins.

TIMERS

The **555 timer** is a very useful integrated circuit which can be used to build lots of different **monostable** and **astable** circuits. You can use a 555 timer without having to understand the detailed function of each pin. When the 555 is used in astable mode it generates a continuous series of pulses. When used in monostable mode it produces a single output. The 555 is capable of driving a wide range of output devices.

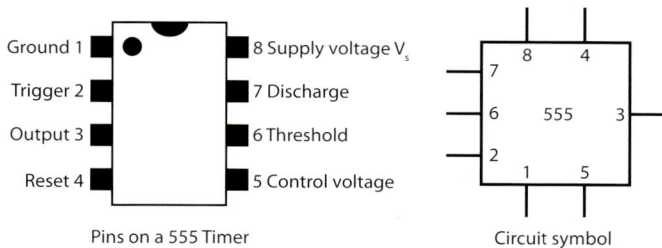

Ground 1   8 Supply voltage V_s
Trigger 2   7 Discharge
Output 3   6 Threshold
Reset 4   5 Control voltage

Pins on a 555 Timer

Circuit symbol

Monostable circuit

A monostable circuit produces a single output pulse when triggered. It is called a **mono**stable because it is stable in just **one** state: **'output low'**. The 'output high' state is temporary. A courtesy light in a car would use a monostable circuit to switch the light on for a certain amount of time and then off.

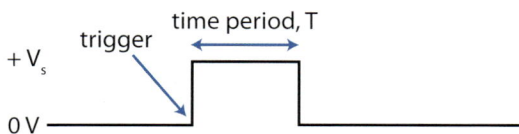

+ V_s trigger   time period, T

0 V

The 555 integrated circuit is in monostable state until pin 2 is triggered by a low voltage. After the time period it always returns to the monostable state.

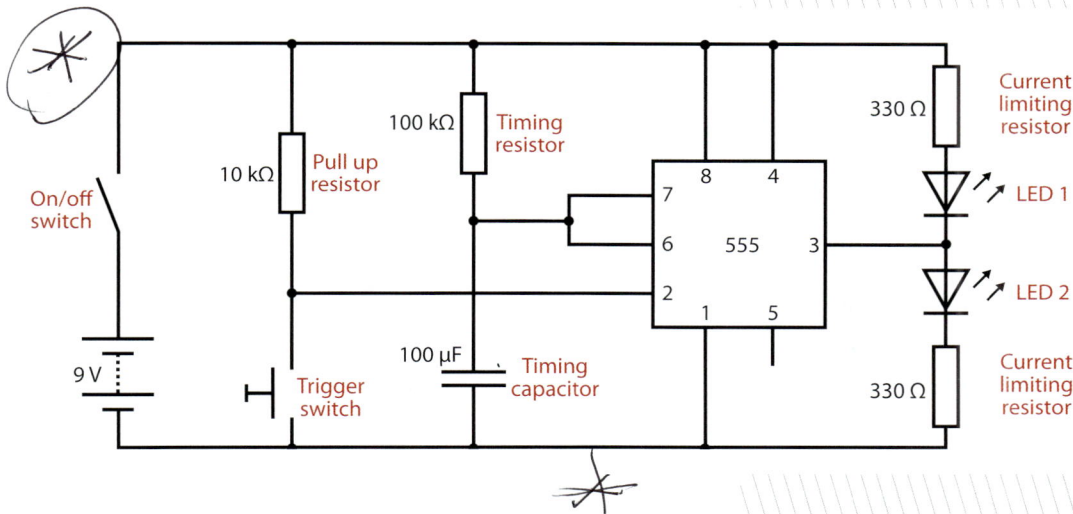

- Pin 2 is a **high** voltage. Pin 3 is a **low** voltage, with current sinking in and LED 1 lit.

- When pin 2 is triggered, by being taken to low voltage by the **switch** (or an electronic signal), the output at pin 3 changes from 0 V to 7 V. It stays in this (timed) state for a set amount of time. Pin 3 is now sourcing current and LED 2 is lit.

- A **timing resistor** and the **timing capacitor** are used to set the monostable time period. They are connected to timing pins 6 and 7.

- When the timed period is complete, the output at pin 3 changes from 7 V to 0 V and stays in the monostable state until the circuit is triggered or switched off.

- The 10 K pull-up resistor connected to the trigger pin is kept **high** until triggered by a **low** input.

- Output is 7 V because the 555 integrated circuit uses 2 V internally.

On/off switch

9 V

10 kΩ   Pull up resistor

100 kΩ   Timing resistor

Trigger switch

100 µF   Timing capacitor

8   4
7
6   555   3
2
1   5

330 Ω   Current limiting resistor

LED 1

LED 2

330 Ω   Current limiting resistor

81

Astable circuit

An astable circuit produces a 'square wave', this is a digital waveform with sharp transitions between low (0 V) and high (+Vs). Note that the durations of the low and high states may be different. The circuit is called an astable because it is not stable in any state; the output is continually changing between 'low' and 'high'. An astable can be used to provide the **clock signal** for circuits such as counters or to switch something on and off continuously, for example, a flashing warning light on a motorway.

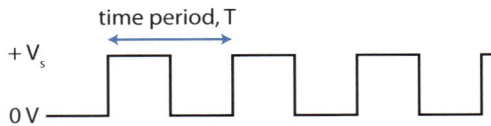

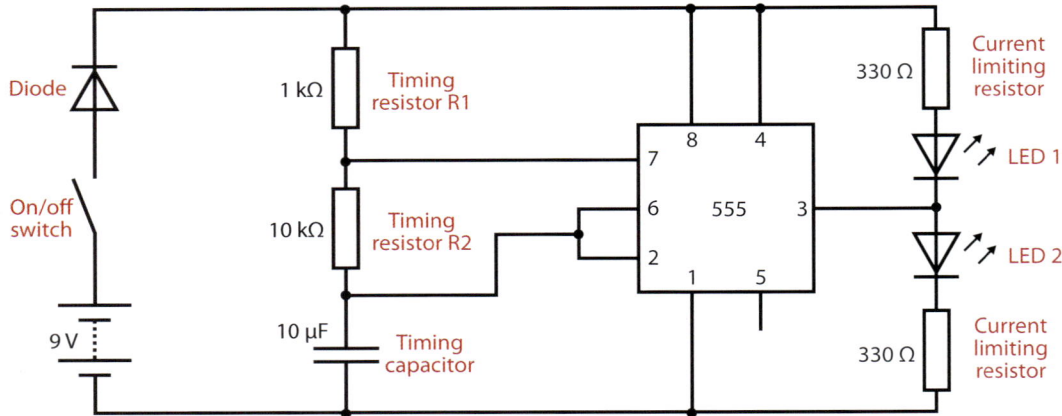

- When an astable circuit is first switched on, the timing capacitor is not charged up. The voltage across the capacitor is less than one third of the battery voltage. This causes the output voltage at pin 3 to be high.

- The capacitor **charges** through the timing resistors R1 and R2 until the voltage across the capacitor is **greater** than ⅔ of the battery voltage. At this point, the output voltage at pin 3 changes from high voltage to 0 V.

- The capacitor then **discharges** through R2 into pin 7 until the voltage across the capacitor becomes less than ⅓ of the battery voltage.

- When this happens, the output at pin 3 changes from 0 V to high voltage and repeats the process until the circuit is switched off.

CAPACITORS

A capacitor is made of two thin sheets of metal (plates) placed close together but not touching. The space between them is filled with air or plastic, non-conducting material. Capacitors are used in electronic circuits to store an electrical charge. The unit of capacitance is Farad (F). The capacitance value and the working voltage are printed on the capacitor. They are able to:

- create time delays (monostable).
- control the frequency of pulse generators (astable).
- smooth the input across a power supply.

Non-polarised capacitors

Non-polarised capacitors can be connected either way round in a circuit. They are normally smaller in size than polarised capacitors and have a capacitance value of less than 1 μF.

Polarised capacitors

There are two main types of polarised capacitors, axial and radial, which must be connected the right way around in a circuit. Polarised capacitors are available in a larger range of values from 1 µF–4,700 µF with ±10–20% tolerance.

Axial capacitor: Leads are attached to each end.

Radial capacitor: Both leads are at the same end. It is a little smaller than an axial capacitor.

Application of capacitors

Capacitors are chosen for use in different applications. They are used to produce steady direct-current voltages by smoothing rectified alternating-current voltages. If a fluctuation occurs within a signal it can be filtered out by a capacitor. Capacitors can also be used to achieve a time delay within a circuit if they are used in series with resistors. A capacitor can be charged instantly by connecting a power supply across its two leads. The capacitor size and the regulating resistor value are relative to the length of time it will take for the capacitor to charge. This is known as the Time Constant.

Time Constant (seconds) = C (Farads) × R (Ohms)

After one time constant the capacitor is charged to about 0.6 of its full charge and would require another four time constants to fully charge.

Time = 0.0047 × 10 000
T = 47 seconds

The voltage across C reaches 6 V in about 47 seconds so requires further time constants to fully charge.

ACTIVITY

- Draw a radial and axial capacitor.
- Sketch the symbols for a polarised capacitor and a non-polarised capacitor.

ACTIVITY

1. What is meant by 'time constant' when referring to capacitors.
2. Calculate the time constant for a capacitor when C = 100 µF and R = 100 K. Show your working out.

INTERFACE

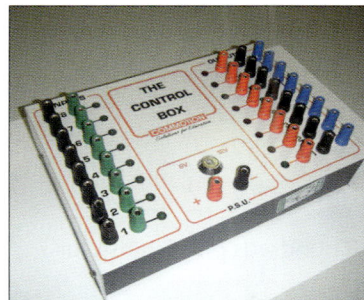

To connect input and output devices to a computer system you must use an interface (control box). It is essential to use an interface to protect you and the computer from damage should you make a wrong connection.

CHECK YOUR LEARNING

Recall a list of possible output devices. Once you have come up with as many as you can think of, check your list on page 41.

DIGITAL SIGNALS

Electronic products are made of electronic circuits. The circuits work by receiving digital signals, but in these circuits there can only be two states: electricity can be flowing or not flowing. When a pulse of electricity is present we call this a '**1**' and when there is no electricity present we call it a '**0**'. This pulse of electricity is a digital signal that a computer will recognise.

A **bit** is the simplest form of information for computer programming. A **byte** is the unit of memory in a computer. It is made up of 8 bits, so a byte can store eight 0s or 1s.

- 1 represents a 'high' voltage level
- 0 represents a 'low' voltage level

This system of 0s and 1s is known as **binary** and is used by computers. It is explained in more detail on the following page.

COUNTING
The base-2 System and the 8-bit byte

In everyday life we use the **decimal (base-10)** number system. Decimal numbers are numbers where each digit can have one of ten possible values (0–9). In the **binary (base-2)** number system each digit can have only two possible values (0 or 1). These two values are called **binary digits** or **bits**. Computers use binary to work with numbers, because it is much easier to implement base-2 with electronic technology.

To understand decimal numbers, think back to how you understand a decimal number such as 6357. We can write each digit under a heading:

Thousands	Hundreds	Tens	Units
6	3	5	7

This means 6 thousands plus 3 hundreds plus 5 tens plus 7 units.

Or $6 \times 1000 + 3 \times 100 + 5 \times 10 + 7 \times 1 = 6357$

Note: that each heading is **10** times bigger than the one to the right, because decimal is a **base-10** number system.

Converting binary to decimal

Now let's consider the binary number 1101. What would this be in decimal? The same concept applies to binary numbers, except that each heading is two times bigger than the one to the right, because binary is a base-2 number system.

Eights	Fours	Twos	Units
1	1	0	1

This means 1 eight plus 1 four plus no twos plus 1 unit.

Or $1 \times 8 + 1 \times 4 + 0 \times 2 + 1 \times 1 = 13$

At GCSE you need to be able to work with binary numbers up to a value of 255. In binary, this is represented as 11111111, which needs eight binary digits, or bits. Eight bits grouped together is called a **byte** in computing. Each of the headings for these eight digits are two times the value of the heading to the right, ie:

128s	64s	32s	16s	8s	4s	2s	1s (Units)

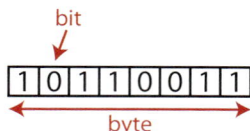

bit

`1 0 1 1 0 0 1 1`

byte

Converting decimal to binary

We can also convert decimal numbers to binary. To do this, start with the leftmost column in the list (at the bottom of the left column), ie 128s. If your number is smaller than 128, then write down '0'. But if it is not, then write down '1' and subtract 128 from your number. Repeat this process all the way to the units column. In this example, we will convert the decimal number 21 to binary:

128s   Is 21 smaller than 128? Yes. Write down '0'.
        0

64s   Is 21 smaller than 64? Yes. Write down another '0'.
        00

32s   Is 21 smaller than 32? Yes. Write down another '0'.
        000

16s   Is 21 smaller than 16? No. Write down a '1'.
        0001
        Subtract 16 from your number 21, which leaves 5.

8s   Is your new number, 5, smaller than 8? Yes. Write down '0'. **00010**

4s   Is 5 smaller than 4? No. Write down a '1'.
        000101
        Subtract 4 from your number 5, which leaves 1.

2s   Is your new number, 1, smaller than 2? Yes. Write down a '0'. **0001010**

1s   Is 1 smaller than 1? No. Write down a '1'.
        00010101
        You are finished.

The answer is **00010101**. However, just like in decimal, we generally leave off any zeros at the start of the number, so we can say that the decimal number **21** is **10101** in binary.

For the exam you must be able to convert decimal numbers from 0 to 255 into binary and vice versa.

ACTIVITY

1. Prove that the binary number 10101 is the same as the decimal number 21 by converting it back to decimal. Show your working out.
2. Copy and complete the list below for decimal numbers 1 to 20. The first 5 have been completed for you.

DECIMAL	BINARY
1	1
2	10
3	11
4	100
5	101

USE AND FUNCTION OF MICROCONTROLLERS (PICs)

A PIC microcontroller is a small electronic integrated circuit, with memory that can be programmed to carry out a wide variety of jobs such as timing or production line control. It has a large number of inputs and outputs. Nearly all electronic devices manufactured today have a PIC microcontroller (Programmable Interface Controllers), which has been programmed using specific software. These include household appliances such as microwaves and washing machines, alarm systems, medical equipment, sub-systems of vehicles and electronic instruments. They are now affordable components that are available as pre-built circuits or kits that are easy to assemble. They can be reprogrammed over and over again, and are extremely versatile. For these reasons they are often used in complex circuits, replacing a large number of components that would be needed without them.

ACTIVITY

Research PIC microcontrollers and produce an A4 information page with the main features of a PIC and images of applications for PICs.

To programme a PIC microcontroller circuit a computer is required to run the software. The computer can be connected to the PIC through the serial or USB port. If the programmer uses software with a simulation feature the program can be checked for faults or the program changed before it is downloaded to the PIC. At the time of writing, the software for PIC programming supported by C2K, the Northern Ireland school IT system, is PIC Logicator. It is pupil friendly computer programming and very like Logicator discussed in Unit 1E, Pneumatic Systems and Control. When the program has been simulated and is ready, it is downloaded to the PIC microcontroller integrated circuit via the USB lead, which can then be disconnected, allowing the PIC circuit to be used independently.

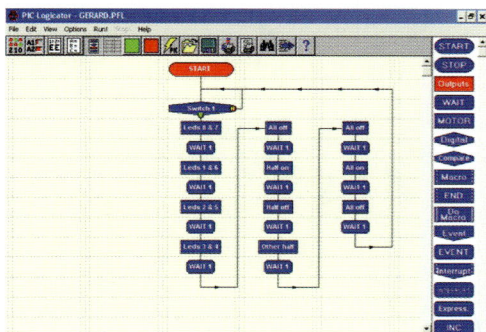

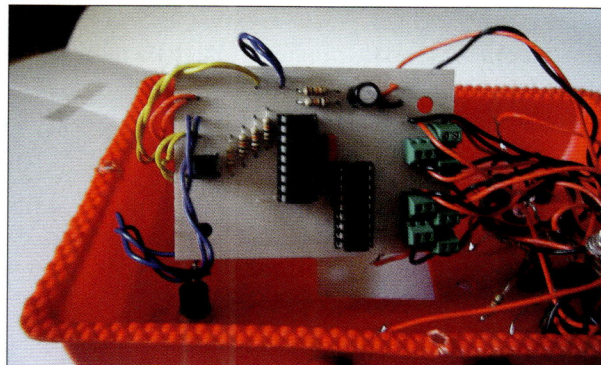

Output devices are controlled within the flowcharts by setting the output patterns to on or off using either a 1 or 0. The diagram shows that the outputs, which are LEDs, are plugged into Port 1 and Port 7, and turned on as the bit patterns for each port are turned to 1, meaning ON.

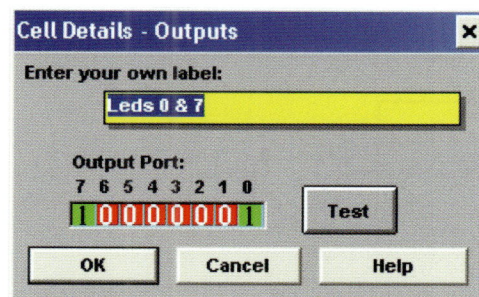

For the exam you must be able to design and interpret circuits which incorporate a PIC with analogue and digital inputs and digital outputs.

Control situations using a PIC

Control situations using a PIC include:

- A car may contain 40 PICs for many purposes, including temperature control for passenger comfort or engine management
- Washing machines
- Microwaves
- Stereos
- Mobile phones
- Toys
- Alarms

Analogue or digital inputs can be received by the PIC and low current outputs can be provided to a maximum of 50 mA, but higher current devices require amplification. Without amplification, the only output device that can be used with a PIC is a LED. This works well, but most T&D projects designed by pupils will need to drive devices such as motors, solenoids and buzzers. These are difficult output devices to drive using a PIC because of the inductive loads created that result in electronics noise. This noise causes the PIC to be unreliable and the program may not work properly. Therefore amplification using additional components, such as transistors, is essential.

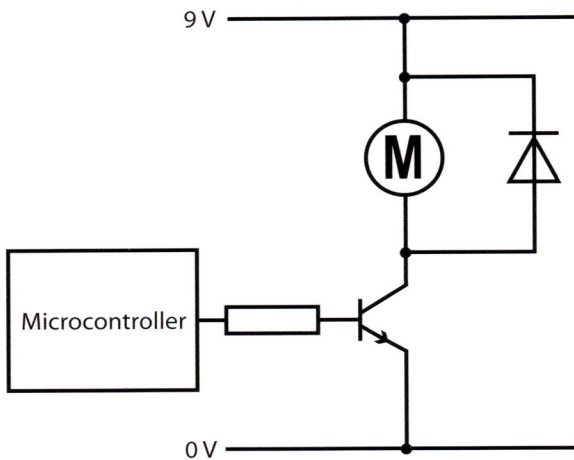

A transistor being used to build an amplifier that allows a PIC to drive a motor.

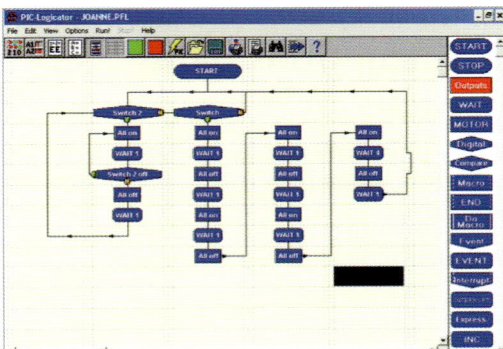

Sample program written on PIC Logicator that could be downloaded on to a PIC.

ACTIVITY

1. Design a control system for a sliding door. When a switch is pressed, the door opens. It stays open for ten seconds and then closes again. The system uses limit switches to sense when the door is fully open and fully closed. The motor is halted in response to the feedback from these microswitches.

2. A keypad is a useful input device. Design a programme that can be used to scan a keypad on which a three digit number has to be entered to open a solenoid-operated lock. Connect the keypad to a PIC microcontroller using inputs and outputs.

KEY WORD CHECK

Revise the key words for Electronics in Unit 1B, page 45, then explain what each of the key words below mean. Remember to add these words to your glossary.

- EMF
- Ohms Law
- Capacitance
- Resistors in parallel
- Pull up resistors
- Pull down resistors
- Resistor colour code
- Ammeter
- Voltmeter
- NPN transistor
- Analogue signal
- Digital signal
- Inputs
- Outputs
- Variable resistor
- Relay
- Solenoid
- Integrated circuit
- 555 Timer
- Monostable circuit
- Astable circuit
- Capacitors
- Interface
- Bit
- Byte
- Binary
- Microcontrollers

Complete the following past paper questions to help consolidate your learning and practice your exam skills.

Formulae for GCSE Technology and Design

You should use, where appropriate, the formulae given below when answering questions which include calculations.

1. Potential Difference = current × resistance $(V = I \times R)$

2. For Potential divider

$$V_2 = \frac{R_2}{R_1 + R_2} \times V_T$$

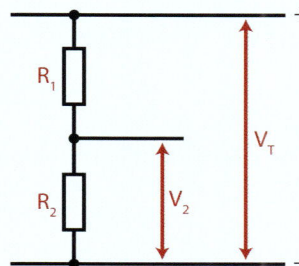

3. Series Resistors

$$R_T = R_1 + R_2 + R_3 \text{ etc}$$

Parallel Resistors

$$\frac{1}{R_T} = \frac{1}{R_1} \times \frac{1}{R_2} \quad \text{or} \quad R_T = \frac{R_1 \times R_2}{R_1 + R_2}$$

4. Time Constant T = $R \times C$

1. (a) Complete the following statements by inserting the missing word:

In an electronic circuit current is a flow of charge carried by _____ [1]

The unit used to measure electrical current is _____ [1]

In an electronic circuit the force which produces a flow of charge is known as _____ [1]

The unit used to measure electrical resistance is _____ [1]

(b) Two resistors are shown in Figure 1 and Figure 2 below. Each resistor has four coloured bands, the fourth band is off-set from the other three bands.

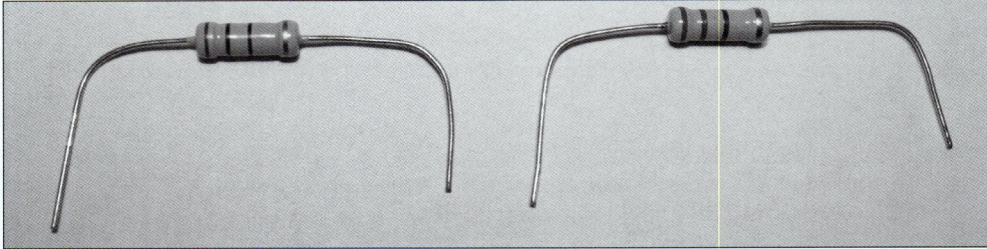

Figure 1 (47 kΩ)   Figure 2 (2.2 kΩ)

(i) State the value of each resistor in Ωs.

47 kΩ = _____Ω   2.2 kΩ = _____Ω [2]

(ii) Use the information below to identify the colours of the first three bands for the resistor in Figure 1.

0 = Black	1 = Brown	2 = Red	3 = Orange	4 = Yellow
5 = Green	6 = Blue	7 = Violet	8 = Grey	9 = White

Band 1 _____   Band 2 _____   Band 3 _____   [3]

(c) (i) If, in Figure 1, the fourth band is coloured silver (10%) and in Figure 2 the fourth band is coloured gold (5%), use notes and calculations to show the information that can be obtained for each resistor. [6]

(ii) If the two resistors illustrated in part (b) are used in a potential divider circuit as shown in Figure 3 calculate the expected output at X. Set out your calculations. [5]

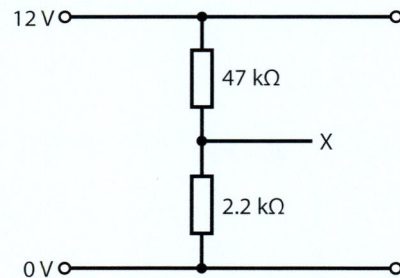

Figure 3

(d) Figure 5 shows a basic circuit layout that requires the components shown in Figure 4 to be located in Figure 5 as follows:

Location	Component
A	SPST
B	LED
C	Variable Resistor
D	Polarised Capacitor

Figure 4

(i) Make a copy of Figure 5 and insert each component symbol in the correct place. [4]

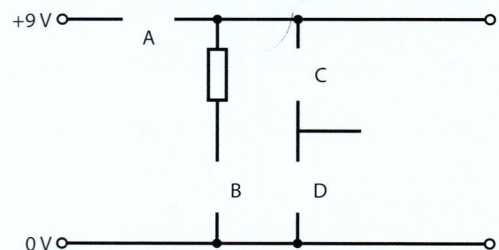

Figure 5

The circuit in Figure 5 is required to operate a relay when a transistor is switched on.

(ii) Complete the circuit in Figure 5 by including the relay and transistor. Include any additional components that are needed for this circuit. [4]

(iii) Outline the purpose of any additional component that you have used when completing (d) part (ii). [2]

(iv) Describe the operation of the completed circuit stating the function of each component. [8]

(v) Suggest **one** possible use for this circuit. [2]

CCEA GCSE Technology & Design Past Paper, Unit 2, Systems and Control, Element 1, Electronic and Microelectronic Control Systems, Summer 2011, © CCEA
For copyright reasons the diagrams in the formulae, Figures 3 and 5 have replaced those from the CCEA past paper.

2. **A typical alarm system uses bits and bit patterns as the method of communication. For example, the plan in Figure 6 shows doors and windows either closed or open. If a door or window is open it is represented as a '1' and if it is closed it is represented as a '0'. Each door or window is identified by a letter.**

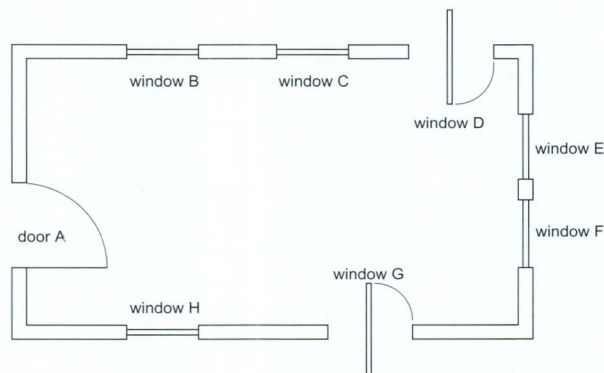

Window and Door Bit Pattern

Figure 6

(a) (i) Complete the bit pattern below to represent the position of the doors and windows in Figure 6. [3]

A	B	C	D	E	F	G	H
	0	0	1	0	0		

(ii) Outline two features of a microcontroller (PIC). [2]

(iii) List two advantages of using a microcontroller compared to an integrated circuit such as a 555 timer. [4]

(iv) List three applications, other than an alarm system that use a microcontroller. [3]

(b) To maintain climate control in a greenhouse a window is opened and closed using a motor operated by a microcontroller. The window opens when a temperature sensor rises to 25°C and closes when the temperature falls below 20°C. Figure 7 shows the cross-section of the window including two limit switches and a temperature sensor.

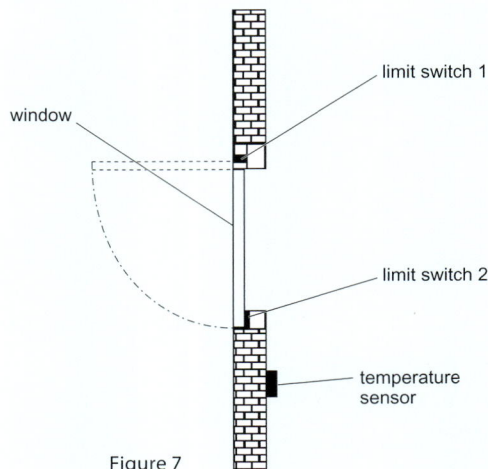

Figure 7

The PIC has 5 inputs (only 3 are used) and 8 outputs (only 4 are used).
A binary '1' indicates that a switch has been pressed or that the temperature sensor has risen to the set temperature.

The input connections are shown in Figure 8.

PIC Inputs	(Not used)	Limit switch 2	Limit switch 1	(Not used)	Temperature sensor
BIT	4	3	2	1	0

Figure 8

The output connections are as shown in Figure 9.

PIC Inputs	(Not used)	(Not used)	Motor		(Not used)	(Not used)	LED	Buzzer
BIT	7	6	5	4	3	2	1	0
Motor clockwise	X	X	0	1	X	X	X	X
Motor anti-clockwise	X	X	1	0	X	X	X	X
BIT	X	X	0	0	X	X	X	X

Figure 9

Two bits are required to control the motor. An 'X' means ignore.
A binary '1' switches the LED or buzzer on.

Construct a series of flowcharts to represent the overall operating routine as follows.
The first flowchart (Figure 10) has been completed for you.

(i) Make a copy of Figure 10 and complete the flowchart and its
   relevant bit pattern to represent the OPEN macro as follows:

   • Motor rotates clockwise to open the window.

   • The motor is turned off when limit switch 1 is activated.

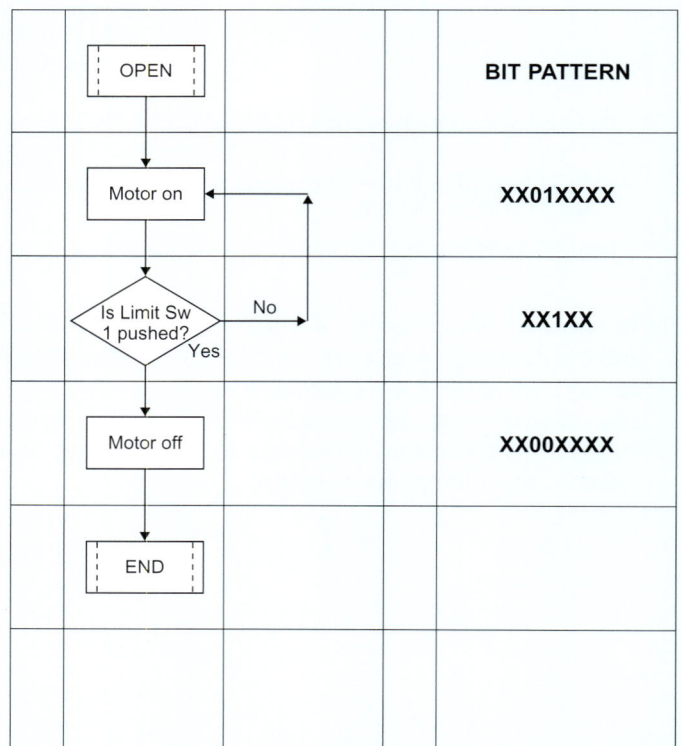

   • The macro ends. [8]

Figure 10

	BIT PATTERN
OPEN	
Motor on	XX01XXXX
Is Limit Sw 1 pushed? No Yes	XX1XX
Motor off	XX00XXXX
END	

(ii) Make a copy of Figure 11 and complete the flowchart and its relevant bit pattern to represent the CLOSED macro as follows:

- Motor rotates anti-clockwise to close the door.
- The motor is turned off when limit switch 2 is activated.
- The macro ends. [8]

	CLOSED			BIT PATTERN

Figure 11

(iii) The system is to be modified by introducing a LED and buzzer to warn that the window is about to open. Using the OPEN and CLOSED macros produced in parts (i) and (ii), make a copy of Figure 12 and complete the flowchart to operate the system as follows:

- When the temperature sensor reaches a temperature of 25°C the LED and buzzer will come on for 3 seconds.
- The OPEN macro operates and then waits until the temperature drops to 20°C before the window closes using the CLOSED macro.
- The system will repeat.

Beside each input and output cell, indicate the relevant bit pattern.

No bit pattern is required for the macros. [12]

	START			BIT PATTERN

CCEA GCSE Technology & Design Past Paper, Unit 2, Systems and Control, Element 1, Electronic and Microelectronic Control Systems, Summer 2011, © CCEA

Figure 12

MECHANICAL AND PNEUMATIC CONTROL SYSTEMS

MECHANICAL ADVANTAGE

Mechanisms will make a job easier to do. For example, a crowbar can be used as a lever to lift a crate or a screwdriver to open a tin of paint. A mechanism gives you a **mechanical advantage (MA)** if you are able to move a large load with a smaller effort.

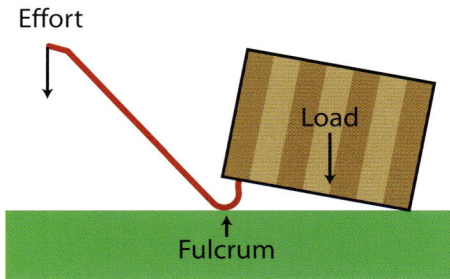

Effort

Load

Fulcrum

KEY TERMS

Load: the weight to be moved.

Effort: the amount of effort used to push down on the rod to move the weight.

Fulcrum: the place the rod pivots or rotates.

The mechanical advantage of a mechanism can be calculated as follows:

$$MA = \frac{Load}{Effort}$$

Effort 8 N

Fulcrum   Load 40 N

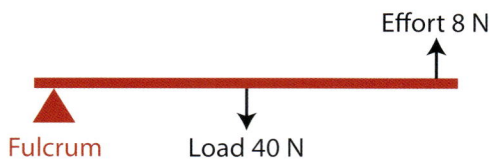

$$MA = \frac{Load}{Effort} = \frac{40}{8} = \frac{5}{1} = 5:1$$

ACTIVITY

Calculate the mechanical advantage for the following diagrams.

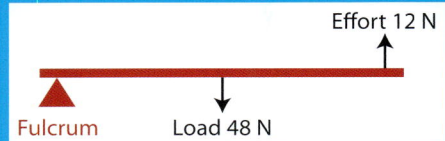

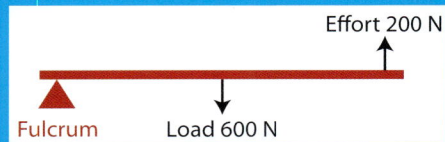

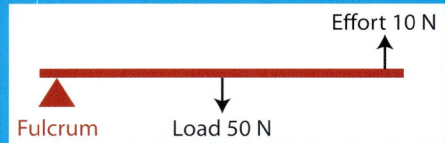

Effort 12 N

Fulcrum   Load 48 N

Effort 200 N

Fulcrum   Load 600 N

Effort 10 N

Fulcrum   Load 50 N

Velocity ratio

The diagram below shows a lever giving a mechanical advantage as a load can be moved using a smaller effort. However, the effort must move through a greater distance than the load.

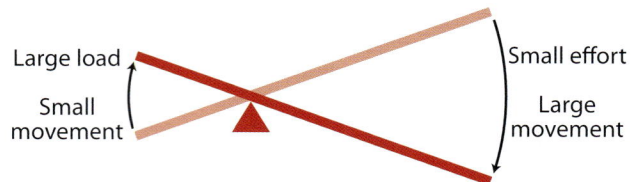

Large load   Small effort

Small movement   Large movement

If the two distances are compared we get the velocity ratio (VR):

$$VR = \frac{\text{Distance moved by Effort}}{\text{Distance moved by Load}}$$

Example:

Distance moved by Load **200 mm**
Distance moved by Effort **1 m**

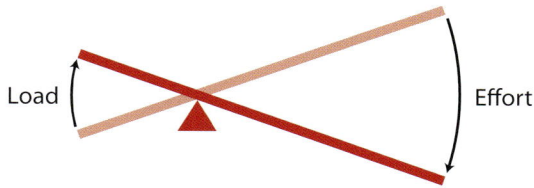

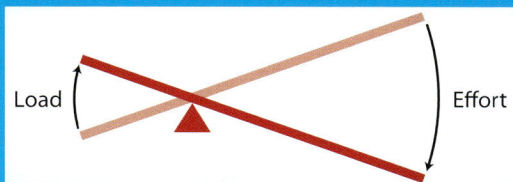

$$VR = \frac{\text{Distance moved by Effort}}{\text{Distance moved by Load}} = \frac{1\text{ m}}{0.5\text{ m}} = 5$$

This means that the effort must move five times further than the load.

ACTIVITY

Calculate the velocity ratio for the following. Remember to change distances into meters first.

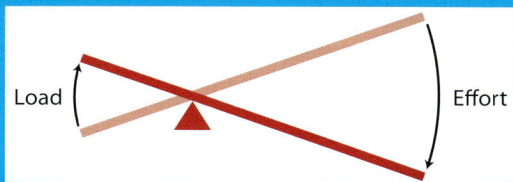

Distance moved by Load **400 mm**
Distance moved by Effort **1 m**

Distance moved by Load **50 cm**
Distance moved by Effort **3 m**

LEVERS AND LINKAGES

Levers

Most mechanisms are designed to make jobs easier, which means that only a small force is needed to apply a larger force to the load. For example, using a small force to turn the handle on a vice means you can apply a large force to hold the work in place.

The handle acts as a lever and the longer the handle the smaller the force needed to turn it. Force is measured in **newtons** (N).

Moment is the name given to the turning force or work done by a lever when it turns on its fulcrum. The following is used to calculate the moment of a lever:

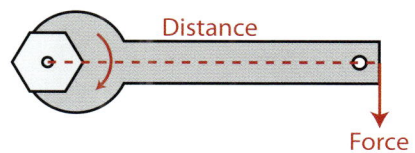

Moment = Force (N) x Distance (m)
Moments are measured in **newton metres** (Nm)

ACTIVITY

Calculate the moments for the following. Remember to change distances into meters first.

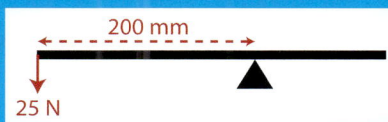

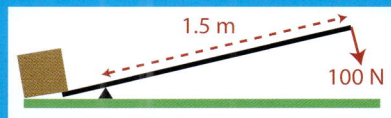

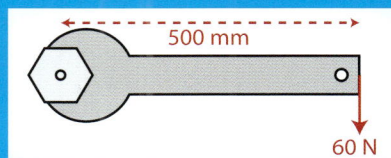

Linkages

A linkage is a mechanism made by connecting levers together. They can do many things, such as change the direction of a force or moment, make two things move at the same time or make objects move parallel to each other.

Bell Cranks

This type of linkage can change the direction of movement through 90°.

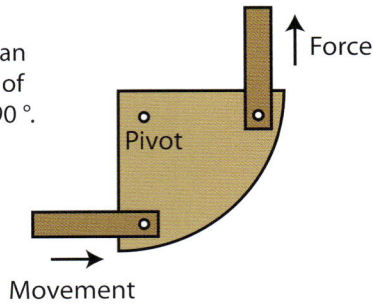

Force

Pivot

Movement

A pedal bin and the brakes of a bicycle both use the bell crank principle.

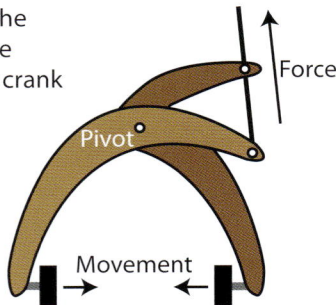

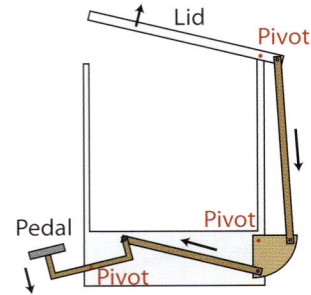

Force

Pivot

Movement

Lid

Pivot

Pedal

Pivot

Pivot

Parallel linkages

Parallel linkages are used in products to make parts move in a line, keeping them at a set distance apart or to repeat movements.

A tool box uses parallel linkages and a shaving mirror uses a series of levers linked.

TRANSMISSION OF MOTION USING GEARS

Gears play an important part in many of the machines that we use in our daily lives. They are used to increase or decrease the speed of motion or to change the strength (torque) of motion. They are also used to change the direction of motion and transfer motion from one axle to another in simple machines.

Real life image	Description	Symbol	Practical applications
	Spur gears: are used to transmit rotary motion in the driver wheel to rotary motion in the driver pinion. They are mounted on parallel shafts.	Side view Top view	• Salad spinner • Windup alarm clock
	Bevel gears: are useful when the direction of a shaft's rotation needs to be changed. They are usually mounted on shafts that are 90° apart. The teeth are cut on a cone instead of on a disc or wheel.	Bevel Gear Meshed Bevel Gear	• Hand drills • Hand whisks • Shaft driven motor cycles
	Worm wheels and worm gears are used when large speed reductions are required. The worm drives the wheel but the wheel cannot drive the worm.	Worm and worm wheel	• Heavy industrial applications requiring gear reductions • Tuning mechanisms on musical instruments • Band hose clamps • Small electrical devices and toys

	Rack and pinion gears change the rotary motion of the pinion to the linear motion of the rack. Often the pinion rotates in a fixed position and the rack is free to move. Alternatively, the rack may be fixed and the pinion rotates, moving up and down the rack.	*Rack and Pinion*	• Pinion fixed - used in the steering mechanism of most cars • Rack fixed – funicular railways • Corkscrew
	Sprockets and chains: are used to transmit rotary motion from one gear to another. A traditional gear train requires many gears arranged to mesh with each other in order to transmit motion. However, the advantage of a chain drive is that it only needs two gear wheels and a chain to transmit rotary motion over a distance. The chain is made up of a series of links joined with steel pins. The sprockets are profiled wheels with teeth that mesh with the chain.		• Machinery • Motorcycles • Car engines

QUESTIONS & ANSWERS

Q. Why do we use gears in machines?

A. Gears are used in machines to:
(a) reverse the direction of rotational motion.
(b) change the speed of rotational motion by increasing or decreasing it.
(c) change rotational motion from one axle to another.
(d) change the direction of and/or strength (torque) of motion.
(e) keep axle rotation speeds synchronised.

Gear trains

A gear train can be defined as two or more gears arranged together to transmit torque or power from one system to another. A feature of gear trains is that adjacent gears turn in the opposite direction. They can vary in size from something as small as a wrist watch to something as large as an industrial gear box. A gear train can be a simple gear train or compound gear train, each is explained in detail below:

Simple gear trains

In a simple gear train there is only one gear wheel on each gear shaft. A simple gear train can be a combination of a very large gear wheel meshing with a very small gear wheel, or very small gear wheel meshing with a very large gear wheel. Combining very large gear wheels can produce very high gear ratios, while combining very small gear wheels can produce very low gear ratios. In a simple gear train the shafts of the input and output must be parallel to each other. An idler gear can be used between two spur gears to make them rotate in the same direction without affecting the gear speed.

Practical applications: • salad spinner • windup alarm clock

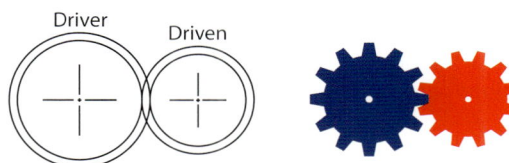

Compound gear trains

In a compound gear train there is more than one gear wheel on a gear shaft. If a combination of large and small gear wheels on the same gear shaft are intermeshed with large and small gear wheels on another gear shaft, a full range of gear ratios can be arranged to meet all requirements. This combination of gears is called a **compound gear train**. The final gear ratio is calculated by multiplying the separate gear ratios by the gear ratios of the adjacent gear wheels throughout the train. Compound gear trains are preferred over simple gear trains if large reduction ratios are required. Unlike the idler gear of a simple train, the intermediate gears of a compound gear train will influence the overall relative speeds of the driver and driven gears. The diagram below shows the intermediate gears.

Practical applications: • grandfather clock

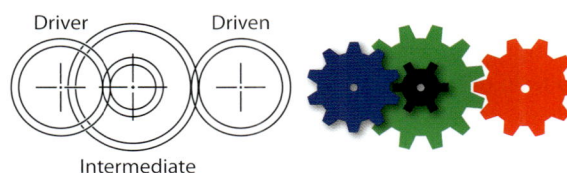

- Research simple gear trains and make a list of products which use them to make them work
- Explain the function of the gear train within the product.
- Now do the same for compound gear trains.

Choosing the arrangement for a gear train depends on:

- the torque to be transmitted.
- the position of the input and output shafts.
- the size of the gear box.

Calculating gear transmissions

In the examination you will need to be able to use given information to complete calculations involving simple and compound gear transmissions for:

1. **velocity ratio**
2. **gear ratio**
3. **transmission speeds**

The following formulae and examples explain how to complete calculations involving simple and compound gear transmissions using a maximum of four gears:

1. Calculating velocity ratios

Simple gear trains

$$\text{Velocity Ratio} = \frac{\text{Number of teeth on driven gear}}{\text{Number of teeth on driver gear}}$$

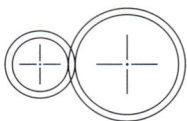

Driver 6 teeth
Driven 12 teeth

$$VR = \frac{12}{6} = \frac{2}{1} = 2:1$$

When you make the calculation you are left with a fraction which is then converted into a ratio. The figure above the line always comes first.

Compound gear trains

Calculating the gear ratio for compound gear trains uses the same principle as for simple gear trains; the number of teeth on the driven gear is divided by the number of teeth on the driver. First work out the velocity ratio for each pair of gears then multiply the answers together to calculate the total velocity ratio of the gear train:

Total Velocity (speed) Ratio = VR1 × VR2 × VR3 × VR4, etc.

Example: In a product like this speed reducer, which is connected to an electric motor, there is a compound gear train made of two pairs of gears.

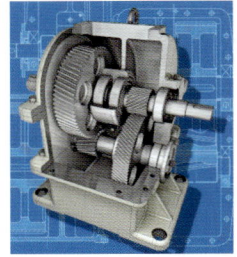

If the velocity ratios of the two pairs of gears are 6:1 and 8:1, then:

Total Velocity (speed) Ratio = 6:1 × 8:1 = 48:1

Therefore it can be said that this speed reducer uses a compound gear train to give an output speed 48 times slower than the motor input speed.

2. Calculating gear ratios:

Simple gear trains

$$\text{Gear Ratio} = \frac{\text{Number of teeth on driven gear}}{\text{Number of teeth on driver gear}}$$

Calculate the gear ratio of the following gear trains.

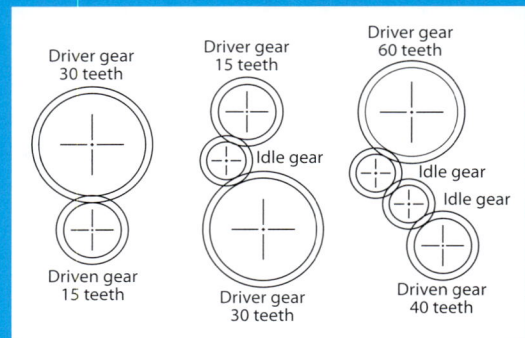

Driver gear 30 teeth
Driven gear 15 teeth

Driver gear 15 teeth
Idle gear
Driver gear 30 teeth

Driver gear 60 teeth
Idle gear
Idle gear
Driven gear 40 teeth

Compound gear trains

The final gear ratio of compound gear trains is calculated by multiplying the separate gear ratios by the gear ratios of the adjacent gear wheels throughout the train. First work out the gear ratio for each pair of gears then multiply the answers together to calculate the total gear ratio of the gear train:

Gear Ratio = GR1 × GR2 × GR3 × GR4, etc.

Driver 10 teeth
12 teeth
Driven 10 teeth
6 teeth

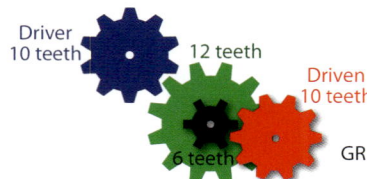

$$GR = \frac{12}{10} \times \frac{10}{6} = \frac{120}{60} = 2:1$$

The driven gear will turn twice for every turn of the driver gear.

Calculate the gear ratio of the following gear trains.

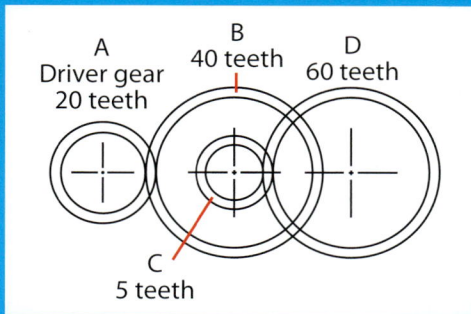

A
Driver gear
20 teeth

B
40 teeth

D
60 teeth

C
5 teeth

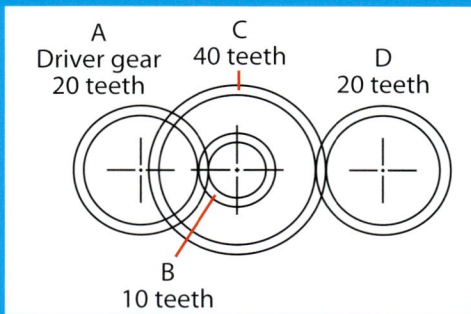

A
Driver gear
20 teeth

C
40 teeth

D
20 teeth

B
10 teeth

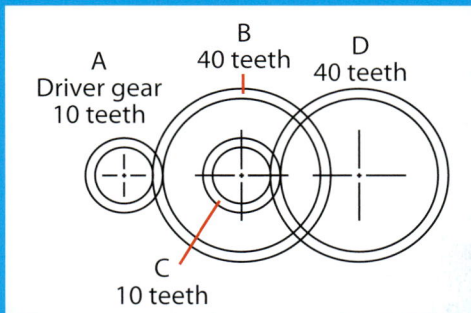

A
Driver gear
10 teeth

B
40 teeth

D
40 teeth

C
10 teeth

Sprockets and chains

When calculating the velocity or gear ratios for a sprocket and chain, ignore the chain. Just find out the number of teeth on the gears and calculate the ratios using the same formulae for simple gear trains.

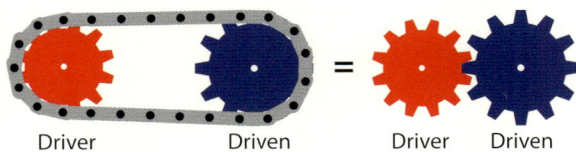

Driver   Driven   =   Driver   Driven

3. Calculating transmission speeds

Driver and driven gears rotate in opposite directions. The relative speed of the gears is calculated by the following equation:

$$\frac{\text{Rev/min of driver gear}}{\text{Rev/min of driven gear}} = \frac{\text{Number of teeth on driven gear}}{\text{Number of teeth on driver gear}}$$

Note: *Rev/min and rpm are both abbreviations for 'revolutions per minute'.*

Example: Calculate the speed of the driven gear if the driving gear is rotating at 120 rev/min. The driven gear has 150 teeth and the driving gear has 50 teeth.

$$\frac{120}{\text{Rev/min of driven gear}} = \frac{150}{50}$$

$$\text{Rev/min of driven gear} = \frac{120 \times 50}{150} = 40 \text{ Rev/min}$$

1. Name the transmission system shown.
2. Calculate the gear ratio of the system.
3. What speed will shaft B rotate if shaft A rotates at 36 rpm?

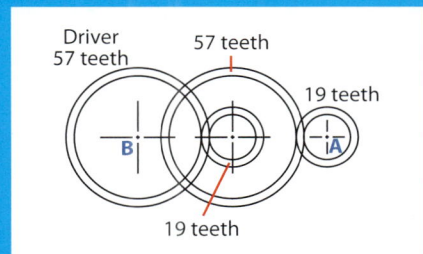

Driver
57 teeth

57 teeth

19 teeth

B

A

19 teeth

Idler gear

If two spur gears are meshed together the driver and the driven gear will rotate in opposite directions. An idler gear can be placed in the middle of the two spur wheels to change the direction of the gears so the driver and the driven gears rotate in the same direction. Using an idler gear will not affect the overall ratio of a gear train or change the velocity ratio.

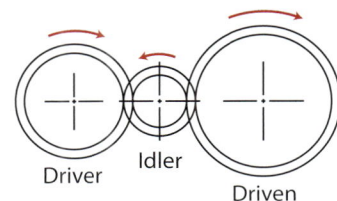

Driver   Idler   Driven

OTHER TRANSMISSION SYSTEMS

Other Transmission Systems		Factors influencing the choice of transmission system	Practical applications
Flat belts		• Belt can slip without damaging the machine. • Cheapest option.	• Washing machines • CD players • Electric generators
Toothed belts		• Belts with teeth cut into the inside of them are used in situations where slippage needs to be avoided for safety reasons. • Used for applications of constant speeds and timing. • Quietest option.	• Car timing belts • Car fan belts

Motor mount adjustment

The belt passed around a pulley must be tensioned correctly. It must not be too tight or it will apply bending forces to the pulley shafts and if it is too slack it will slip or come off the pulley. Correct tightening of the belt can be achieved by mounting the motor so it can slide to increase the tension.

This is a motor mount with fixing holes that allow the motor to be moved slightly for belt tensioning.

Jockey pulleys

If it is not practical to move the drive source to increase tension then a jockey pulley is used.

Sprung self-adjusting jockey pulley

A sprung self-adjusting jockey pulley has a strong spring which keeps the wheel firmly against the belt. This type of jockey pulley is used when belt slip is desirable or stretching of the belt is a problem.

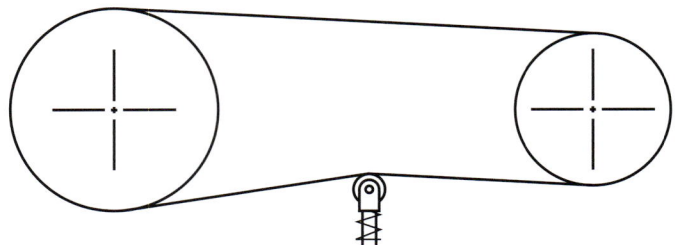

Fixed jockey pulley

A fixed jockey pulley has a slot in the bracket and a nut that loosens. These allow the jockey pulley to slide to increase or decrease the tension on the belt. The nut is then tightened to maintain the tension.

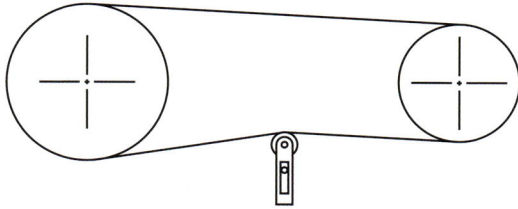

The main advantages of belt and pulley transmission systems are that they are quiet in operation, require no lubrication and are relatively cheap to produce. This is why they are used in domestic appliances.

CONVERSION OF MOTION

Cams and followers

Cams are mechanisms that change one type of motion into another type of motion. The cams below are rotary cams that **convert rotary motion into linear motion**.

You should be able to sketch, describe and compare the following cams and common followers.

Eccentric or circular cam	Heart shaped cam
The follower rises and falls at a uniform rate.	The follower rises to a height which remains constant until the follower reaches the groove, when it falls sharply at a uniform rate before rising again.

Pear shaped cam	Snail cam
The follower rises rapidly as it comes into contact with the bump part of the cam. The rise and fall of the follower will happen with equal speed but for half of the revolution it does not move.	The follower rises slowly then falls sharply into the step.

The profile of a cam will determine the distance travelled by its **follower**.

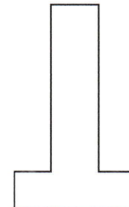

Knife follower   Flat follower   Roller follower

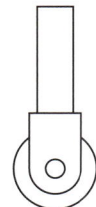

Many machines that have moving parts use cams, including:

- A motor car engine uses cams to open and close valves, contact breaker points and operate fuel pumps.

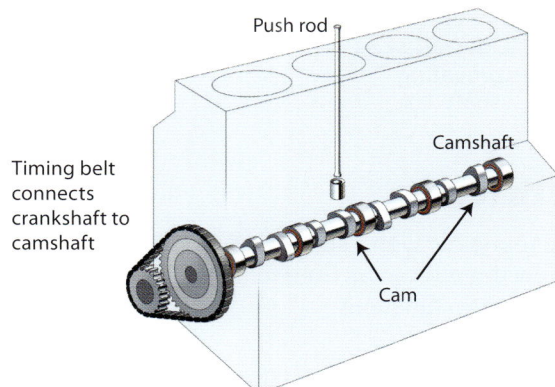

Push rod

Camshaft

Timing belt connects crankshaft to camshaft

Cam

- Children's toys sometimes use cams to make parts of the toy move when it is pulled along.

Crank and slider mechanisms

The **crank** uses the wheel and axle principle. The length of the handle increases the leverage and allows more force to be used to turn the shaft. The pedals on a child's tricycle are cranks. Several crank handles can be put together to form a crank shaft.

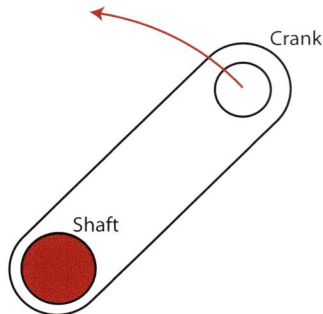

When a crank is connected to a slider it is known as a **crank-slider mechanism**. The crank rotates while the slider reciprocates. The longer the crank the further the slider will move. The two main uses are:

- **To change reciprocating motion into rotary motion**

  In a car engine the reciprocating motion of the piston, caused by exploding fuel, is converted into rotary motion as the rod moves the crankshaft around.

- **To change rotary motion into reciprocating motion**

  An air compressor uses this principal in reverse. An electric motor turns the crankshaft and the piston moves up and down to compress the air.

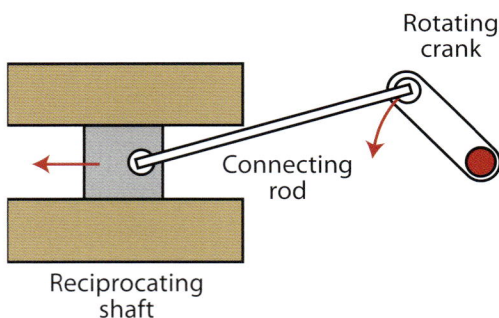

Screw threads

A **screw** is a round bar with a spiral groove cut into its surface. Screw threads can be used to transmit motion. They have two main functions:

- It converts rotary motion into linear motion.
- It prevents linear motion without the corresponding rotation.

The linear motion is produced as the threads of the screw climb on top of each other and is determined by the pitch of the thread. For each complete rotation of the thread, a nut, for example, will move a distance equal to the pitch of the thread.

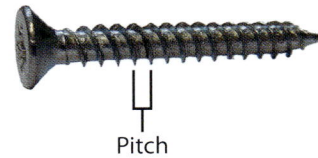

Ratchet and pawl mechanisms

A ratchet mechanism uses a wheel that has teeth cut out of it and a pawl that follows as the wheel turns. As the ratchet wheel turns, the pawl falls into the 'dip' between the teeth. The ratchet wheel can only turn in one direction. Ratchet mechanisms are very useful devices that can be used in systems for lifting heavy weights. They are also used in mechanical clocks.

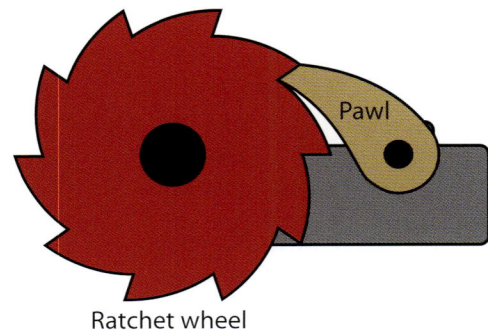

PNEUMATIC PRINCIPALS

Pneumatic systems use the energy stored in compressed air to do work. By controlling the release of the air to pneumatic cylinders, we can turn that energy into movement. Compressed air is the normal air that you breathe, put under pressure by being forced into a small space. A compressor is used to compress air.

Here are some basic pneumatic symbols. More components will be described in later sections:

Symbol	Meaning
	Pressure source
	Exhaust
- - - - - - - - - - -	Pilot
	Pipeline junction
	Pipeline not connected
	3/2 valve
	Spring return
	Single acting cylinder
	Reservoir
	Shuttle valve

The force you get out of a cylinder depends on the air pressure inside it, and the size or area of the piston.

Calculating force output:
The force you get from a piston is measured in Newtons (N).

Force (F) = Pressure (p) × Area (a)

Pressure is measured in N/mm² (0.1 N/mm² = 1 bar) and **area** is measured in mm²

Note: *We acknowledge that while these are not SI units, they are the industry standard.*

Working out the pressure:
If pressure is shown in **bar** you must convert it to N/mm². To convert bars to N/mm² simply **divide by 10**.
For example: 5 bar = 5 ÷ 10 = 0.5 N/mm²

Working out the area:

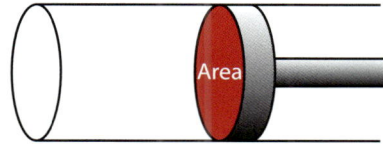

The area is the surface area of the piston. As every piston is round, you may have to calculate the area of the circular piston from the radius. Use the formula for the area of a circle to do this:

Area = π × radius² (taking π to be 3.14)

For example: if a piston has a radius of 30 mm, the surface area of the piston is: **3.14 × 30² = 3.14 × 30 × 30 = 2826 mm²**

QUESTIONS & ANSWERS

Q. A piston has a radius of 20 mm and the pressure in the cylinder is 4 bar. Calculate the force output from the cylinder.

A. Convert the units of pressure:
Pressure = 4 bar = 0.4 N/mm²

Work out the area: **Area = 3.14 × 20 × 20 = 1256 mm²**

Now you can calculate the force output from the cylinder: **Force = 0.4 × 1256 = 502.4 N**

Now rearrange the formula so it can be used to find the pressure or surface area of the piston.

ACTIVITY

1. What force is produced by the piston shown here if the air pressure is 0.3 N/mm²?

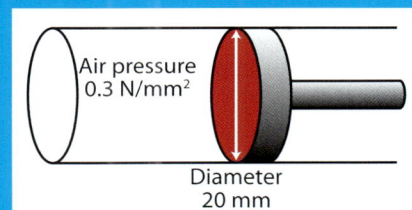

Air pressure 0.3 N/mm²

Diameter 20 mm

2. If the air pressure is 0.4 N/mm² calculate the force of the piston.

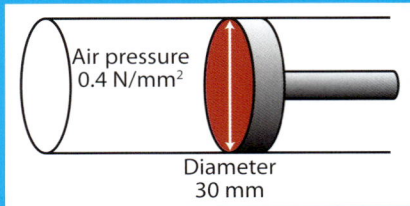

Air pressure
0.4 N/mm²

Diameter
30 mm

1. What is the key formula in pneumatics?
2. What is the value of 10 bars of pressure in Newtons/mm²?
3. What is the surface area of the piston if the radius is 25 mm?
4. If a piston has a radius of 10 mm and a pressure of 4 bar, what is the force?

DOUBLE ACTING CYLINDER

In the examination you may need to identify a double acting cylinder and its circuit symbol. These are shown below.

Real life

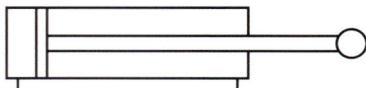

Symbol

The movement of the piston in and out of a double acting cylinder is controlled by compressed air. It does not have a return spring like the single acting cylinder you studied in Unit 1E, Pneumatic Systems and Control. The double acting cylinder has two ports through which compressed air can enter. Compressed air entering the back port will make the piston out-stroke or go positive (+). Compressed air is also needed to make the piston in-stroke or go negative (−) again. This is shown in the diagram at the top of the next column.

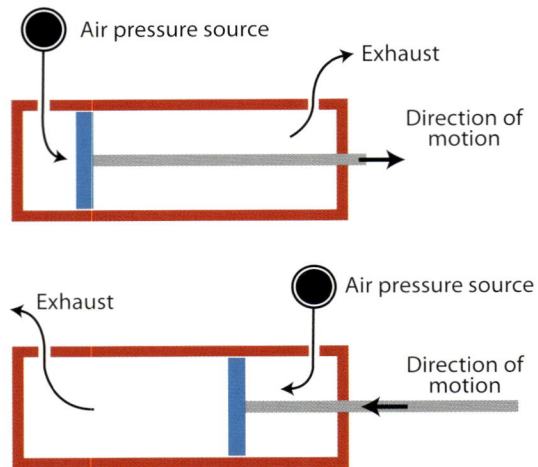

Air pressure source

Exhaust

Direction of motion

Exhaust

Air pressure source

Direction of motion

5/2 VALVE

Symbol

The **5/2 valve** is used to control items such as double acting cylinders which have two inputs. The diagram below shows how it does so.

• The compressed air supply is connected to **port 1**.

• Air can be directed from the valve through **ports 2 and 4** to other components or used to direct exhausted air to **port 3 or 5**.

• **Ports 3 and 5** are used to release exhausted air to the atmosphere.

• The number 5 in a 5/2 valve signifies that the valve has five ports, whilst the number 2 signifies that the valve has 2 directions or states.

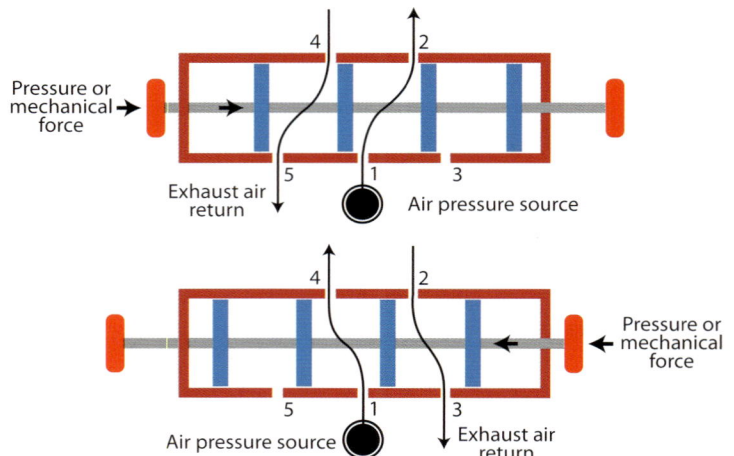

Pressure or mechanical force

Exhaust air return

Air pressure source

Pressure or mechanical force

Air pressure source

Exhaust air return

ACTUATORS

In Unit 1E, Pneumatic Systems and Control you studied mechanical actuators that actuated 3/2 valves. These can also be used to actuate 5/2 valves. Actuated means turned on and this can be achieved by the following methods:

Symbols

Push   Roller   Lever   Plunger

A real life roller actuator on a 3/2 valve.

Air actuated valves

Another actuator you need to know is a pilot actuator. A 5/2 pilot or pilot valve can also be used to control a double acting cylinder. The dashed lines of the symbol indicate the valve is operated by air pressure rather than by manual or mechanical means, as would happen if any of the actuators above were used. The air pressure is called *signal air*. Air actuated valves are often utilised in industry, where high pressure systems are used, and are essential to keep the operators away from danger.

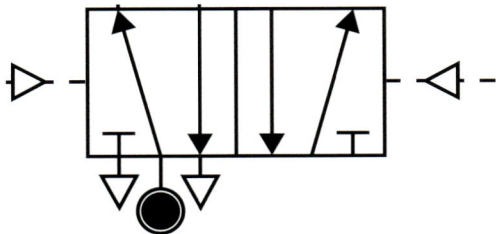

Symbol

BIDIRECTIONAL AND UNIDIRECTIONAL FLOW CONTROL VALVES

Unidirectional flow control valves

Symbol

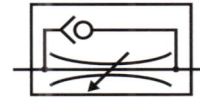

A unidirectional flow control valve is used in a pneumatic circuit when the flow of air needs to be controlled only in one direction. A screw adjuster is turned into the valve to reduce the rate at which the air is flowing by blocking the airway inside the valve. In the image below you can see that the restriction of air is only happening in one direction, from right to left. The air from right to left has been blocked as the sprung valve is acting as a stop, so air is forced to pass through the restricted channel. The air flow meets resistance as it flows from left to right, causing pressure to build, which forces the sprung valve backwards and allows more air to move over the valve.

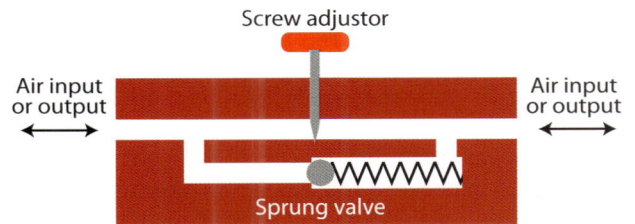

A unidirectional flow control valve can be used when the speed of a piston out of the cylinder needs controlled.

Practical applications: A unidirectional flow valve can be used to control the speed of a piston which gently pushes a product onto a conveyor belt. However, the piston also needs to be able to move back quickly in preparation to push the next product along.

Bidirectional flow control valves

A *bidirectional (two-way) restrictor valve* will control both the speed of the piston moving out of the cylinder going positive (+) and the speed of the piston moving back into the cylinder going negative (−). This is because the air going down the pipe is restricted equally in both directions.

Symbol

PNEUMATIC CIRCUITS

Pneumatic circuits can be designed to be semi-automatic or fully automatic. A semi-automatic circuit requires a valve to be actuated manually for the circuit to begin. To design a pneumatic circuit to operate automatically, the valves need to be placed in a position where they can be turned on by the piston rod as it reaches the end of its movement.

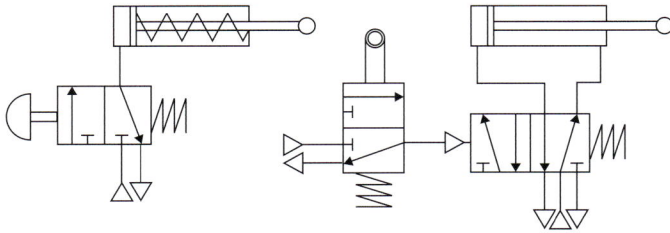

Semi-automatic circuit

Automatic circuit with a five-port valve

As the piston of the double acting cylinder moves back in going negative (–) it activates the roller control, this allows air to pass through the 3/2 roller spring return valve.

The air output from the 3/2 roller spring return valve activates the left side of the 5/2 pilot/pilot valve as represented by the dashed lines in the diagram below. This causes air to be released at the top left of the 5/2 pilot/pilot valve, making the piston move outwards going positive (+). Air at the front of the piston is exhausted and this exhaust air is used to control the speed of the piston moving outwards by the unidirectional flow control valve.

When the piston has moved out completely it actuates the plunger of the 3/2 plunger spring return valve, which sends out a signal.

The right side of the 5/2 pilot/pilot valve is activated by the air that has been released by the 3/2 plunger spring return valve. They are connected by the dashed lines. This signal causes air to be released from the top right of the 5/2 pilot/pilot valve, making the piston return into the cylinder going negative (–). The cycle repeats as the piston operates the roller trip control.

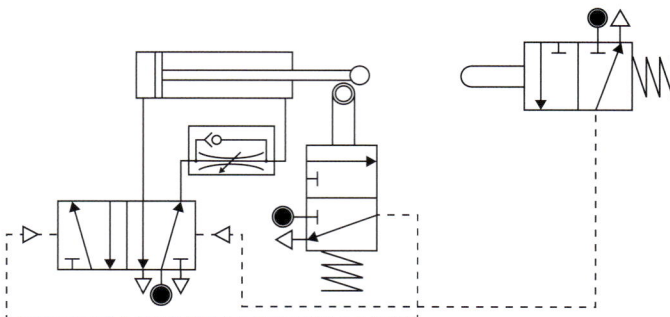

An automatic circuit with a 5/2 pilot/pilot valve

SENSORS: FEEDBACK SIGNAL

At this stage of your study of pneumatic control systems you should have a sound understanding of the use of a various 3/2 valves and 5/2 valves to produce controlled motion for semi-automatic and automatic circuits using a range of actuators. Remember pneumatic circuits are used as control systems so like all systems they will have an input, process and output.

Within a pneumatic system there may also be feedback given by air signals. These air signals are air under pressure, and are used to actuate valves and cause the processing within the pneumatic system to continue.

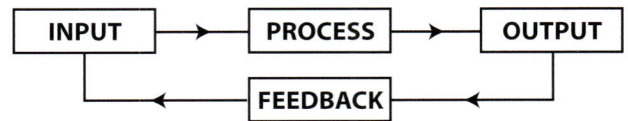

Using pressure sensing is another way to achieve a fully automatic pneumatic circuit. Low-pressure, air operated valves can be used to sense when a piston has reached the end of its movement. The dashed lines of the symbol indicate that the valve is air operated. These air signals are then fed back to the valves, allowing the processing of the pneumatic circuit to continue.

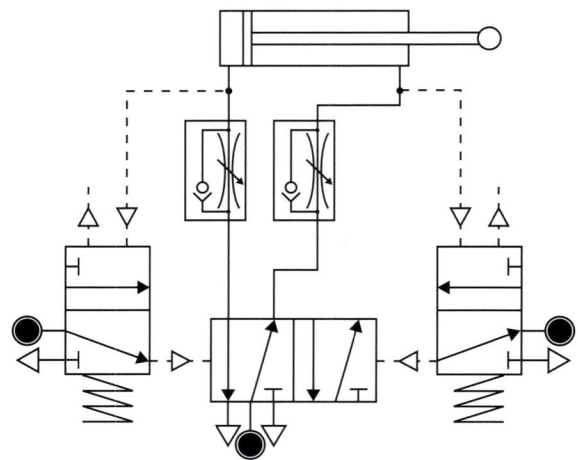

Circuit that senses end of piston movement

TIME DELAY CIRCUITS

A pneumatic circuit with a time delay is shown in the diagram below. Using a time delay in a pneumatic circuit allows a delay to occur between a valve being operated and the piston moving. Time delays are achieved by connecting a **unidirectional flow control valve** and a **reservoir** in series. A reservoir is an empty container or bottle that will fill with air.

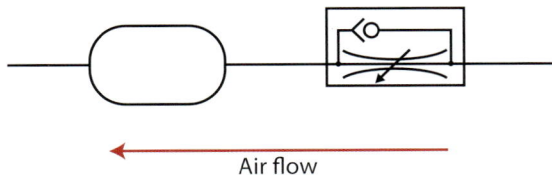

Air flow

Look at the circuit below. Once the push button of the 3/2 valve is actuated, the unidirectional flow control valve restricts the air flow and it slowly enters the reservoir. The time delay is caused by the pressure in the reservoir building up slowly. Only the 5/2 valve will operate and cause the release of air, making the piston outstroke and go positive (+) when the pressure in the reservoir is high enough. When the push button is actuated on the other 3/2 valve, the 5/2 valve will switch, causing the release of air that makes the piston in-stroke and go negative (–).

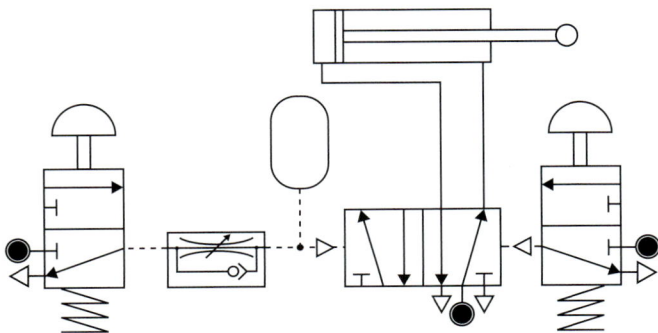

Semi-automatic circuit with a time delay

Do not confuse a time delay within a pneumatic circuit with speed control. Speed control slows the speed of the piston down whereas a time delay gives several seconds delay before the piston moves.

AUTOMATIC RECIPROCATION

To achieve automatic reciprocation a circuit can be designed with positional feedback to activate a pilot air operated 5/2 valve, controlling two double acting cylinders incorporating speed control (no more cylinders are required).

This diagram of a pneumatic circuit shows automatic reciprocation within a machine that stamps shapes onto wooden blocks in a continuous process.

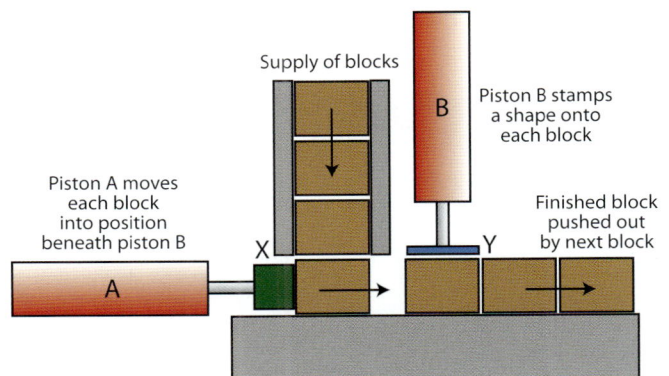

Blocks are fed in at X and out at Y.
Pistons A and B go out-stroke (+) and in-stroke (–) in a specific sequence: **A+ B+ A– B–**

- If piston A moves outwards, going positive (+) it pushes a wooden box into place, then pilot valve A2 (in the diagram overleaf) is activated sending an air signal to control valve C (connecting port 1 to port 4).

- This makes piston B go positive and stamp the block. When fully positive, piston B activates pilot valve B2 sending an air signal to control valve D (connecting port 1 to port 4).

- This makes piston A go negative. When fully negative, piston A activates pilot valve A1 sending an air signal to control valve C (connecting port 1 to port 2).

- This makes piston B go negative. When fully negative, piston B activates pilot valve B1 sending an air signal to control valve D (connecting port 1 to port 2).

- And so on continuously ...

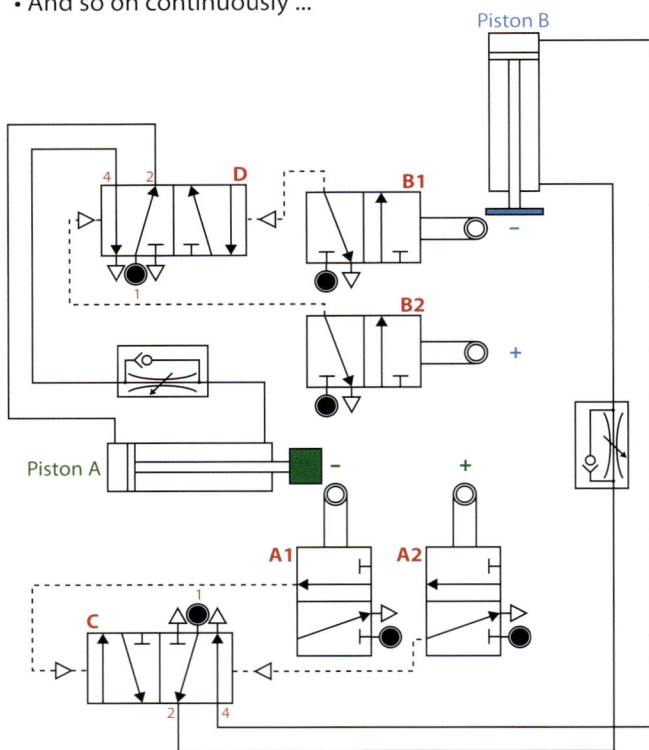

ACTIVITY

The following pictures are examples of real life applications. Design pneumatic circuits for the safe operation of each system shown in the images below:

- Tipper trolley

- Paper guillotine

- Factory ventilator hatch

ACTIVITY

The following scenarios are examples of real life problems that could be solved by pneumatic circuits. Design pneumatic circuits for each.

- In a factory, some parts need to be drilled on a production line but they must be held securely in place for safety reasons. The operator wants to be able to activate and deactivate a pneumatic clamp that will hold the part to be drilled in a jig. Before the drilling cycle starts the clamp must be in place and the part unclamped at the end of the drilling cycle.

- A factory requires a pneumatic circuit to be designed to operate a stamping machine but also reduces potential safety hazards. They need the parts to be stamped in place, the clamps activated and the safety guard closed before the stamping machine can be started.

- In a factory finished products are building up at the end of a conveyor belt. The products need to be moved on to another conveyor, which will move them to the quality control and packaging areas. The operator wants to be able to activate and then release a device to transfer the products from one conveyor belt to another connected conveyor that is powered by a pneumatic cylinder.

Revise the key words for Mechanisms in Unit 1C, page 55 and Pneumatics in Unit 1E, page 67, then explain what each of the key words below mean. Remember to add these words to your glossary.

- Mechanical advantage
- Load
- Effort
- Fulcrum
- Velocity ratio
- Moment
- Lever
- Linkage
- Bell Crank
- Parallel Linkage
- Spur gear

- Bevel gear
- Worm wheel and worm gears
- Rack and pinion
- Gear train
- Simple gear Train
- Compound gear Train
- Gear ratio
- Idler gear
- Pulleys
- Cams

- Cam followers
- Crank and slider mechanisms
- Screw threads
- Ratchet and pawl mechanisms
- Pneumatic systems
- Pressure
- Force
- Double acting cylinder
- 5/2 valve

- Actuators
- Pilot valve
- Unidirectional flow control valve
- Bidirectional flow control valve
- Time delay
- Speed control
- Automatic reciprocation

EXAM FOCUS

Complete the following past paper questions to help consolidate your learning and practice your exam skills.

1. **Metal parts are to be dipped in a degreasing solution for a given time before painting. The pneumatic cylinder used in this process is shown in Figure 1.**

(a) (i) Name the type of cylinder shown in Figure 1. [1]

  (ii) The cylinder is required to raise a maximum load of 300 N. Calculate the cross-sectional area of the piston required.
  Supply pressure = 0.6 N/mm^2.
  Cross-sectional area of the piston rod = 100 mm^2. [5]

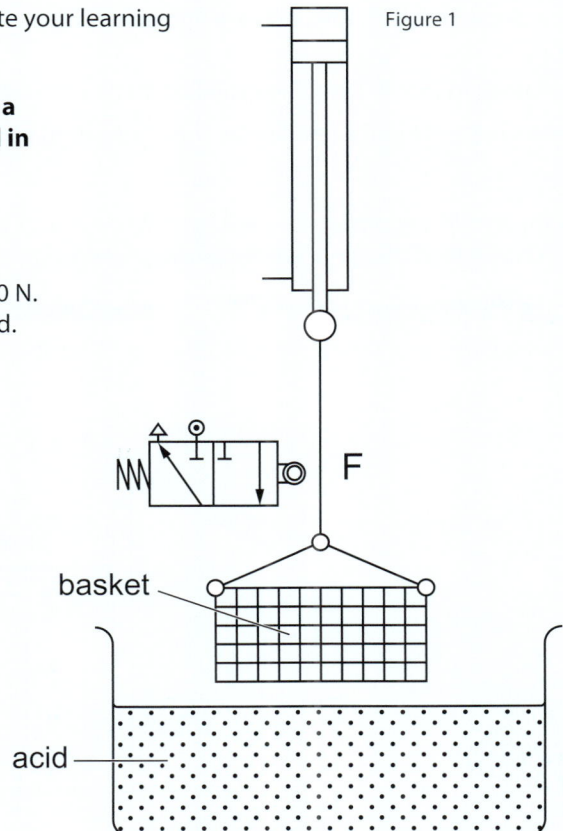

Figure 1

start button A

basket

acid

F

(b) The pneumatic circuit used to control the cylinder in Figure 1 is shown in Figure 2.

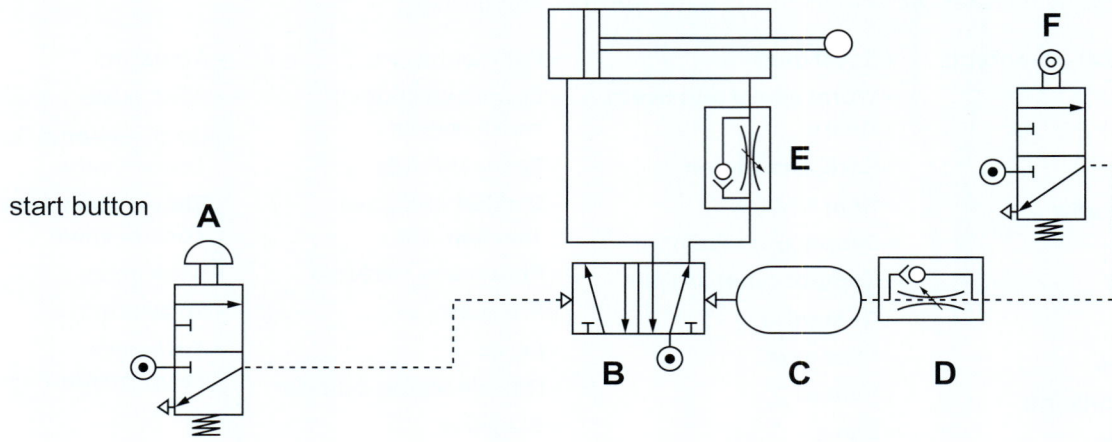

Figure 2

(i)   Name the components A, B, C and D. [4]

(ii) Describe briefly how the circuit operates when the start button is pressed. [6]

(iii) State how each of the following could be changed.
   • The rate of immersion of the parts. [3]
   • The depth to which the parts are immersed. [3]

(iv) The circuit in Figure 2 is to be modified so that the start signal can be given from either of two positions.
    Make a copy of Figure 2 and show the connecting pipes and additional valves needed to achieve this. [6]

(c) Figure 3 shows a lifting device for packages. When a start button is operated for an instant the package is lifted by cylinder A. Cylinder B then pushes the package onto a gravity-roller conveyor. Both cylinders then return to their initial position.

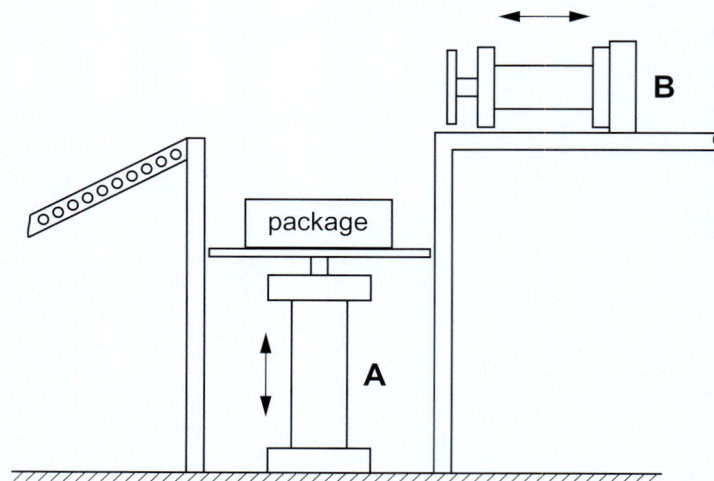

Figure 3

Part of the pneumatic circuit for Figure 3 is shown in Figure 4.

    (i)   Complete the pneumatic circuit in Figure 4 by adding the pipework to give the required sequence. [8]

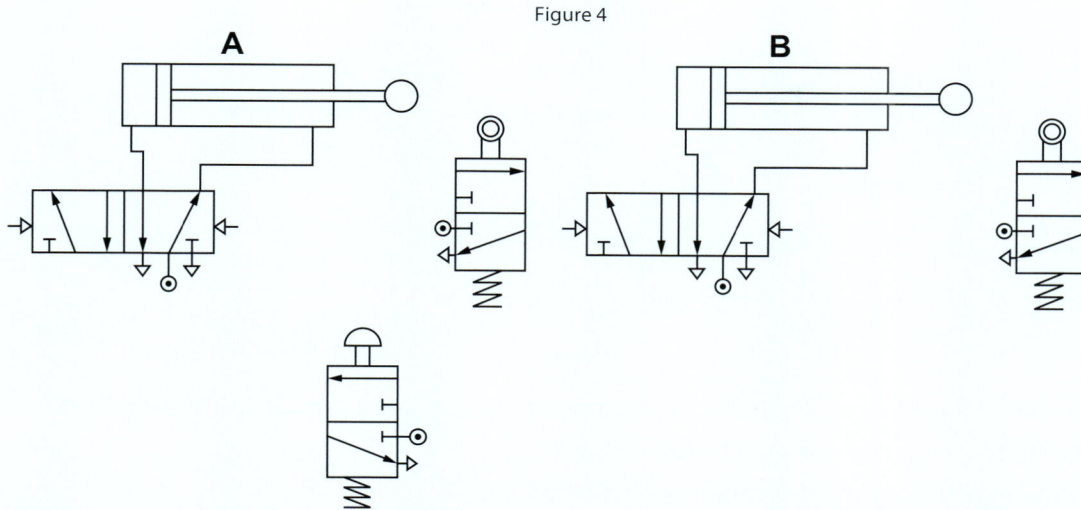

Figure 4

    (ii) The circuit is to be modified so that the signal to outstroke cylinder A cannot be given unless cylinder B is fully retracted. Explain briefly how this could be achieved. [4]

CCEA GCSE Technology & Design Past Paper, Unit 2, Systems and Control, Element 1, Electronic and Microelectronic Control Systems, Summer 2011, © CCEA

2.   **Figure 5 shows four different mechanisms. Make a copy of the table. You do not have to draw the diagrams in the mechanism column but can identify them by (i), (ii), (iii) and (iv) instead.**

    (a)   Complete the table by inserting the correct name for each mechanism and the appropriate letter from the list beside it to describe its function. Each letter may be used only once. [8]

Figure 5

Mechanism	Name	Function
(i)		
(ii)		
(iii)		
(iv)		

A To make large speed changes.

B To allow rotation in one direction only.

C To change the direction of movement through 90 degrees.

D To convert rotary motion to rotary motion at right angles with a large speed reduction.

(b) Power is to be transmitted from Motor A to Shaft B parallel to the motor as shown in Figure 6.

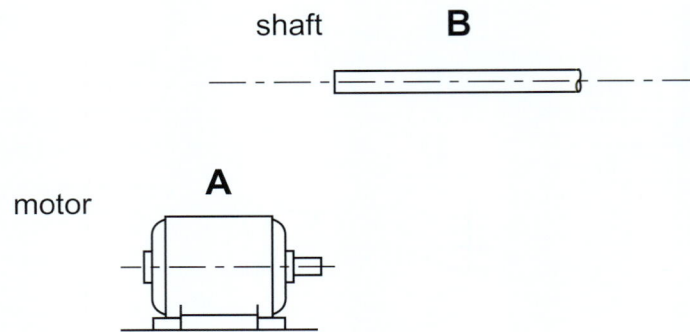

shaft   **B**

motor   **A**

Figure 6

(i) State two factors, other than cost, which should be considered in selecting a method to achieve this. [4]

(ii) Name two methods which could be used to achieve this. [4]

(iii) Give one advantage and one disadvantage of each method. [4]

(c) Figure 7 shows a mechanism, used on a machine in which the lever is rotated to produce movement M.

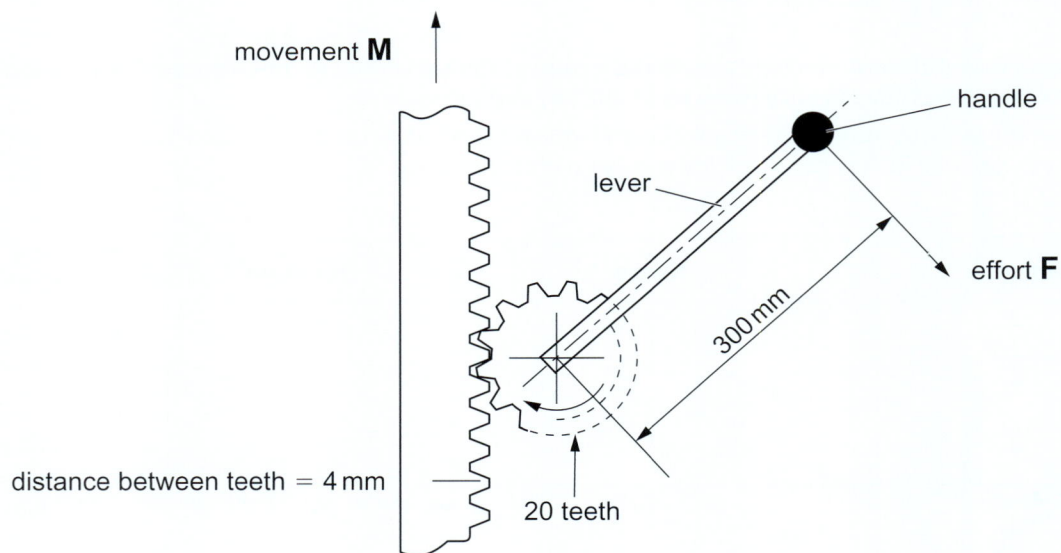

movement **M**

handle

lever

effort **F**

300 mm

distance between teeth = 4 mm

20 teeth

Figure 7

(i)   Name the mechanism in Figure 3. [2]

(ii) State the type of input and output motion for the mechanism. [4]

(iii) Describe briefly a sustainable method for attaching the handle to the lever. [4]

(iv) The effort F is applied to a handle at the end of a lever 3000 mm long.

     If the lever is turned through 90 degrees calculate:
     (Circumference of a circle = π x diameter)

     • The distance moved by the effort F. [4]

     • The distance moved by M. [4]

     • The velocity ratio. [2]

CCEA GCSE Technology & Design Past Paper, Unit 2, Systems and Control, Element 1, Electronic and Microelectronic Control Systems, Summer 2011, © CCEA

UNIT 3

PRODUCT DESIGN

This unit is a choice for students.
In this chapter you will be studying:

Your school will advise you on whether
you will be studying this unit.

Designing and innovation

Materials, components and fabrication

Manufacturing practices

Social responsibility of product design and market influences

Product design is complex and involves more than sketching a concept and hoping it can be manufactured. The design must be innovative, look good, work well, be comfortable to use, be manufactured to high quality from the most appropriate materials and still be affordable. It also needs to be a potential best seller, which can be difficult in a highly competitive market, and a product designer must research market influences to ensure the product is what the consumer wants.

The four elements in this unit will help you understand product design in greater detail.

3A DESIGN AND INNOVATION

MARKET/DEMAND PULL AND TECHNOLOGY PUSH

If the terms market/demand pull and technology push are understood you will be able to discuss why a product is developed.

Market/demand pull

Market/demand pull is when consumers see a product they want to buy. The market place creates the consumer demand that results in development and expansion of the product.

Consumer demand can be increased by manufacturers developing new products. The technology for a product such as the 1970s Sony Walkman had been available prior to its manufacture but when the company developed a product that enabled people to listen to music on the go, the consumer demand soared. The product developed continuously into the products we have today, from CD walkmans to MP3 players.

ACTIVITY

List other products you think have developed from market/demand pull.

Technology push

Technology push is when a technological advance such as new materials or a production method exists that pushes the development of new products. Designers then think of a use for the new material developed by a scientist.

Example:
PTFE (polytetrafluroethylene) resin was discovered during research at DuPont by a chemist. The material is known as Teflon, which is heat tolerant and stick resistant. It is used on saucepans and frying pans to make them non-stick.

ACTIVITY

Research other products that have been developed as a result of a technological advance.

CHECK YOUR LEARNING

Explain briefly how market pull can create the development of a new product.

ROLE OF THE CLIENT, USER, DESIGNER AND MAKER

It is important that you are able to demonstrate an understanding of the main roles of the client, user, designer and maker, and how they interact in commissioning, design, manufacture and evaluation of a product.

The client: is usually the person or company who commissions the design by providing the designer with the problem or need, a clear brief, completes the market research and has the money for the project.

The designer: is the person who solves the problem or need by designing a product following the design process.

The maker: is the manufacturer who plans and manufactures safely and efficiently a quality end product that will make a profit.

The retailer: gives customers what they want reasonably.

The user: is the person who will be getting a high quality product that functions well, has fulfilled a need and is value for money.

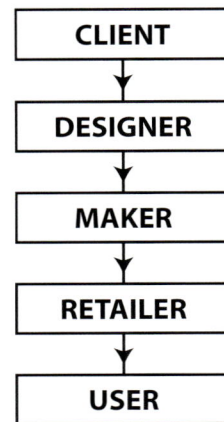

```
┌─────────────┐
│   CLIENT    │
└─────────────┘
       ↓
┌─────────────┐
│  DESIGNER   │
└─────────────┘
       ↓
┌─────────────┐
│   MAKER     │
└─────────────┘
       ↓
┌─────────────┐
│  RETAILER   │
└─────────────┘
       ↓
┌─────────────┐
│    USER     │
└─────────────┘
```

All of these roles interact during the design process to bring a design solution to a need or problem, which is manufactured to the highest standard to be a fully functional and desired product for use by the user. Good communication between the roles is essential at all stages of the design process.

IDEA GENERATION AND DEVELOPMENT TECHNIQUES

The designer works for the client designing a product for the user that solves the original design brief. They use the following techniques to generate and develop ideas:

1. Brainstorming
2. Morphological analysis
3. Disassembly of existing products

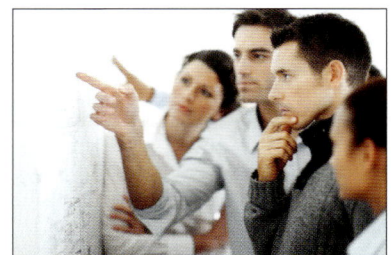

Brainstorming

This is when you think up any questions, key words and initial thoughts you have about your problem, idea or product. Write down everything initially as ideas can be disregarded later.

Morphological analysis

This means breaking the ideas into features and designing the product in different ways. Look firstly at the technology, then at aesthetics, then at materials and dimensions, and so on. It is a way of exploring lots of ideas.

Example:
You could carry out a morphological analysis to design a new lamp. The properties of a lamp might be power, light intensity, type of bulb, size, style, finish, material, shade, etc.

The features or properties should be set out as column headings in a table and the variations of each brainstormed. This table is sometimes known as a 'Morphologial Box' or 'Zwicky Box', after Fritz Zwicky, the scientist who developed the technique in the 1960s.

Power Supply	Light Intensity	Style	Finish
Mains	Medium	Antique	White
Battery	Low	Modern	Black
Solar	High	Roman	Metallic
Generator	Variable	Art Nouveau	Terracotta
Crank		Industrial	Enamel
Gas		Ethnic	Natural
Oil/petrol			Fabric
Flame			

Material	Size	Bulb Type
Ceramic	Large	Bulb
Metal	Very Large	Halogen
Concrete	Medium	Daylight
Bone	Small	Colored
Glass	Hand held	
Wood		
Stone		
Plastic		

The results of products designed from this analysis may or may not be practical. An interesting example would be a solar powered/battery, medium intensity, daylight bulb, which could be used in clothes shops to allow customers to see the true color of clothes.

ACTIVITY

Use the information in the morphological box to find other combinations for possible new light designs. Sketch and annotate them with notes to explain the new design.

Disassembly of existing products

This means taking an existing product apart. It will help you find out how a current product is made and how it works. It will also give you information about the processes and materials used and how the user's needs have been met.

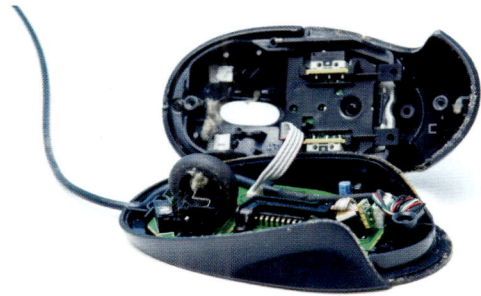

Disassembly of a computer mouse.

CHECK YOUR LEARNING

List and explain three ways a designer could generate ideas or develop a product.

PRODUCT ANALYSIS

Another aspect of product design is product analysis. Without looking at what other designers have done with existing products you will not be able to design a good product. You will be a better designer if you analyse existing products to find out what makes the design good and work well.

Product analysis should help you:

1. Think about what makes a design good.
2. Think about the manufacturing methods used.
3. Understand the uses of different materials.

4. Identify examples of good or bad designs, manufacture and material choices.

5. Get ideas you can use in your own designs, or to make modifications to an existing design.

6. Make better decisions about what people want and might buy.

Fitness for purpose

To analyse whether a product is fit for a purpose or not you need to ask some questions, such as:

1. Has the design need or situation been met? Refer back to the initial need or situation, and ensure your product is fulfilling this need.

2. Are the needs of the intended users being met?

3. Find out if the product user is satisfied with the final product. Question the user: Does it suit the situation or environment it is to be used in? Is the cost appropriate?

4. Is the product fit for the purpose it was designed and manufactured for? Does it do what it was intended for?

Quality

Consumers will demand quality when they buy a product, and this can refer to:

Design quality: Has the product been designed to meet the needs of the intended user?

Manufacturing quality: How well has the product been made?

A product can be designed well, but not well manufactured; or well manufactured, but badly designed. So to determine product quality you need to think about the user's needs, the materials chosen, the accuracy of manufacture, and the maintenance and the disposal of the product. You might like to consider some of the following questions:

User's needs: Have the intended users' needs been met by the product?

Material choice: Are the materials chosen for manufacture suitable?

Manufacture: Is it well manufactured? Was it checked for quality during manufacture?

Maintenance: Will the product be easily maintained or replaced if necessary?

Disposal: Will the product be easily disposed at the end of its life without causing damage to the environment?

Specification

A specification is a detailed list of everything a product should do or have. A product designer must be able to develop a specification by looking at a product and use factors such as these examples to write it:

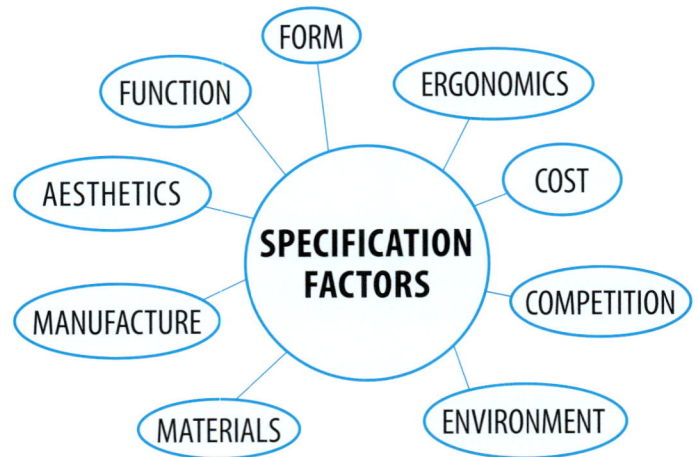

When you are writing a specification it is important that you state what the factor is and why it should be considered.

114

entertainment section of the local supermarket, with an aim of increasing sales and profits for the client.

Cost:
The display unit must be designed and manufactured to be cost efficient in terms of the amount of material required, the manufacturing processes chosen and overall must be affordable for the client.

Materials:
The material for the display unit should compliment the product it is holding. It should have a high quality finish that will look professional and be in keeping with other furniture and display cabinets within the supermarket. It should machine well and be available in the school workshop. The material chosen must be affordable.

Evaluation

Evaluating your own product is not really any different from judging or evaluating products that you buy. As part of your product analysis try to evaluate the product using the specification criteria, consider each specification factor and score it. A sample of possible users could also score the product to help your evaluation. It may be useful to put this information into a table format, such as the one below, where it can be easily analysed and comments can be made about how the product has met the specification criteria.

	Colour	Material	Function	Size	Shape	Safety	Cost	Aesthetics	Ergonomics	Fun factor	/100 Score	Comment
Example of a scoring technique to help evaluate products.												
	8	10	8	6	6	8	5	6	8	0	65	From my scoring I feel this product fulfils its need as it functions well as a bicycle mirror, improving cyclist's safety. It was expensive at £19.99 and the mirror is slightly small, reducing rear views for the user. It was easily adjusted so it was ergonomically designed but it is not an attractive or fun product. It was only available in black. The choice of material made it lightweight.

Historical influences and trends

When completing a product analysis consider how historical influences and trends can have an effect on the design of a product. You should be aware of the following:

Design movements
Design movements are distinct styles that emerged at

certain times in history due to influences such as:

- fashions
- trends
- iconic products
- the development of new materials
- the developments in manufacturing and technology
- the latest thinking

The influences of nature: were seen in the Arts and Crafts movement of the 1890s, founded by William Morris, and the Art Nouveau movement that was popularised between 1890 and 1914. Both were influenced by natural patterns and forms.

The influences of industry resulted in the Modernist movement, who used geometric shapes in their designs.

- The **Bauhaus** movement of 1919–1933 was a German school of art and design that produced the first design for mass production. It was also the origin of many classic designs.
- The **Art Deco** movement, popular during the 1920s and 1930s, used geometric shapes.
- The **DeStijl** movement of the mid 1920s used extreme geometric shapes and primary colours that inspired brand new furniture and architectectural designs.

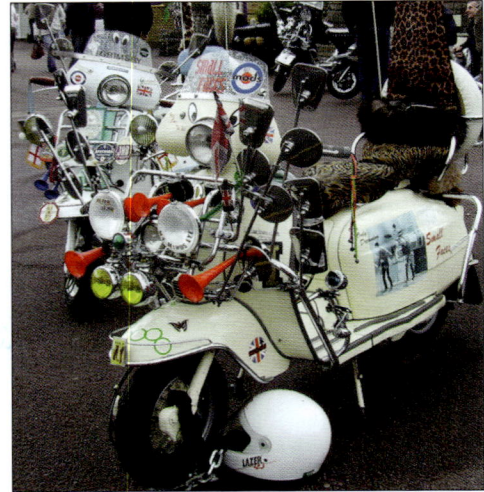

Art deco detail of the upper tower of the Chrysler Building, New York City.

DeStijl movement 'Red and Blue Chair', designed by Gerrit Rietveld in 1917.

During WW2, post war and the 1960s: designs could be manufactured cheaply, as new materials and production methods were developed. The three main influences that caused this were:

1. The increased interest in science.
2. Rapid growth in transport design.
3. The challenge to get the first man on the moon.

The 1960s saw a big growth in consumers wanting new ideas. The teenage consumer market also developed for the first time with the 'Mods'. 'Mods' is short for Modernist. In the late 1950s to their peak in the mid 1960s, 'Mods' could be defined as a young subculture in Britain, which originated in London. They had their own fashion sense, style of music, and motorcycle scooters. This group of people became a new teenage consumer market.

Many Mods owned scooters and often treated them as a fashion accessory.

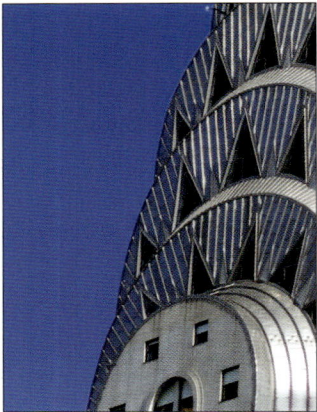

From the 1970s onwards the following trends developed:

- By the 1980s consumers were putting importance on brand and designer names, not just within fashion but also with a wider range of products.
- Packaging and promotion became part of the whole product.
- The Memphis Group of the early 1980s brought designs that were an alternative to minimalism. They were highly decorated with laminate surfaces, bright patterns and bold colours.
- A current trend in product design is Blobism were curves are very apparent in designs. This has been aided by developments in CAD that has helped with design and manufacture of such products.

A Memphis Group room.

Research the following influences on design to help you understand more about the history of product design:

- The Arts and Crafts movement of the 1890s, founded by William Morris.
- The Art Nouveau movement, including designers such as Charles Rennie Mackintosh and Louis Comfort Tiffany.
- The Bauhaus movement. The Classic Design website (www.classic-design24.com) gives some examples of Bauhaus design.
- Gerrit Rietveld
- Mary Quant and Alec Issigonis. What did they design in the 1960s?
- Use 'google images' to find a range of Memphis designs.

Now produce a time line of historical influences in product design, with one image that represents each era.

MODELLING

Modelling is an essential part of the development process. The following modelling types can be used:

- mock-ups
- prototypes
- computer modelling

Models are very important to help judge proportion. They can be either full size or scale models, and a variety of model types are available such as card, foam, corrugated paper, Styrofoam and CAD prototypes. They all have different benefits and limitations:

Mock-ups

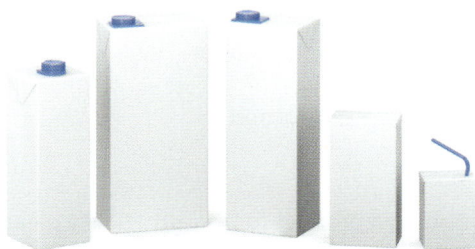

Mock-ups can be used to experiment with different sizes and shapes.

Mock-ups can be used to help evaluate a design. They allow the dimensions and human factors to be examined, and market research can be used to test consumers' impressions. They also enable designers to try out features that cannot be visualised from initial sketches such as the final colours, finish and design details.

Prototypes

Prototypes are models built early in the design process to help the designer find out how the real product will look and work. They can be made quickly and either very simply or as full size models. A prototype will have some functioning within it to allow a design to be tested.

Computer modelling

CAD can be used to make computer simulations of designs. Solidworks is an example of a software package used for computer modelling. The disadvantage of computer modeling is that the model cannot be held or passed around designers in a group to handle.

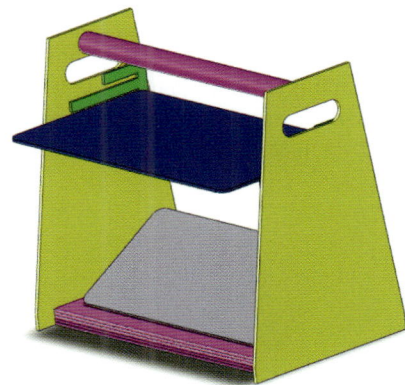

An example of a product designed using 3D solid modelling.

1. Name three types of modelling that can be used as part of the development process in product design.
2. Explain the difference between mock-ups and prototypes.

COMMUNICATION OF IDEAS

Communication of ideas is a vital part of a designer's work and there are numerous communication methods that can be used when generating ideas creatively.

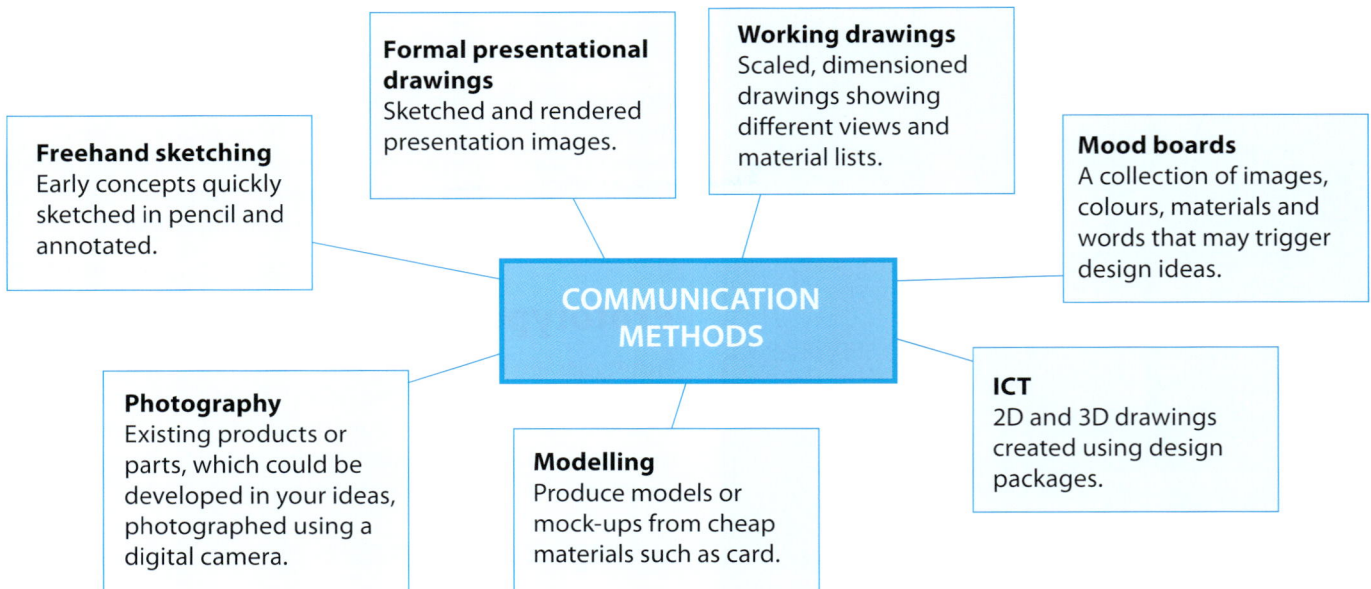

Formal presentational drawings
Sketched and rendered presentation images.

Working drawings
Scaled, dimensioned drawings showing different views and material lists.

Freehand sketching
Early concepts quickly sketched in pencil and annotated.

Mood boards
A collection of images, colours, materials and words that may trigger design ideas.

COMMUNICATION METHODS

Photography
Existing products or parts, which could be developed in your ideas, photographed using a digital camera.

Modelling
Produce models or mock-ups from cheap materials such as card.

ICT
2D and 3D drawings created using design packages.

AESTHETICS

The term 'aesthetics' concerns our senses and our responses to an object. If something is aesthetically pleasing to you, it means you like it. If it is aesthetically displeasing to you, it means you do not like it. Aesthetics involves all of your senses and your emotions. As a product designer you must be able to demonstrate an understanding of the main visual elements of product design that add to the aesthetic appeal of a product:

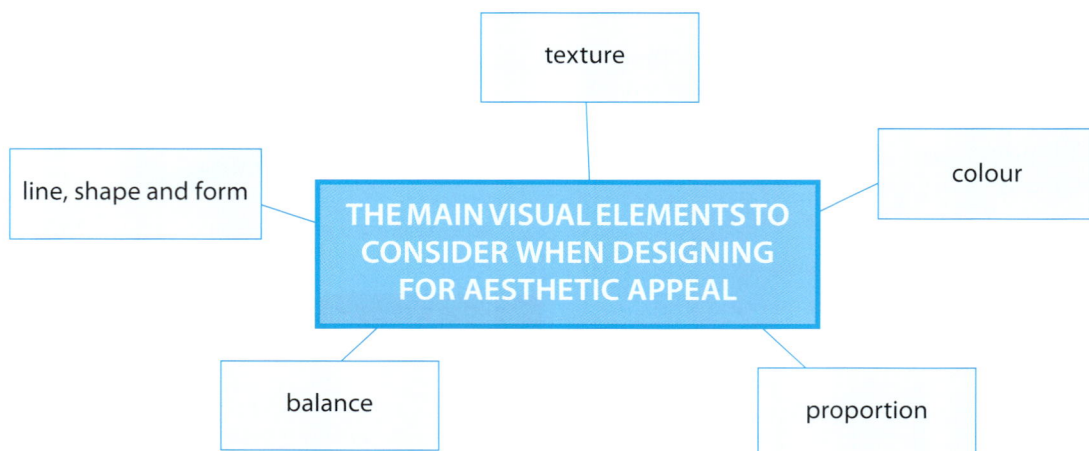

texture

line, shape and form

colour

THE MAIN VISUAL ELEMENTS TO CONSIDER WHEN DESIGNING FOR AESTHETIC APPEAL

balance

proportion

These are the visual factors that a product designer will consider when designing a product to be aesthetically pleasing. They contribute to your perception of a product, and to your opinion of whether it is aesthetically pleasing to you.

ERGONOMICS AND ANTHROPOMETRICS

The role of a product designer no longer solely focuses on aesthetics. They now also need to integrate the science of ergonomics into the products they design to meet the changing demands of consumers.

Ergonomics is the study of people in their environment. It means making the product fit the user.

Consumers demand a product that functions; they expect it to be usable and are looking for a product that gives them other feelings or emotions. It will be the aesthetics of the product – the way it looks, the feel of the material, the tactile response evoked by controls on a product or more abstract feelings – that will give pleasure. Remember this when designing and that the best design occurs when aesthetics, ergonomics and technology are considered together from the start of the design process.

As a product designer you must understand the relationship between people and products so you need an awareness of ergonomics and anthropometrics.

The following ergonomic factors are important considerations for a designer when trying to make things easier, more comfortable and safer to use:

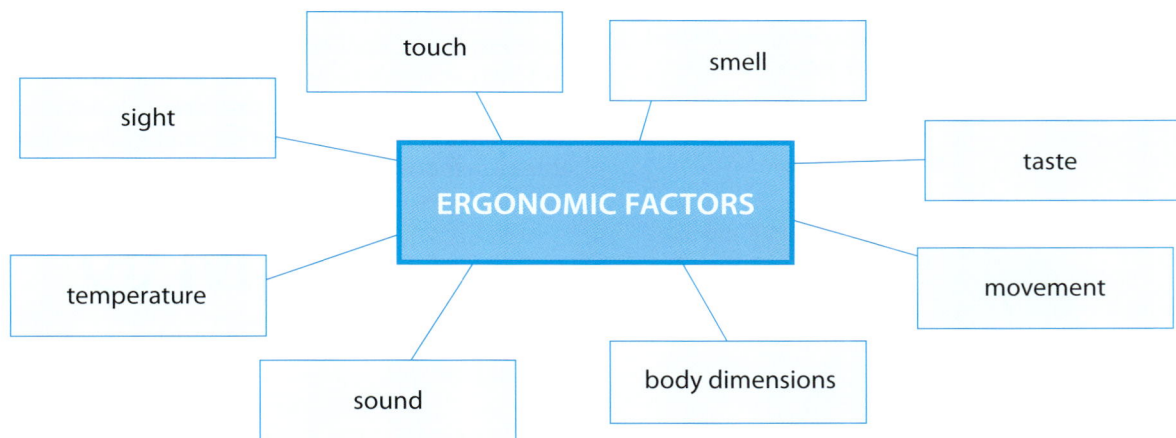

touch   smell
sight   taste
ERGONOMIC FACTORS
temperature   movement
sound   body dimensions

Sight, touch, taste, smell and sound are *psychological factors* concerned with how the brain works. Designers need to understand how people think and react to these senses when designing products.

Sight: is a major consideration for designers, as how people see and react to visual information such a signs, symbols and displays is very important. Designers use colour to make a product attractive, as using different colours and shapes creates feelings within people, can alert us or suggest issues such as gender or cleanliness.

Touch: is a key factor in products as it can be designed to give the user texture, warmth or coolness, or be controlled by touch such as a computer mouse or games console.

Smell: is an important consideration in the development of products like cosmetics and household fragrances. Our sense of taste is influenced by smell.

Taste: is another valuable consideration in the design of products intended to appeal to this sense, such as toothpaste and lip products.

Sound: is used by designers in warning products such as security and fire alarms, alarm clocks and car horns, as humans react to noise.

Anthropometrics

Anthropometrics is the study of the human body and the movement of each part. As a product designer you must consider the person or people who are your intended user(s). There is a wide variation in size amongst people so anthropometric data is collected and collated.

119

Anthropometric data is measurements that have been taken from a wide sample of people of various sizes and shapes and collated in charts. This anthropometric data is used by designers to design products that are ergonomical. There is a lot of data, so most designers' work from the 5th to the 95th percentile, which ensures they are designing for 90% of the population. The graph below gives you a visual idea of what the 5th to the 95th percentile means. This graph represents height measurements and it is evident that most of the people measured in the sample were of average height. If a designer decides to take height measurements into account in a product they are designing, they will design for the majority of the people. In this example, the majority are all of average height and the designer will not design for those people who fall into the extremes, the extremely tall or small, which only account for 5% each.

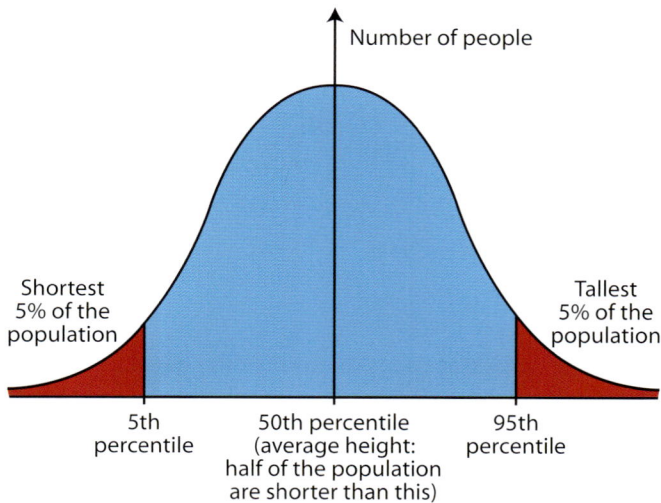

Number of people

Shortest 5% of the population

Tallest 5% of the population

5th percentile

50th percentile (average height: half of the population are shorter than this)

95th percentile

1. Make a list of possible communication methods a product designer could use.
2. Explain the term 'aesthetics'.
3. List five visual elements to consider when designing for aesthetic appeal.
4. What does the term anthropometrics mean?
5. What does it mean if a designer uses data from the 5th to 95th percentile when designing a product?

1. Make a list of six colours and suggest what the designer would be trying to achieve by using this colour.
2. List a range of products that depend on the sense of touch being considered.
3. Do a website search for sites that provide anthropometric data. Evaluate them and find a simple but effective site that could be useful for T&D projects in school. Share your findings with your peers.

INTELLECTUAL PROPERTY

As a designer you will have great design ideas that you want protected. Intellectual property is a designer's idea and this can be protected by law to stop others copying it. **Intellectual property legislation** includes copyrights, trademarks and patents. As a product designer you must be able to demonstrate knowledge and understanding of their main features:

© TM ®

• **Copyrights:** are used for protecting building plans and publications.

• **Trademarks:** are registered and they protect logos, symbols and names.

• **Patents:** are used to protect new inventions, processes or technologies. Patents can be restricted to certain countries or worldwide.

The logos used by large companies to identify themselves and advertise their brand will have registered trademarks that prevent them being copied or used without permission. Think of companies such as Coca-Cola and McDonalds who use the registered trademark symbol within their logos. There are many thousands more registered trademark symbols that are on products you use every day, so open your eyes and start being aware of the intellectual property that is all around you.

KEY WORD CHECK

Below are some key words, explain what each means. Remember to add these words to your glossary.

- Market/demand pull
- Technology push
- The client, user, designer and maker
- Brainstorming
- Morphological analysis
- Disassembly of existing products
- Product analysis
- Fitness for purpose

- Quality
- Specification
- Evaluating
- Historical influences
- Mock-ups
- Prototypes
- Computer modelling

- Communication of ideas
- Aesthetics
- Ergonomics
- Anthropometrics
- Intellectual property
- Copyrights
- Trademarks
- Patents

EXAM FOCUS

Complete the following past paper questions to help consolidate your learning and practice your exam skills.

1. (a) Figure 1 shows a typical mobile phone which is designed to be easy for the operator to use.

Figure 1

Outline one aesthetic and one ergonomic factor a designer would consider in the development of a new mobile. [2]

(b) Many new products are marketed by companies each year.
Explain, giving one example for each, what is meant by the terms 'Demand Pull' and 'Technology Push' in relation to the development of new products. [4]

(c) Outline two ways a patent may protect a new product. [2]

CCEA GCSE Technology & Design Specimen Paper, Unit 3, Product Design, 2011, © CCEA
For copyright reasons the image in Figure 1 has replaced the one from the CCEA past paper.

2 Figure 2 shows a bicycle.

Figure 2

A sample designer's specification point for the bicycle could be:
To provide a method of guarding the chain from contact with clothing.

(a) Outline three other specification points. [3]

(b) Computer modelling is commonly used by designers.

    (i) State one other type of modelling used by designers. [1]

    (ii) Describe one advantage and one disadvantage associated with computer modelling. [2]

(c) A designer may disassemble a product to analyse how it has been manufactured.
    Describe two other areas they may be searching for in the disassembly of a product. [2]

CCEA GCSE Technology & Design Specimen Paper, Unit 3, Product Design, 2011, © CCEA
For copyright reasons the image in Figure 2 has replaced the one from the CCEA past paper.

When studying this section try to remember the theory you learned for the 1A Manufacturing section of Unit 1. There is some overlap between the two sections as it is essential that you have the knowledge and understanding of materials, components and how they can be fabricated together when designing and developing products.

MATERIAL SELECTION

Think carefully about the materials you choose to use in your project work. Your final choice will depend on a number of factors and you should be able to make a good choice if you consider the following:

Intended use

- What will it be used for?
- Where will the product be used (inside or outside)?
- How long will it last (if the material will corrode)?
- What does it look like?
- Does it need a particular style or look to fit into a certain environment?

Economics

- How much will it cost for the size of product planned?
- What is the scale of production (will it be expensive if the product is mass produced)?

Properties

- Does the material you are thinking of using for a product have the properties needed?
- See opposite for an extensive list of all the material properties you can check for.

Availability

- What is available?
- What sizes are available in stock?
- Is it only available in a standard size or form?

Manufacturing method

- How easy is it to work or join?
- Is the material suitable for the method of production?

Function of its finish

- Does the product need a finish for aesthetic reasons or protection?
- What finish could be chosen for the material you propose to manufacture with?

MATERIAL PROPERTIES

Strength: The ability of a material to stand up to forces being applied without it bending, breaking, shattering or deforming in any way. There are five types of strength:

- **Tensile strength** – The ability of a material to *stretch* or *pull* without breaking or snapping.
- **Compressive strength** – The ability of a material to resist *squashing* forces.
- **Bending strength** – The ability of a material to resist *bending* forces.
- **Shear strength** – The ability of a material to resist *sliding* forces.
- **Torsional strength** – The ability of a material to resist *twisting* forces.

Hardness: The ability of a material to resist *scratching* from wear and tear, *bending* and *indentation*.

Brittleness: Brittle materials cannot withstand much *stretching*. They will *crack* or *break* rather than change shape.

Toughness: The ability of a material to resist *breaking* or *shattering*. The opposite of brittle.

Plasticity: A material has good plastic qualities if it can change its shape *permanently* without *breaking* or *cracking*.

Durability: The ability of a material to withstand *repeated use,* wear and tear, weathering and corrosive attack.

Pliability: The ability of a material to be *shaped, bent* or *drawn out*. For example, ductile copper or malleable metals such as gold.

Malleability: The ability of a material to be *reshaped* in all directions without *cracking*.

Elasticity: The ability of a material to absorb force and flex in different directions then *return to* its *original position*.

Ductility: The ability of a material to *change shape* (deform) usually by stretching *along its length*.

Heat conductivity: The ability of a material to *conduct heat*.

Electrical conductivity: The ability of a material to *conduct electricity*.

Corrosion-resistant: The ability of a metal or alloy to *resist being destroyed* by oxidation or chemicals.

CHECK YOUR LEARNING

1. When selecting a material what six factors must be considered to ensure you make a good choice?

2. Choose the right form of strength to complete the sentences below:

(i)   A material that can withstand pulling forces without breaking has _____ strength.

(ii) A material that can withstand squashing forces without breaking has _____ strength.

(iii) A material that can withstand twisting forces without breaking has _____ strength.

(iv) A material that can withstand forces trying to bend it without breaking has _____ strength.

(v)   A material that can withstand sliding forces without breaking has _____ strength.

3. What term describes a material that can change its shape, without it cracking or breaking?

4. What is the opposite of brittle?

5. Explain the term 'hardness'.

6. How can a material that will resist wear, tear, weathering and corrosive attack be described?

7. Explain each of the following technical terms:

   a) Tensile Strength

   b) Compressive Strength

   c) Hard

   d) Tough

   e) Brittle

   f) Pliable

   g) Malleable

   h) Corrodible

   i) Durable

   j) Heat conductivity

   k) Electrical conductivity

SHAPES OF AVAILABLE MATERIALS

When selecting materials be aware there are a wide range of commonly available shapes. These include, sheet, bar, tubes, angled, U-shaped channel and I-shaped sections. Different materials come in different shapes.

Metal: is extracted as metal ore from the earth. It is then refined and processed into useable materials in a wide range of shapes. Common shapes include flat sheet, solid bar, tubes, angled, U-shaped channel and I-shaped sections as shown below. Metal tubing and pipe are available in round, rectangular and hexagonal shapes, also shown below.

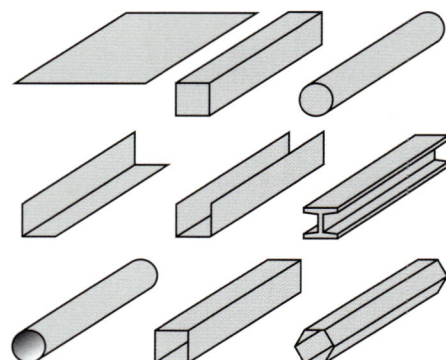

Plastic: is also available in different forms, including, granules, pellets and liquids before processing, which are used for processing products from films, rods, sheets, and extruded mouldings.

Plastic pellets.

An extruded plastic moulding.

WOOD

If considering using wood during the development of an idea it is important that you can demonstrate an understanding of the main characteristics and uses of hardwood, softwood and manufactured boards. This will enable you to compare the wood available and make informed choices about the type you select for the manufacture of a product.

Hardwoods

Usually hardwood trees have broad leaves and are deciduous, shedding leaves each year. They are slow growing, not reaching maturity until 100 years, so they are more expensive than softwoods. Examples include mahogany, beech, ash, oak and elm.

Ash

Ash wood is generally light in colour and highly grained. It is strong and flexible so can withstand pressure, shock and splintering, and can be steam bent into curved outlines without breaking or losing strength. Ash wood is used for sports equipment, furniture, wood floors, musical instruments and many construction materials.

An electric guitar made from ash.

Oak

Oak is a very strong, hard, light brown wood with open-grain. It is easy to work with and is often used in high quality furniture, as its grain pattern is very aesthetically pleasing. For the same reason, it is also chosen for veneers. Other uses include building beams of timber framed houses and flooring.

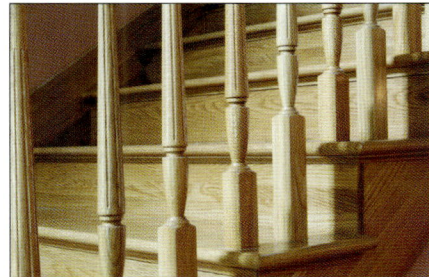

Stairs made from oak.

Softwoods

Most softwood trees are coniferous (bear cones), grow in colder climates, have needle-like leaves and are evergreen. They are fast growing trees, reaching maturity by 30 years and are easily replaced. This usually makes them cheaper than hardwoods and better for the environment. Examples include cedar, pine and yew.

Parana pine

Parana pine is a pale yellow colour with red-brown streaks. It is hard, fairly strong and durable, and the grain is quite straight, with few knots. It is quite expensive and usually used for furniture and interior fittings such as doors and staircases.

Cedar

Cedar has many qualities that make it a good choice of wood for manufacturing. It is lightweight, smooth in texture, with a grain that is fine and straight. This makes it easy to cut, saw and nail with regular tools, and its surface easy to plane smooth or to machine into different patterns. It has

a cell structure that speeds up the drying out process, so it rarely rots, and it remains straight and dimensionally stable when lying flat, making it resistant to splitting, cracking and checking. It emits a pleasant smell that people like but which deters attack from insects and other wood pests, making it popular for many purposes, such as patio furniture, panels, ceilings, doors, windows, posts, beams and cupboards.

Manufactured boards

Manufactured boards are timber sheets produced by gluing together wood fibres or layers. Waste wood materials are often used for the manufacture of these boards, making them more affordable than real wood. However, they do not have the same aesthetic appeal. To improve their appearance sometimes a thin layer of real wood called a **veneer** is used to cover the boards. A veneer can also be applied to a manufactured board to give it more strength.

As you learned in Unit 1A, Manufacturing, there is a wide range of manufactured boards available, including MDF, chipboard, plywood, blockboard, laminboard and hardboard. Plywood, blockboard and laminboard are discussed in more detail in the table below.

Manufactured Boards	Qualities	Properties	Uses
Plywood	• Appearance can be improved with a veneer of good quality wood. • Very strong for its weight and thickness, compared to solid wood.	• Odd numbers of layers that are glued with their grain at 90° to each other, making it very strong. • Different grades suit a variety of situations: 1. Marine plywood that is moisture resistant. 2. Weather and boil proof plywood. 3. Boil resistant plywood. 4. Interior plywood.	• Building work, general construction, boat building, furniture making.
Blockboard and Laminboard	• Similar construction. • Cheap substitute to plywood when a thicker board is required but not as strong.	• Strips of softwood such as pine or spruce are glued side by side and sandwiched between two veneers for added strength and aesthetics. **Blockboard strips are 5–7 cm** **Laminboard strips are 7–25 mm**	• Shelving, worktops and furniture backs.

Timber defects

Timber is prone to **defects** which can sometimes cause difficulties when it is being worked:

- **Dry rot**
- **Wet rot**
- **Insect attack**
- **Splits**
- **Shrinkage**
- **Knots**

If left unprotected the strength of the wood can be weakened by insect and fungal attack. In addition, when working with wood it is important that you are aware of the difficulties that can be encountered due of its considerable affinity for moisture. Shrinking and expansion of wood are dimensional changes caused by loss or gain of water.

Shrinkage

Shrinkage causes more problems than expansion. Wood is made up of fibrous cells that contain water. However, each cell is not uniform, nor is the shrinkage across a piece of wood, so some parts may lose water moisture content whilst other parts do not. This causes splits in the wood, as shown in the image below. Warping and bowing can be caused when parts of a piece of wood are different thicknesses. There is more shrinkage from the thicker parts than the thinner parts, again causing uneven shrinkage and possibly resulting in some of the following types of warping:

bow	crook	kink	cup	twist

Wood with splits

Expansion

Expansion or swelling occurs as wood gains moisture, when it moves from 0 to 25–30 % moisture content, which is the fibre saturation point. This causes an increase in the dimension of the wood.

Remember all wood is different and will both lose and absorb moisture in different ways and at different rates. The drying process should be slow and controlled to avoid drying defects. Appropriate storage is also a consideration for timber.

When choosing wood for a specific purpose, consider the **natural characteristics:**

- **Grain pattern:** the growth ring marks visible on the surface.
- **Colour:** different tree species differ greatly in colour.
- **Texture:** surface and cell texture varies with different species.
- **Workability:** some are easier to work with than others.
- **Structural strength:** weak to very strong.

METAL

If considering using metal during the development of an idea it is important that you can demonstrate an understanding of their main characteristics and uses. Some metals are pure and others are alloys. An alloy is a mixture of more than one metal so the alloy will have the properties of the different metals it has been made from. There are two basic groups of metals: ferrous and non-ferrous.

Ferrous metals

Ferrous metals contain iron. Generally they tend to corrode so need some form of protection against corrosion. Almost all are magnetic. High carbon steel and stainless steel are detailed below but you will also have learned about mild steel in Unit 1A, Manufacturing.

Ferrous metal	Properties	Uses
High carbon steel	Harder than mild steel and can be tempered and hardened. It will rust and it is not that easy to work.	Used for saws, files, chisels, drill bits.
Stainless steel	A hard metal that will not rust but is more expensive.	Used for sinks, kettles, medical equipment, cutlery.

Recall the properties and uses of mild steel.

Non-ferrous metals

Non-ferrous metals do not contain iron. For example: aluminium and copper.

Non-Ferrous Metals		
	Aluminium	**Copper**
Properties	• Light, soft, easily shaped and silvery in colour. • Conducts heat and electricity well. • Corrosion resistant but expensive. • Polishes well.	• Malleable and ductile. • Tough but easily shaped and soldered as relatively soft, malleable and ductile. • Conducts heat and electricity well. • Quite expensive.
Uses	Used for window frames, saucepans, cooking foil, cans and aircrafts.	Used for water pipes, wires and cisterns.

Alloys

An alloy is a mixture of two or more metals. The use of alloying is to produce a mixture that is a new material with different working characteristics and properties. Steel and brass are alloys.

Steel

Steel = iron + carbon (ferrous alloy)

Brass

Brass = copper + zinc (non-ferrous alloy)

Brass has a number of practical properties which make it useful for a variety of products:

- It is malleable and machines well.
- It is harder than either of its components and casts well.
- It is a dull yellow colour and does not tarnish as it resists corrosion. For this reason it is often used for decoration such as door handles, knockers, letter boxes, name plates and coins.
- It has low friction so is used in applications where the surface of material comes in contact with another surface such as gears, bearings, door locks and valves. Also screws, hinges, water fittings and electrical parts are available in brass.
- It has good acoustic properties making it ideal for a range of musical instruments including trumpets, horns, tubas and trombones.

Heat treatments

Heat can be used to change a metal's characteristics and properties. The following heat treatments are used for softening or toughening metals:

- **Annealing** – metal can be softened by this process by heating it and leaving it to cool.
- **Hardening** – metal can be hardened by heating it to its upper critical temperature then rapidly cooling it by plunging it into cold water. The metal can be left brittle so it is followed by tempering.
- **Tempering** – metal can be toughened by this process to make it less likely to break.

A piece of steel will change colour the hotter it is heated, from a pale straw colour to blue. The colour indicates how tough it has become, as shown in the diagram.

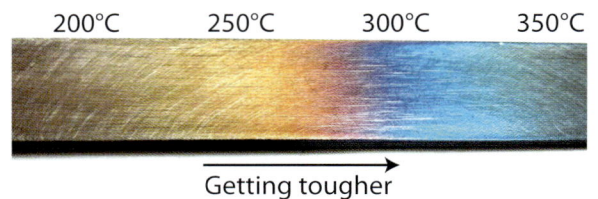

200°C	250°C	300°C	350°C

Getting tougher

PLASTICS

You may design products that will require you to demonstrate your understanding of the main characteristics and uses of different thermosetting plastics and thermoplastics (also knows as thermoforming plastics). The following will help you to make informed choices when selecting a plastic for a product.

Thermosetting	*Thermoplastics/thermoforming*
When thermosetting plastics 'set' they cannot be softened, shaped or moulded by reheating. They cannot be reshaped or recycled because of the three dimensional cross-linking of the molecules within these plastics. This arrangement makes a very strong bond between the molecules. • Cannot be recycled. • Resist heat and fire well. • Undergo significant chemical change when heated making them hard and rigid.	Thermoplastics/thermoforming plastics can be reheated, allowing them to be shaped and moulded in different ways. The molecular bonds are weak and are weakened further when reheated, which allows reshaping. These plastics are made up of 'long chain monomers'. • Can be recycled. • Do not resist heat well. • Do not undergo significant chemical change when heated.

Epoxy resin		**Acrylonitrile butadiene styrene (ABS)**	
Epoxy resin is a resin and a hardener mixed to produce a cast. It has good chemical and heat resistance (better than other adhesives), and very good mechanical, electrical insulating and adhesion properties. Araldite is the trade name of the epoxy adhesive used in schools.	Used for: • Surface coatings on 'white goods' such as washing machines, driers, etc, by plastic powder coating to give appliances colour. • Applied to give metals corrosion resistance in the gas and oil industry. • When used as a primer it aids the adhesion of paint to metal car and marine parts. • Electrical components such as PCBs. • Structural adhesives where high performance is needed such as the car and aircraft industries.	ABS is impact resistant, tough and lightweight so processes well by injection moulding and extrusion. The advantage of ABS is its combination of strength and rigidity from the acrylonitrile and the toughness from the butadiene rubber. It is more expensive to produce than polystyrene but it is superior because of its hardness, gloss, electrical insulation and toughness.	Used for: • Toys including Lego bricks, drain-pipes, protective headgear, musical recorders and plastic clarinets. • Golf club heads and car bumpers due to its good shock absorbance. • Car trims. • Electronic boxes. • Whitewater canoes. • Luggage and protective carrying cases. • Small kitchen appliances.

Thermosetting	Thermoplastics
Urea formaldehyde	**Nylon**

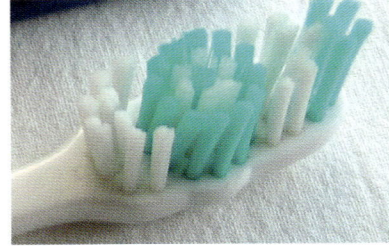

A colourless polymer* that can be coloured with artificial pigments.	Used for: • Electrical fittings and switches. • Cupboard and door handles.	Nylon has good wear resistance, especially when oil is added. It is also a good heat resistor.	Used for: • Gears, bearings and mechanical parts in cars. • Fabrics, toothbrush bristles, fishing lines and cable ties.

* Polymers are long chains of molecules that occur when synthetic plastics are manufactured using a process known as polymerisation. Synthetic plastics are the most common plastics and are manufactured chemically from carbon based materials such as crude oil and natural gas. Natural plastics are amber and latex, a type of rubber.

SMART MATERIALS

As a product designer you need to be aware that there are developments being made in materials all the time. Smart Materials are new materials that have been developed by scientists, which have new properties. These materials respond to changes in their environment which cause changes to their properties.

Smart Materials	Main properties	Uses
Biodegradable plastic	Biodegradable plastic is more environmentally friendly than the usual non-biodegradable plastic made from chemicals. Biodegradable plastic is made from natural food sources such as wheat or corn starch. The structure of these natural products are easily attacked and broken down by microbes. However, biodegradable plastic is up to ten times more expensive to produce than chemical based non-biodegradable plastic.	• Mulch film for farming, which can be ploughed into the ground after it has been used on the crops. • Agricultural mulch. • Plant pots that can be planted. • Disposable food industry items. • Organic fruit packaging. • Collection bags for leaves and grass trimmings.

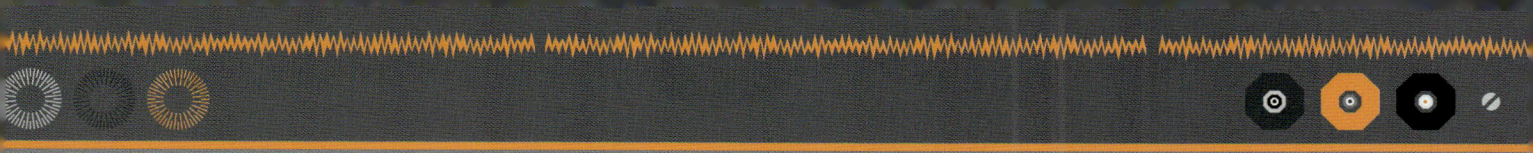

Thermochromic pigments	Thermochromic pigments are sensitive to temperature and change colour when they heat up or cool down. They can be added to polymers.	• Kettles. • Heat warning patches in baby food products.
Shape memory alloy (nithinol)	Nithinol is a 'shape memory alloy'. When cool it is easily shaped but if the material is heated to a certain temperature it will return to a 'remembered' shape. This is due to its superelasticity.	• Eyeglass frames. • Sunglasses. • Wires of teeth braces. • The antennas of old mobile phones. • Trick spoons from magic shops. • The medical industry.
Polymorph	Polymorph is a new type of plastic smart material. It is ideal for model making or prototyping. It is as strong as a normal plastic at room temperature but at 62°C it becomes soft and can be moulded. Hot water, a hairdryer or a heat gun will heat it quickly. Food dye can be used to colour polymorph and it is biodegradable in soil. When fully cooled it is very similar in appearance and physical properties to polythene but is slightly stiffer, stronger and tougher than the polythene used in domestic products. As it is a thermoplastic it can be re-heated and thermoformed repeatedly.	• One-off moulds. • Vacuum form moulds. • Specialised prototyping. • Orthopaedic splints. • General DIY material. • Children's moulding material. • Trainer/shoe components. • Hot-melt glue. • Sports protective clothing. • Components for other plastic. • Applications requiring high mechanical strength.

ACTIVITY

Carry out some research on smart materials. Make a list of any other products that are manufactured from:

• biodegradable plastic   • thermochromic pigments   • nithinol   • plymorph

JOINTING FORMS

If you decide to design products that use wood these may need to be jointed, so it is important that you are able to demonstrate knowledge and understanding of the following forms of jointing:

Jointing Forms		Uses
Stopped housing — Through housing	**Housing joints:** are strong as they have a large gluing area.	Used for shelving as the shelf is supported across its full width. This image shows a housing joint used in a child's toy.
	Dovetail joints: are very strong and are attractive to look at. They are difficult to construct by hand but a jig can be used to help.	Used for drawer construction.
	Mortise and tenon joints: are really strong. They are cut with a tenon saw and mortise chisel.	Used in the manufacture of tables, chairs, other furniture and gates.
Joints with more surface area such as housing, dovetail and mortise and tenon are stronger joints.		
	Mitred joints: are cut at a 45° angle. They are a more attractive joint than the butt joint.	Used for picture frames.
	Lap joints: have increased surface area for gluing so are slightly stronger than butt joints.	Used for boxes and drawers.
Mitred and lap joints are less secure but are often cheaper to manufacture.		

KEY WORD CHECK

Below are some key words, explain what each means. Remember to add these words to your glossary

- Hardwoods
- Softwoods
- Manufactured boards
- Veneer
- Timber defects
- Ferrous metals
- Non-ferrous metals
- Alloys
- Annealing
- Hardening
- Tempering
- Thermoplastics
- Thermosetting
- Smart Materials
- Joints

ACTIVITY

To help your understanding of the various types of wood joints, produce a sample of each of the joints in the table opposite using waste wood cut offs.

EXAM FOCUS

Complete the following past paper questions to help consolidate your learning and practice your exam skills.

1. Figure 1 shows a soldering iron used to manufacture electronic circuits.

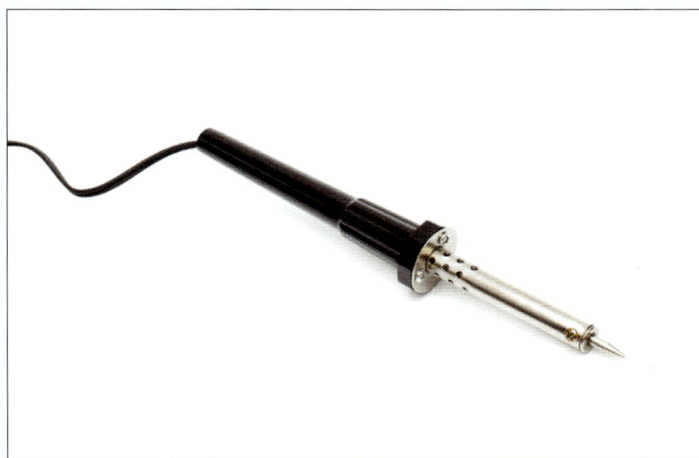

Figure 1

(a) (i) Name a suitable plastic that could be used for the manufacture of the handle. [1]

(ii) Identify **two** material properties necessary for the plastic handle of the soldering iron. Give one reason for each material property you have identified. [4]

(b) Tempering is a treatment applied to metals.

(i) What effect does tempering have on a metal? [1]

(ii) Outline **two** main stages in the process of tempering metals. [2]

2. Figure 2 shows part of a prototype outdoor domestic mail box.

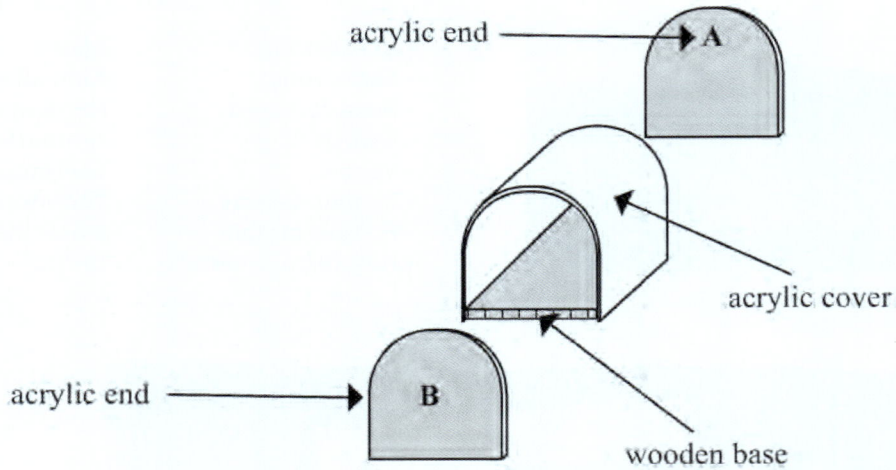

(a) The mail box has a wooden base and is to be made from cedar.
Give one reason why cedar has been chosen for the base. [1]

(b) Acrylic end B is to be replaced with wood and is to be joined to the base with dovetail joints.
Using an annotated sketch, outline the main features of a dovetail joint. Show how the dovetails interlock. [4]

CCEA GCSE Technology & Design Specimen Paper, Unit 3, Product Design, 2011, © CCEA
For copyright reasons the image in Figure 1 has replaced the one from the CCEA past paper.

3. (a) Two main types of plastic are thermosetting plastic and thermoplastic. Explain the main characteristic of each type. [2]

(b) Select from the two plastics named below, the most appropriate plastic for the manufacture of the socket shown in Figure 3. [1]

Urea formaldehyde or acrylonitrile butadiene styrene (ABS)

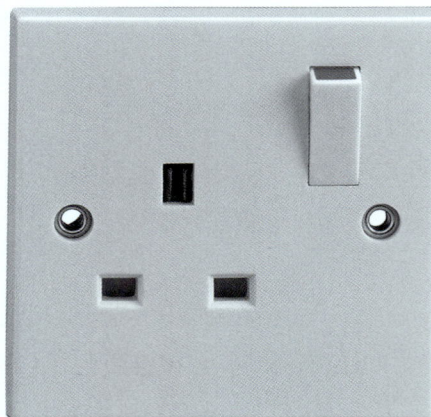

Figure 3

(c) (i) State the plastic manufacturing process that would be used to produce the plastic socket. [1]

(ii) Describe two steps in the manufacturing process used to produce the plastic socket. [2]

CCEA GCSE Technology & Design Past Paper, Unit 3, Product Design, Summer 2011, © CCEA

For copyright reasons the image in Figure 3 has replaced the one from the CCEA past paper.

4. Figure 4 shows two types of chisel.

Figure 4a   Figure 4b

(a) (i) Name each chisel shown. [2]

   (ii) Select either chisel and describe a practical use for it in the school workshop. [2]

(b) The point of the chisel is hardened and tempered. Outline four main steps in this process. [4]

CCEA GCSE Technology & Design Past Paper, Unit 3, Product Design, Summer 2011, © CCEA

5. Figure 5 shows a design for an ornamental wheelbarrow to display flowers in a garden.

handle

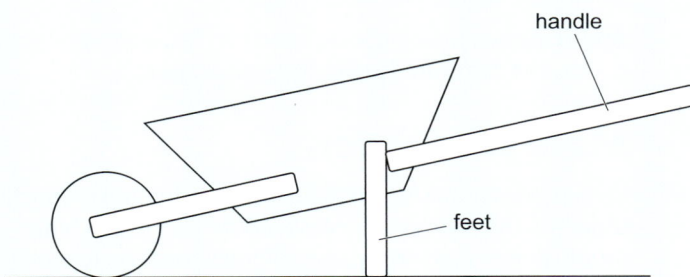

feet

Figure 5

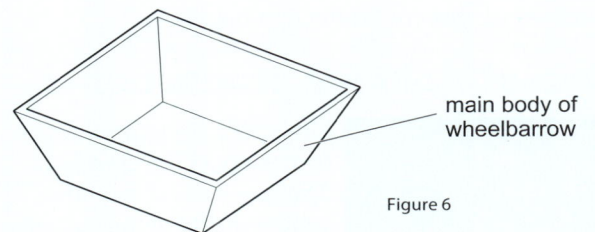

main body of
wheelbarrow

Figure 6

(a) Give two reasons why you should choose solid timber compared to a manufactured board for the wheelbarrow. [2]

(b) The main body of the wheelbarrow shown in Figure 6 is to be joined using mitre joints. Using annotated sketches, outline the main features of a mitre joint. [3]

(c) During quality assurance and control testing it was found that the mitre joints were weak and unsatisfactory. Explain with sketches how the mitre joint could be improved. [3]

CCEA GCSE Technology & Design Past Paper, Unit 3, Product Design, Summer 2011, © CCEA

MANUFACTURING PRACTICES

When designing a product you must be able to confidently demonstrate how your design proposal could be manufactured. You need an awareness of the quantity to be produced and an understanding of the main features and applications of different processes and tools that would be necessary for manufacture. How the production process for your product could be computerised is another consideration. Finally, you must be able to consider how the product would be manufactured in industry: the different manufacturing systems available, the use of standard components or sub-contracting and the quality of the end product. Knowledge and understanding of all these areas will help you with your product designs.

SCALE OF PRODUCTION

Scale of Production is about the quantity of products to be manufactured from one-off products to the continuous production of a product. You should be able to compare the advantages and disadvantages associated with the four commercial types of production below:

One-off/jobbing production

One-off/jobbing production is making a single product. The specific and individual requirements of the customer have to be met, so every item will be made differently. It requires a highly skilled workforce and is very labour intensive.

Applications: bridges, one-off structures such as the Eiffel Tower, racing car engines, one-off furniture or jewellery pieces.

Batch production

Batch production is when a specific quantity of a product is made, between two and one hundred. A production line is set up where each worker completes one task then passes it along the production line to the next worker. The workers are either semi-skilled or unskilled but must be able to switch from one part of the production line to another. This is known as a flexible workforce. The production line needs to be easily and quickly changed, so that different products can be made. Generally batches of product are produced for a period of time and then the product is changed. It is common for individual parts of the product to be purchased from other companies and assembled on the production line.

Applications: baked goods, sports shoes, clothes, electrical goods, DIY furniture, books and newspapers.

Mass production

Mass production is the high volume production of products, usually in their hundreds. Mass production uses a high proportion of machinery and energy in relation to workers, and is highly automated. The initial cost of set-up is high for machinery and energy, but when this cost is spread across a very large number of products, the cost per unit is reduced greatly. With the high setup costs, there needs to be some assurance that the product produced will make profit.

Applications: electrical goods and cars.

Continuous production

Continuous production is uninterrupted, non-stop, 24/7 mass production of tens of thousands of identical products. A semi-automated production line is set up using computer control and a combination of skilled and unskilled workers. The workers are less flexible than those working in batch production, as the product seldom changes. However, they also require little training, as the product and equipment change slowly, and training is only needed when new equipment is introduced or new staff begin. Quality control occurs at every stage of production and sampling takes place at various stages. A high level of investment in machinery and equipment is needed for continuous production.

Applications: petrol and oil products, many food products, electronic components, chemicals, paper products, cars and bricks.

PLANNING FOR PRODUCTION

Good working practice is essential when planning for and managing production. The Gantt Chart method is a tool often used to achieve good planning, laying out what has to be done and in what order. Project stages are plotted against time. When completing projects you must be realistic about the time tasks will take. Within a Gantt chart some tasks will overlap, meaning you can get started on a task before a previous task is completed. Other tasks will not overlap and will continue one after another. A Gantt chart allows you to monitor your progress.

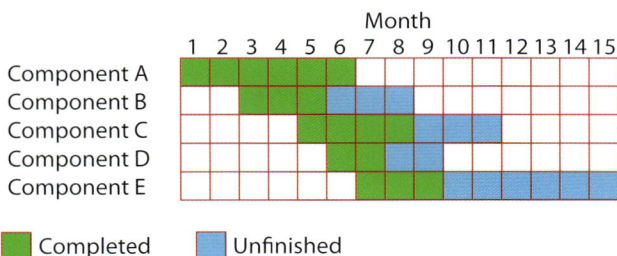

	Month
	1 2 3 4 5 6 7 8 9 10 11 12 13 14 15
Component A	
Component B	
Component C	
Component D	
Component E	

■ Completed ■ Unfinished

PROCESSES

When designing a product you need an understanding of the main features and applications of the processes below. This will enable you to demonstrate how a design proposal could be manufactured.

Reforming

Reforming is when plastics or metals are liquefied with heat and pressure, then shaped with a mould. The following processes use the reforming technique:

Injection moulding

Injection moulding moulds plastic or metal by forcing the molten material into a closed mould. There are heaters to melt the material within the machine.

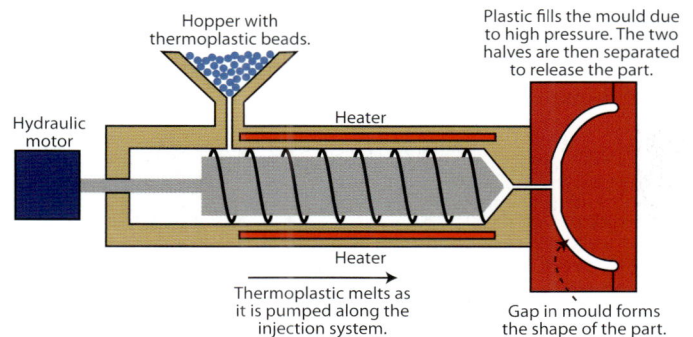

Hopper with thermoplastic beads.

Plastic fills the mould due to high pressure. The two halves are then separated to release the part.

Hydraulic motor

Heater

Heater

Thermoplastic melts as it is pumped along the injection system.

Gap in mould forms the shape of the part.

Advantages:
- High production rates are achievable as the process is automated and continuous. The cycle for a 3 mm thick part could be completed in 40 seconds.
- Products can be produced with a good surface finish and a consistent quality.

Disadvantages:
- Initial set up is very expensive as the tools, such as the dies or moulds, are produced to a high degree of accuracy and surface finish.

Applications:

Plastics: Injection moulding is used to produce bottles, sand buckets, wire spools, packaging, bottle caps, dashboards in cars, bins, one-piece chairs and small tables, storage containers, mechanical parts including gears, and most other plastic products available today.

Metal: Injection moulding is used to make electrical components such as connectors and switches, firearm components, parts of automotive systems such as steering columns, seating mechanisms, solenoids, fuel injectors, orthodontic braces in the dental industry, medical instruments for surgery, lock parts such as lock cylinders and bolts, and computer and electronics parts including disk drive components.

Die casting

Die casting is a process used to mould thermoplastics and metals. The material is melted and poured into a mould that is the required shape of the product.

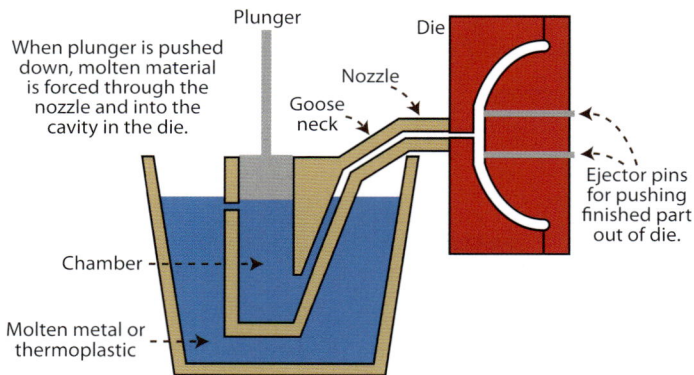

Advantages:

- Die casting production is fast. A small component can be cast in less than one second whilst a larger component weighing 2 kg may take 2–3 minutes.

- Die casting produces parts that are durable and have high dimensional accuracy, while maintaining close tolerances.

- Die casting provides the widest range of possible shapes available from any manufacturing technique.

- Thinner walls (between 0.6 mm–0.8 mm) are achievable with a high quality mould.

- The assembly of die cast parts can be simplified by casting parts with external threads or holes.

- The parts have a good surface finish, as they can be finished smooth, textured or can be easily plated with little preparation.

- Plastic die parts are stronger than plastic injection mouldings with the same dimensions.

Disadvantages:

- The initial costs of moulds to achieve a good surface finish and machine set up are high.

- A large production volume is required to make the process cost effective.

- Some empty spaces occur in die casted material.

- Only non-ferrous metals with high fluidity such as zinc, aluminium, magnesium, copper, lead and tin can be die casted.

- Castings must be smaller than 600 mm and the thickest wall section should be kept below 13 mm.

Applications:

Die casting is commonly used to produce industrial kitchen equipment and castings for the car industry.

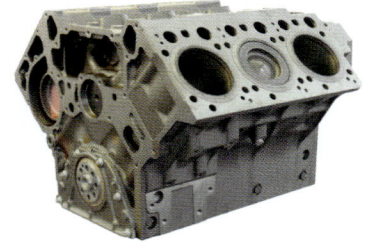

Extrusion

Extrusion is used for thermoplastics and some metals. The material is forced through a nozzle under high pressure into a mould. The process produces long continuous strips of the moulding in the shape of the nozzle it leaves. Thermoplastics such as polythene, PVC and nylon; and metals such as aluminium, copper, lead, tin, magnesium, steel and titanium are materials commonly used for extrusion.

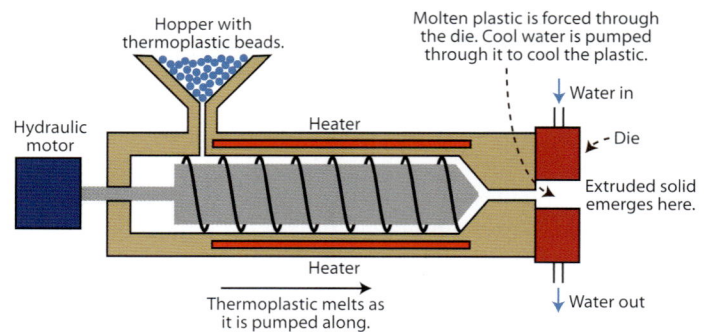

Advantages:

- Products with very detailed cross-sections can be processed.

- High production rates are achievable as the process is automated and continuous, so cost per unit is low.

- Products are manufactured with a very good surface finish.

- Many types of raw materials can be extruded.

Disadvantages:

- Complex parts cannot be produced.
- Only shapes with uniform cross-sections can be produced.

Applications:

Plastic: Extrusion is used to make sheets of plastic for fabrication, pipes, tubes, spouting, plastic covered wire, plastic bag ties.

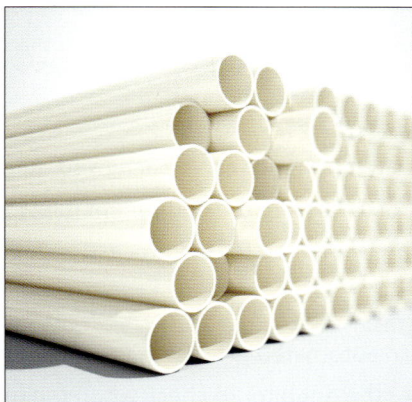

Metal: Extrusion is used to mould copper for pipes, wire, rods, bars and tubes; magnesium and titanium for structural parts in the aircraft industry; and zinc for rods, bars, hardware components, fittings and handrails, aluminium edging, flat ribbon multi-conductor cables, appliance cords and TV aerial cables.

Example of an extruded product with a uniform cross-section.

Deforming

Deforming is when the shape of a material is changed. The following processes use the deforming technique:

Blow moulding

Blow moulding uses air to blow plastic into a solid mould. A tube of hot plastic is extended down the centre of a mould and when the mould closes around the plastic, compressed air is blown into the centre. This forces the plastic out to the side walls of the mould, where it swells out, filling up the whole mould forming the part. PVC, polythene and polypropylene are common blow moulding materials.

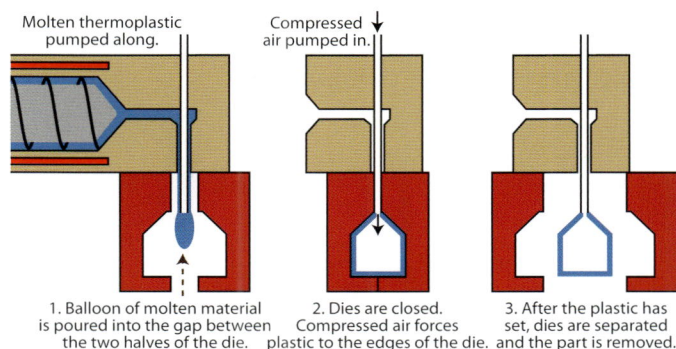

Molten thermoplastic pumped along.   Compressed air pumped in.

1. Balloon of molten material is poured into the gap between the two halves of the die.
2. Dies are closed. Compressed air forces plastic to the edges of the die.
3. After the plastic has set, dies are separated and the part is removed.

Advantages:

- Blow moulding is a less expensive process to run than injection moulding.
- Production is fast, with high volume outputs achievable.
- The need for using adhesives is reduced, as one piece construction is achieved by the process.
- New blow moulding machines have been developed that allow 3D products to be produced, such as plastic pipes for the automotive industry.

Disadvantages:

- The process can only be used to manufacture hollow products.

Applications:

Bottles for food and drinks, cosmetics bottles, hollow toys, plastic pipes, writing tools and bowls.

Vacuum forming

A sheet of plastic is clamped and heated until it is soft. A mould is placed into the machine onto the vacuum bed. The material is then either pulled over or into a mould using a vacuum. The mould can be covered with a release agent to make the removal of the mould from the plastic sheet easier. In school, talcum powder can be used as a release agent on wooden moulds when vacuum forming. After the plastic sheet has cooled, the part is cut from the sheet with a trim-die or, in school, a gerbil cutter. Acrylic, polystyrene and PVC are typical vacuum forming materials.

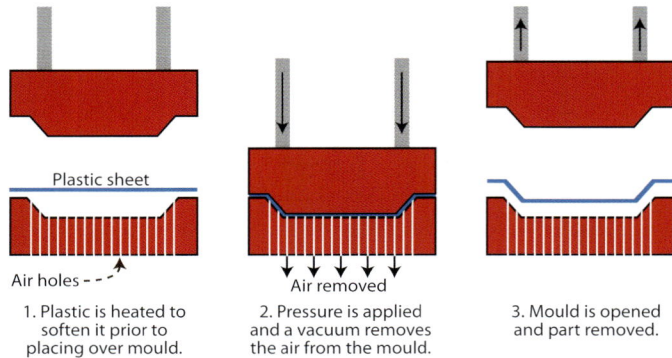

Air holes - - -

1. Plastic is heated to soften it prior to placing over mould.

Air removed

2. Pressure is applied and a vacuum removes the air from the mould.

3. Mould is opened and part removed.

Advantages:
- Large, irregular shaped mouldings can be produced, such as chocolate box liners and egg trays, which cannot be produced by any other plastic forming process.
- The equipment is cheaper than other plastic processing machinery.
- Vacuum forming requires the use of only one mould.

Disadvantages:
- Vacuum forming only works with thin plastics and moulds that have tapered sides and rounded corners, as otherwise the finished product could not be released from the mould.
- It can only be used for forming detail on the outside of the finished product.

Applications:
- Vacuum forming is often used to produce packaging with high visibility to showcase products, for example, plastic trays for cosmetics and yoghurt containers for the food industry.

Line bending
A sheet of thermoplastic material (for example, acrylic, ABS, polycarbonate) is heated in a strip along its length. It becomes flexible when heated, allowing it to be bent to the required shape. It can be bent by hand or more precisely by using a jig to achieve the required bend. Once cooled, the bent material retains the formed shape.

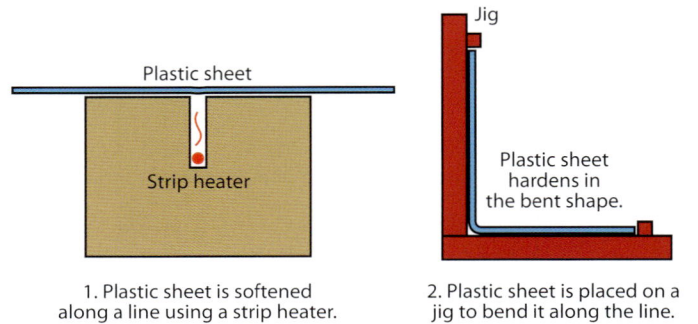

Plastic sheet

Strip heater

1. Plastic sheet is softened along a line using a strip heater.

Jig

Plastic sheet hardens in the bent shape.

2. Plastic sheet is placed on a jig to bend it along the line.

Advantages:
- Efficient straight bends can be achieved quickly.
- The cost of setting up the equipment is low.
- No tooling is required for the process.

Disadvantages:
- It is not an automated process in the school workshop.
- It requires the operator to check when the material is flexible enough for bending, as the plastic can overheat and burn quite easily.

Applications:
- Line bending is used to make display units, picture frames and holders for displaying newspapers, magazines or advertising leaflets.

Metal folding

Metal folding can be used to shape sheet metal such as tin plate or aluminium. A sheet metal folder, folding bars, formers and mallets can all be used to fold the metal sheet to the desired shape.

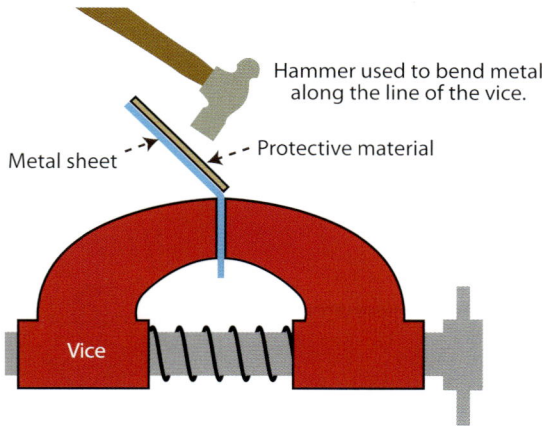

Hammer used to bend metal along the line of the vice.

Metal sheet

Protective material

Vice

Advantages:

- It does not damage the surface of the sheet.

- Large sheets of metal can be folded.

- It is a cost effective process if low or medium quantities of a product are required, as there is little tooling required.

- The process can be automated if required. Computer Numerically Controlled sheet bending is a precise and fast automated process that can give excellent reproduction of the required bend.

Disadvantages:

- The process of metal folding will not produce a completed product, as the corners or edges will still need a method of joining such as riveting, soldering or brazing.

Applications:

- Metal folding is used to make metal boxes, rectangular ductwork, gutters and rails.

Laminating

Laminating is the process of constructing a material with two or more layers together. Thin strips of wood can be glued together into a sandwich, which is kept in shape using a jig until the glue dries. Plywood is a good choice of material for laminating with. Sometimes when the process of laminating is used in industry, the wood veneers would be softened with steam first in a steam chamber. Next they would be clamped into shape until dry and glued together.

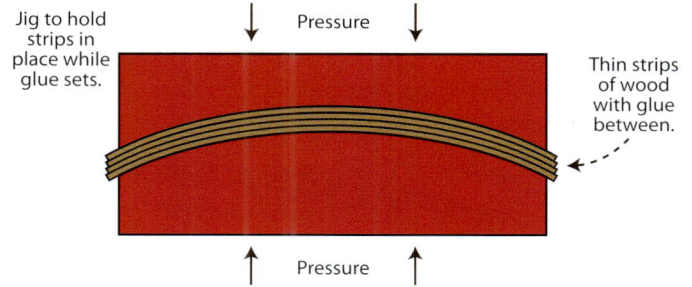

Jig to hold strips in place while glue sets.

Pressure

Thin strips of wood with glue between.

Pressure

Applications:

Laminating is used to produce items such as table and chair legs, rocking chair runners and roof beams.

Press moulding

Press moulding is used to force sheet metal into 3D shapes. The metal sheet is placed between two moulds, which are forced together until the sheet metal takes the shape of the moulds. Press moulding is also used to shape thermosetting plastics by placing powder form plastic into a 'female' mould and pressing a 'male' former onto it. This pushes the plastic into the mould. High temperatures and pressure liquefies the powder and it sets into a permanent shape.

WORD BOX

MALE AND FEMALE MOULDS

Moulds in manufacturing processes are sometimes referred to as male and female moulds. Male moulds are usually pressed into the female mould, which is a cavity. The male mould is known as a positive shape and the female mould a negative shape. The analogy comes from the male and female anatomy.

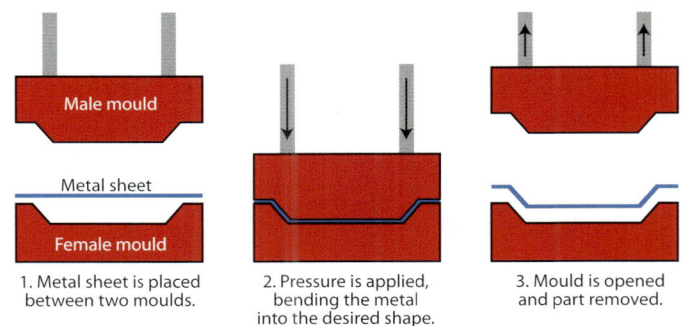

Male mould

Metal sheet

Female mould

1. Metal sheet is placed between two moulds.

2. Pressure is applied, bending the metal into the desired shape.

3. Mould is opened and part removed.

Applications:

- Press moulding is used to make products such as electrical and electronic components, and PVC machine guards, protective visors, safety screens, signage and decorative cladding.

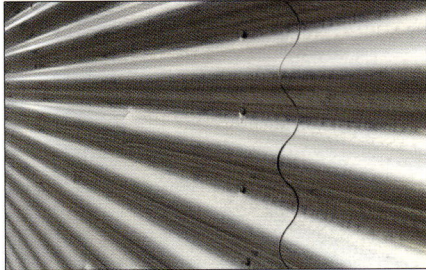

HAND TOOLS

Hand Tools: are used when manufacturing processes have to be completed manually, by hand, for example, when a prototype has to be manufactured. You must be able to demonstrate an understanding of the main features and applications of the following types of hand tools:

- **Saws**
- **Drills**
- **Hammers**
- **Planes and files**
- **Chisels**

Saws

Different saws have teeth designed for cutting different materials. The blade teeth must be kept sharp by sharpening or replacing.

Tenon saw: is a midsized back saw used for cutting wood. It has a stiffening cap over the top edge of the blade, which prevents it flexing and provides good control when cutting. They are available with rip-filed teeth for rip cutting and cross-cut for cutting across the grain. The teeth are quite fine and can be sharpened. It is used for general bench work and cutting out joints.

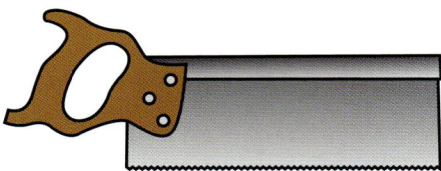

Coping saw: has a very thin metal blade, which is stretched on a U-shaped metal frame. A swiveling clip at each end of the frame holds the ends of the blade and can be loosened to allow the blade to be replaced. A hardwood or plastic handle allows the blade to be turned during the cut to cut round curves. Coarser and finer blades are available for specialised jobs. A coping saw is only used to cut wood or plastic sheet. A piercing or jewellers saw should be used to cut sheet metal.

Rip saw: is a *specialised* handsaw used to manually cut wood in the direction of the grain. It has teeth that are perpendicular to the blade and act like chisels, actually shaving wood away during the cut. The blade below the handle is called the heel and the other end is called the toe. Rip saws are used to cut straight lines in large sheets of wood.

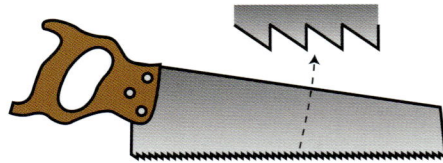

Hacksaw: has fine teeth and is used to cut metal and plastic, but not normally wood. The blade is held in tension in a steel frame by tightening the wing nut. This keeps the blade rigidly straight when cutting. The blades are available in 250 mm and 300 mm lengths, and the frame usually adjusts to hold either length. Blades are referred to by the number of teeth they have per inch (tpi), which range from coarse to fine (an inch = 25 mm). A medium blade would be 18 (tpi), made of high carbon steel and used for general purpose cutting. Coarse blades are used for cutting hard, extra-tough steel, so they would have 24 (tpi) and be made of high speed steel. The blades should always be fitted into the frame with the teeth facing away from the handle.

Drills

Drills are used to make holes in materials by rotating the drill bit clockwise and pressing it into the material. It is important to match the correct drill bit to the material being cut.

Hand drill: is a hand tool for drilling holes.

Bradawl: is a hand tool used to make a small dent hole in wood, which can be picked up by the drill bit for drilling a hole.

Chuck and key: are the parts of the drill that hold the drill bit. The chuck holds the bit whilst the key is used to open and close the chuck to insert and remove different drill bits.

Drill bit: is usually made from carbon or high speed steel and is used to drill small holes (0–13 mm) in wood, plastic and metal.

Flat bit: is used on wood and plastics to drill large flat bottomed holes. It is very good for the quick cutting of holes with a power drill, but it is not the most accurate, and produces a lot of splintering when it emerges from the workpiece.

Countersunk bit: is used to allow a countersunk screwhead or rivet to sit flush with the surface of the material.

Hammers

Hammers are hand tools designed to deliver impact during a variety of different jobs which require hitting or pounding. These include driving in nails, fitting parts, forging metals and breaking up objects. They have a heavy head mounted at right angles to a handle. Different varieties and head sizes are available:

Claw hammer: is heavy and can drive large nails through timber. Bent nails can be removed with the claw.

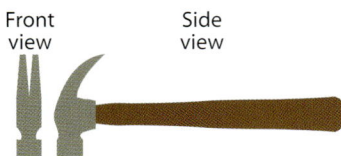

Front view   Side view

Pin or cross pein hammer: is used to start small nails and pins, which are held between the fingers.

Ball pein hammer: has a rounded pein as the rear face. It is used for rounding or spreading rivet heads and other pieces of metal. It is also available in large sizes for heavy duty work such as hot metal working.

Planes and files

Planes and files are used for shaping and smoothing.

Bench plane: uses a wedge-shaped cutting blade to shave off thin layers of wood and some plastics.

Flat file: is one of the fastest cutting general purpose files you can use. It has a broad surface and removes wood or metal quickly. It is useful to have flat files with different cuts.

End view   Face

Single cut: is used when a smooth finish is required.
Double cut: is used for removing wood or metal at a fast rate, leaving a rough surface.

Second cut: is used for roughing out hard metals and plastics and finishing soft metals and plastic.

Smooth cut: is used to finish a rough surface, for example, after using a double or second cut file.

Half-round file: is a good general purpose file. It has a flat face for flat filing and a curved side for filing curves. This file can also be obtained in different grades of coarseness.

End view   Face

143

Round hand file or 'rat-tail' file: is round and tapered toward the end. It is used to enlarge holes and for filing small half-round curves.

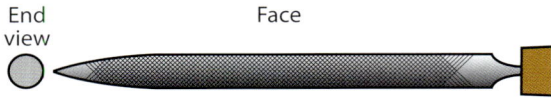

End view   Face

Chisels

A chisel is a cutting tool for cutting or caving wood and metal. It has a shaped cutting edge and a sharp edge to slice across the grain. There are four types of wood chisel:

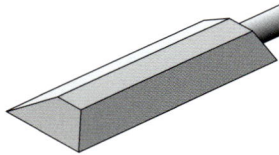

Firmer chisel: is a general hand tool.

Bevel-edged chisel: is used for corners less than 90° such as a dovetail joint.

Mortise chisel: is a strong, thick chisel used for chopping deep holes for joints.

Gouger: is used for carving as it has a curved blade.

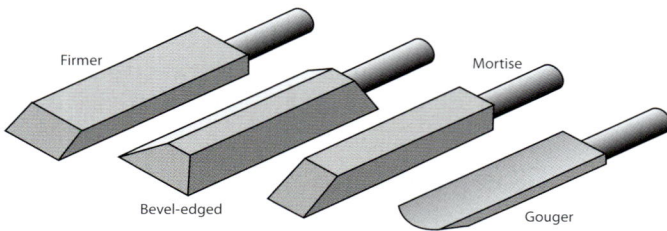

Firmer

Mortise

Bevel-edged

Gouger

Cold chisel: is used for cutting cold metals. It is made of tempered steel and is used to remove waste material when a smooth finish is not required and in situations where the work cannot be done with other tools such as a hacksaw, file or power tools.

Chiseling actions

There are three basic chiseling actions:

Horizontal paring: is cutting across a joint to clean out waste.

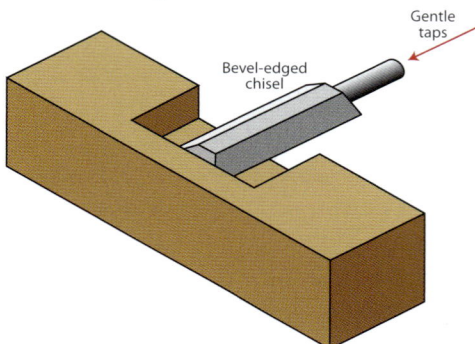

Gentle taps

Bevel-edged chisel

Vertical paring: is pushing down onto a waste surface to shape the end of a piece of wood.

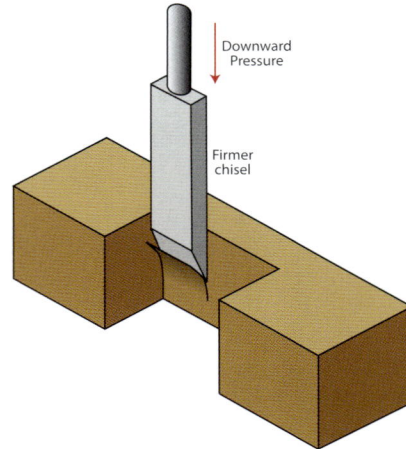

Downward Pressure

Firmer chisel

Chopping: is digging out waste from mortise by cutting the fibres into short lengths.

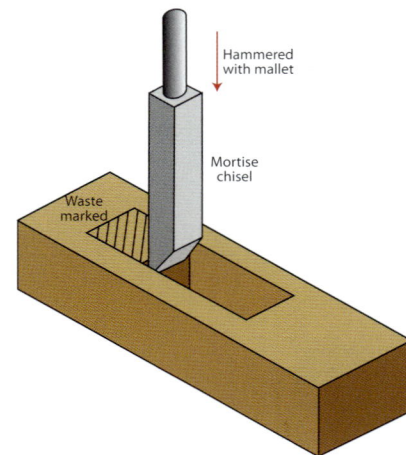

Hammered with mallet

Mortise chisel

Waste marked

MACHINE AND POWER TOOLS

Machine and power tools are used to manufacture products more quickly, efficiently and accurately than hand tools. You must be able to demonstrate an understanding of the main features and applications of the following types of tools:

- **Circular saw**
- **Band saw**
- **Pillar drill**
- **Bandfacer**
- **Lathe**
- **Milling machine**

Power saws such as circular and band saws have a fast moving blade that cuts the material it is in contact with. They are used for cutting plastic and timber. Pupils in schools are not permitted to use the circular saw or bandsaw, as operators must have a Health and Safety Certificate to certify training. These saws are instead used by teachers and technicians in the T&D department to cut material for pupil use.

Circular saw: rotates and the material is moved across the blade.

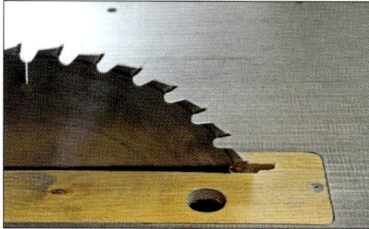

Band saw: rotates a continuous strip of saw blade that is a long flexible loop. It only makes straight cuts.

Pillar drill: can be bench or floor mounted. They allow the safe and easy drilling of material that can be lifted onto the drilling table. A vice or cramp should be used to firmly hold the material during drilling. All types of material can be drilled if the correct drill bit is used.

Bandfacers: have a revolving belt of abrasive material powered by an electric motor. Material is removed evenly and quickly because all parts of the belt are moving at the same speed. The dust is drawn away by an extraction system. For safe operation:

- Keep the workpiece flat on the worktable.
- Keep your fingers behind the workpiece.
- Never try to shape metals on a bandfacer.
- Never try to shape small pieces of material.

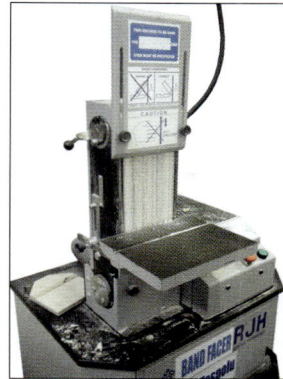

Bandfacer

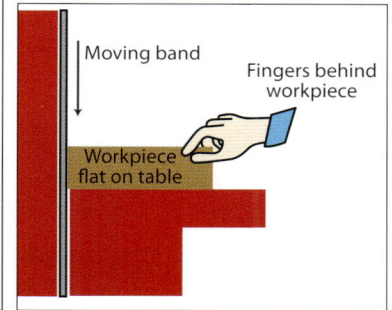

Lathe: An engineer's lathe or centre lathe, as it is more commonly known, is used for working metal but wood lathes are also available to turn wood. The material is held and rotated, whilst a cutting bit is pressed onto the material to cut it. They are used to produce round objects from metal and plastic. A manual lathe is controlled by the operator turning the handles of the top and cross slides to make the product. A chuck or headstock is part of the lathe that holds the material to be cut by the cutting bit. The speed of the chuck can be controlled by turning the gear levers on the top of the headstock, which contains all the gears controlling the lathe.

Wood lathe

Milling machine: is used to machine solid material such as aluminium and mild steel, as well as plastics such as perspex and nylon. The material rotates as it is pushed against the cutting tool. The machine is available as a vertical or horizontal model. The material and the cutting tool are both controlled very precisely by slides and lead screws. The machine should be set to cut away only small pieces each time to prevent the tools being damaged, as they are very expensive. A milling machine can be operated manually, mechanically or by computer control, and is available in different sizes, from bench top products up to full room size. It can produce a wide range of operations from simple slot cutting to complex contouring, using different shapes of cutting tools that are made from high speed steel. The cutting tools are threaded at one end so they can be screwed into the chuck. Cutting fluid can be used to cool and lubricate the tool and wash away debris or waste known as swarf, from the cutting operation.

It will help your understanding of machine tools if you are familiar with what each piece looks like and how it operates.

- Working in small groups, choose one piece of machinery and produce an A4 factsheet on the machine using ICT.
- Include a picture labelling each part, a procedure on how to use it, the materials it can machine and any safety issues.
- Each group should make a copy of their factsheet for each member of the class.

Power tools

Power tools are hand-held motorised tools that are powerful and portable. They have the advantages of machine tools and the convenience of hand tools. Safety precautions must be adhered to when using any of these powerful tools. Make sure you read any instructions and are given training or a demonstration on how to use a tool before beginning a manufacturing task. Also, make sure you use a circuit breaker, wear goggles and clamp work in place.

Jigsaw: is a power tool with a thin blade that reciprocates and moves front to back at various speeds. It is used for cutting arbitrary curves and custom shapes into wood and other materials, they are ideal for cutting thin man-made boards such as MDF and plywood. Different blades are available for different types of cutting. The metal plate at the bottom of the saw is an adjustable foot, which will pivot between 0 and 45°. This will allow you to make angle cuts in the wood. As you cut your line with a jigsaw, the wood particles tend to build up in front of the blade, obscuring the cutting line. A blower will blow these wood particles away allowing you to see the cutting line. There is a little roller on the back by the blade that helps support it while using the tool. It helps reduce flex in the blade, which provides straighter cuts and increases blade life. Most models also have a tool free blade changing system, which will hold the blade in the arm no matter how much pressure you put on the tool when using it. This means the blade can be changed without the use of tools such as allan keys. A jigsaw is an extremely versatile tool, as it can be used as a portable band saw and scroll saw. Always keep the guard in place when cutting.

Power drill: is available as a mains powered tool and a cordless tool, making it convenient and portable. A mains power drill can have a hammer action. The tool has various speed settings for different materials and the direction of the drilling can be easily changed from forward to reverse. Safety chucks that are self-locking mean the drill bit can be changed without a chuck key. The chuck and barrel of the drill are turned in opposite directions by hand to open and close the chuck for easy drill bit changes.

Electric sander: is used to sand or smooth wood. The sandpaper sheets are clipped in place to the base, which vibrates and smooths the material beneath it. If the surface is rough, start sanding with the coarse paper. Most models have a dust extraction system such as a bag to collect the sawdust.

Power planer: is for rough shaping or reducing material to a required size, by removing shavings of wood just like a bench plane is used for. It is not as accurate as a bench plane but it is faster and requires less effort.

It will help your understanding of the safety issues associated with power tools if you have an in-depth look at each power tool available in your school workshop.

- Under supervision use each tool on some waste material.
- Make your own notes about each piece and record any safety features it has or safety precautions you should follow when using the tool.

COMPUTERISED PRODUCTION

Computerised production is when the manufacturing process becomes automated by using computer-aided design (CAD) and computer-aided manufacturing (CAM) to produce products on computer numerically controlled (CNC) machines. Computerised production is being used more and more in T&D, even in school workshops with the use of CNC laser cutters and milling machines. It is therefore important to be familiar with some of the types of computerised production available. This section will recap on the main features of CAD and CAM, which were already discussed in 1A Manufacturing (pages 19–23), and will look at the main characteristics of each stage in the production process using CIM (Computer Integrated Manufacture).

WORD BOX

CAD
Computer-aided design is using a computer for designing.

CAM
Computer-aided manufacture is using a computer to control the machines making a product.

CAD/CAM
Computer-aided design and manufacture is the process of joining CAD and CAM systems together using specialised software which can convert drawing data into instructions for machining.

CNC
Computer numerical control is used to link the different stages of designing and manufacturing.

CIM
Computer integrated manufacturing runs computer-controlled machines.

CAD

CAD stands for **computer-aided design**. It is particularly good for producing **working drawings** and **3D computer models**.

Advantages:
Although CAD systems are relatively expensive they have a number of advantages over manual drawing methods:

- They produce high quality and consistent drawings.
- Information can be stored easily electronically and transmitted, for example, e-mailed.
- Complex assembly drawings can be produced quicker once the user gets used to the package.
- Standard parts can be accessed from a library, reducing the time it takes to draw them.
- Changes to drawings can be easily made and instantly seen on screen.
- Components are dimensioned automatically with most CAD packages.
- Solid modelling allows the product to be viewed from various angles and a 3D image gives a more realistic view than a 2D image.
- Images can be scanned into the system or photos imported, which is beneficial to project work.
- Drawings can be e-mailed.

Disadvantages:
However, there are also some disadvantages to using CAD systems:

- They are not a substitute for freehand sketching, which is quick and essential at the initial design and development stages of a design project.
- The initial set up cost can be expensive, as a computer is essential, some software is expensive and operators need to be trained to use it.

CAM

CAM stands for **computer-aided manufacture.** It is a process that converts drawings produced by CAD into actual products.

CAM involves a **range of machines**, most commonly lathes, routers, milling machines and laser cutters. These machines are **controlled by a computer** that guides the machine through an entire manufacturing process – computer numerical control **(CNC)**. A drawing produced by CAD is only a picture so it needs to be converted into numbers or co-ordinates that can be used by a CNC machine. A computer cannot be plugged directly into a CNC machine, it needs to be connected through an interface. In most CNC machines used today, interfaces are part of the machine. Older versions of CNC machines often have the interface in a separate box. The interface sends the CNC machine the information as digital signals so they can be recognised and manufacturing can begin.

Advantages:
Although relatively expensive to set up, once the CAM systems are programmed the advantages are considerable:

- They have a high production speed, ideal for large volume production.
- Machines can work 24/7 with little human intervention.
- They ensure products are produced accurately consistently.

- They are reliable.
- They are flexible as they can be reprogrammed.
- CAM systems require less skilled operators than traditional manufacturing that is not computerised.

Disadvantages:
- Initial set up costs are high.
- Training is required for operators.
- CAM systems can be slower than traditional methods of manufacture for one-off or low volume production.

CNC Machine	Materials cut	Applications
Laser Cutters	• Plastic • Wood card	• Intense beam of light used to cut • No clamping of material required • Simple and complex shapes can be cut
Lathes	• Wood • Metal • Nylon	• Accurate and complex shapes produced that would be difficult to produce on hand operated lathes
Milling Machines	• Acrylic/plastic • Wood • Metal	• Produce flat and complex curved shapes • In industry fine tolerances can be worked to
Routers	• Foam • Wood • Metal	• Similar to milling machines but using softer materials • Can cut 2D and 3D shapes • Used for block modelling

CIM

Computer Integrated Manufacturing is the central computer system used in industry to link together all the different stages of the design and manufacturing process.

A central computer database is used in CIM to coordinate all the different stages in the process. Usually many different people are involved in manufacturing even simple products, so everyone needs to know what the others are doing. Nothing happens in isolation, so using this central computer system makes communication easier.

The software used will automatically update any changes made and inform all the related stages. Time is saved and expensive mistakes avoided if, for example, a change is made in a CAD program, as the software has the ability to automatically change the related CNC program that is controlling the machines that manufacture.

Advantages:
- Costs can be lower than using just CAM for production, as there is less need for a separate, specialised machine tool for each product.
- Human error is reduced and the product can be quickly and easily changed without retooling the machinery, which would cost time and money.

Disadvantages:
- Initial set up costs for machinery and operator training are high.
- Fast special purpose machines may be cheaper to run for large-scale production runs than CNC machines.

The following manufacturing systems are used widely in industry:
1. In-line assembly
2. Flexible manufacturing systems
3. Just-in-time manufacture (JIT)

In-line assembly

In-line assembly is used for mass production, as most of the production line is automated. Unskilled labour is used mainly for assembly, whilst some semi-skilled workers make sure there is a continuous flow along the production line.

Advantages:
- As tasks are mainly carried out by machinery, human error and variation is reduced.
- A company can produce a larger quantity of one product at a lower cost than using traditional, non-linear methods because labour costs are reduced and production rates increase.

Disadvantages:

- The system is inflexible because it is difficult to alter a design or production process after the production line has been implemented.
- The system can lead to a lack of variety, as products are all produced on one production line so they are identical or very similar, making it difficult to cater for individual needs or wants.

Flexible manufacturing systems

Flexible manufacturing systems (FMS) use semi-skilled workers who are able to do a variety of jobs. The approach is based on the idea that a flexible workforce and flexible machinery is the key to successful manufacturing.

Advantages:

- FMS is useful for batch production where change and flexibility are essential.
- Manufacturing time is reduced per product.
- Cost per unit is reduced.

Disadvantage:

- FMS requires a great deal of pre-planning and organisation prior to production starting.

Just-in-time manufacture

Just-in-time manufacture (JIT) requires a high level of forward planning, as materials and components are only bought as and when needed. Modern manufacturing plants will use sophisticated production scheduling software to plan production, which includes ordering the correct stock. Supplies are delivered directly to the production line as they are needed. If JIT is implemented successfully it can improve a manufacturer's profits, quality and efficiency by continuous improvement, as it is a very responsive method of production.

Advantages:

- Resources are not stockpiled which saves warehouse space and money.
- It reduces the likelihood of stock perishing, becoming obsolete or going out of date.
- It avoids the build-up of unsold finished products as demands change.

Disadvantages:

- There is little room for mistakes as minimal stock is kept for re-working faulty products.
- Production is very reliant on suppliers and if stock is not delivered on time, the whole production schedule can be delayed.

- There is no excess finished product available to meet unexpected orders, because all products are made to industrial practices.

INDUSTRIAL PRACTICES

A company will use the following practices to increase their efficiency and productivity in the very competitive manufacturing industry that exists today:

- Standardised components, assemblies and bought in components.
- Sub-contracting.

Standardised components, assemblies and bought in components

Standardised components, assemblies and bought in components are the building blocks of much more complex products. Components include nuts, bolts, screws and rivets, all made to the same specification, with standard sizes and weights, and of the same material and quality. This allows manufacturers to order the components required for their products with the confidence that they have been manufactured to a very high specification.

Integrated circuits (ICs) are assemblies of electronic components that are bought in and used by the manufacturers of products such as washing machines, microwaves, mobile phones and dishwashers. The electronics boom of the 1950s and 1960s was a result of the mass production of standardised electronic components, such as resistors, transistors and diodes. Today, mass production would be impossible without the use of standardised components, assemblies and bought in components. They allow manufacturers to concentrate on product development, rather than wasting time designing and manufacturing every component needed for a product.

Advantages:

- It speeds up manufacturing and reduces manufacturing and maintenance costs, as the same units can be purchased and used all around the world.
- It means manufacturers do not have to create everything from scratch themselves. Pre-manufactured parts can be bought in by a manufacturer for use in their product. For example, a car manufacturer may buy in the headlights from another supplier rather than make them themselves.

Disadvantages:

- The manufacturer is depending on other manufacturers to supply them, which has the potential to be a less reliable system if delivery dates are not adhered to. Production may slow or cease if a manufacturer is waiting for a delivery of standardised components, assemblies or bought in components.

Sub-contracting

Sub-contracting is when part of a job or manufacturing process is contracted out to another source or company to complete. It can happen if a manufacturer has too much work. This occurs when machines and operators are working to full capacity and production is at its full efficiency but orders are still being placed. The manufacturer's ability to produce products is thus exceeded by the time available, if quality is to remain the same. On-time delivery to customers becomes unachievable if there is a back log in the manufacturing process, which can affect customer service. To avoid this happening but without having to refuse orders, the manufacturer will sub-contract.

Advantages:
- It provides relief to the manufacturer and prevents the manufacturing plant from becoming over burdened.
- It can improve efficiency by ensuring manufacture of the product is optimised.
- It helps manufacturers meet delivery dates without compromising on quality.

Disadvantages:
- It can be time consuming waiting for the sub-contractors to get the work completed and returned.
- It can be difficult to ensure quality when different manufacturers are responsible for different parts.
- Tracking parts can be an issue.

QUALITY ASSURANCE AND QUALITY CONTROL

Manufacturers can be put at a competitive disadvantage if their products are of poor quality, therefore they put a lot of effort into ensuring a high quality product is manufactured. Improved quality should result in the improved image and reputation of a company, which in return should result in:

- there being a greater demand for the product.
- there being an increase in the production volumes required.
- unit costs being reduced, as there will be less waste and less products rejected.
- the selling prices have the potential to be higher, as fewer products need to be discounted.

- customer satisfaction improving, as less customer complaints will be made.

ACTIVITY

Think of several examples from your own experience of when you have come across poor quality.
- Name the product and state why you thought it was not good quality.
- State whether you think the problem was a design or manufacturing quality issue.

Quality Assurance and Quality Control are implemented during the manufacturing processes and when a product is completed.

Quality assurance

Quality Assurance (QA) is about **setting standards** and meeting them. When QA is completed well by a company, they are awarded an international standard of quality known as 'ISO9000'. To achieve this ISO, a company will monitor products for quality through all stages of production, from design and development through to performance and customer satisfaction. Constant checks are made of equipment, materials and staff training. The two main principles of QA are **'fit for purpose'**, meaning the product should be right for its intended users and **'right first time'**, meaning mistakes should be eliminated.

Quality control

Quality Control (QC) is how you **check those standards.** Quality Control ensures that a product:

- does the job it was designed to do.
- conforms to the design specification.
- meets the relevant criteria of standards institutions such as BSI and CE.
- gives customer satisfaction.

It achieves the above by testing a sample of a part at every stage of production. It ensures specific tolerances are worked to.

CHECK YOUR LEARNING

1. What is Quality Assurance?
2. What is Quality Control?
3. How does Quality Assurance differ from Quality Control?

Sample testing

Costly waste can be reduced or prevented when testing is carried out as faults with machining and tool settings can be found and corrected. Types of testing include:

1. Measuring
2. Non-destructive testing
3. Destructive testing

Measuring

A limit gauge: Measuring can be completed with a micrometer but this can be costly as it is time-consuming. Instead a limit gauge could be used. A limit gauge is a double sided gauge machined to the upper and lower limit. If a component fits through the upper but not the lower it is said to be within the acceptable range.

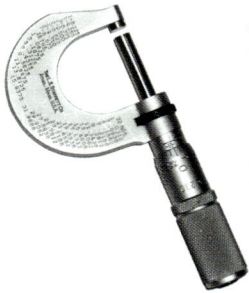

A micrometer: is used for precision measuring and is accurate up to 0.001 mm. However, it can only measure outside dimensions. It has a ratchet mechanism to prevent the jaws being pushed too hard.

A vernier gauge: is a very accurate measuring tool used for measuring both the inside and outside dimensions of material or products precisely.

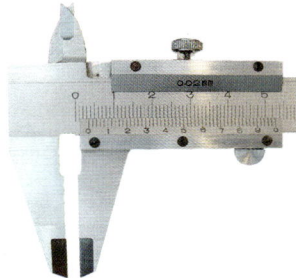

This diagram shows a vernier gauge being used to measure the outside dimension of a ball.

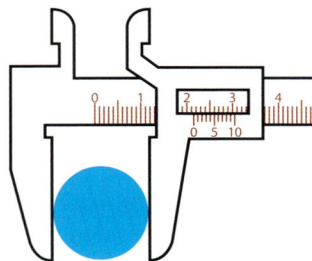

This image shows a vernier gauge being used to measure the inner diameter of a contact hole.

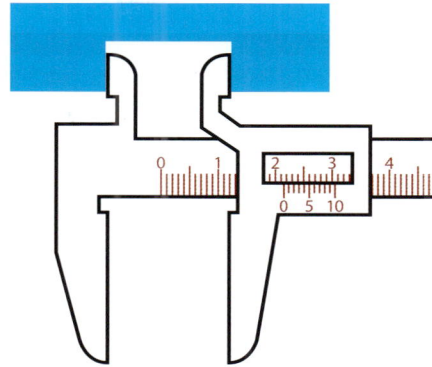

Non-destructive testing

Non-destructive testing does not damage the sample, as the testing is visual and could include using x-rays or penetrative dyes to find defects. The dye method is used to test for surface defects such as hairline cracks in castings, forgings and welds.

Destructive testing

Destructive testing is physical and destroys the product being tested to discover how the product would collapse or how fractures develop. It is only economical to carry out destructive testing on mass produced goods, where the cost to destroy a small number of goods is insignificant.

Tolerance

Tolerance in testing a sample is the amount of error allowed. It is expressed as an upper and lower deviation (+/−). Tolerance can be defined as the variation allowed on a dimension or surface. It is equal to the difference between the minimum and maximum limit of a specific dimension. For example, if a length of tubing was supposed to measure 150 mm +/− 2 mm then the lengths of tubes that would pass a Quality Control test would be:

150 + 2 mm = 152 mm Maximum length limit allowed

150 − 2 mm = 148 mm Minimum length limit allowed

All lengths of tubes that measure within the tolerance range of 148 mm to 152 mm would pass. Any tubes larger than 152 mm or less than 148 mm would be rejected.

ACTIVITY

If a plastic beam must measure 500 mm ± 1 mm calculate what lengths of the product will pass quality checks for dimensional accuracy.

KEY WORD CHECK

Below are some key words, explain what each means. Remember to add these words to your glossary.

- **Scale of production**
- **One-off/jobbing production**
- **Batch production**
- **Mass production**
- **Continuous production**
- **Gantt chart**
- **Reforming**
- **Injection moulding**
- **Die casting**
- **Extrusion**
- **Deforming**
- **Blow moulding**

- **Vacuum forming**
- **Line bending**
- **Metal folding**
- **Laminating**
- **Press moulding**
- **Hand tools**
- **Machines**
- **Power tools**
- **CAD**
- **CAM**
- **CNC**
- **CNC machines**

- **CIM**
- **In-line assembly**
- **Flexible manufacturing systems**
- **Just-in-time manufacture**
- **Quality**
- **Quality assurance**
- **Quality control**
- **Tolerance**
- **Micrometer**
- **Vernier gauge**
- **Non-destructive testing**
- **Destructive testing**

EXAM FOCUS

Complete the following past paper questions to help consolidate your learning and practice your exam skills.

1. Gantt charts are used to plan and manage the production of products.

Complete the Gantt chart shown below based on the following information:

1. Cut block of wood to shape (time – 25 mins)

2. Drill holes in wood (time – 10 mins)

3. Sand block of wood (time – 20 mins)

4. Paint wood (time – 15 mins)

Figure 1

Gantt Chart	5 mins	10	15	20	25	30	35	40	45	50	55	60	65	70
Cut block of wood to shape														
Drill holes in wood														
Sand block of wood														
Paint wood														

2. Figure 2 shows a piece of wood which has been marked out for cutting and drilling.

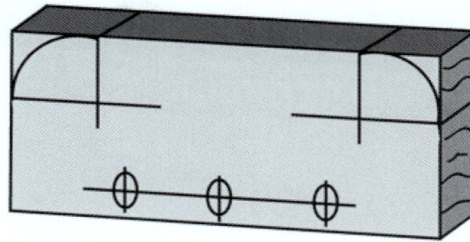

Figure 2

(a) Thirty completed pieces of wood are required.
What is the scale of production? [1]

(b) Name a power tool which could be used to cut the curves in the wood. [1]

(c) Tolerances are part of quality control.
Give one example of dimensional data, from the piece of wood on Figure 2, where tolerances could be applied. [1]

(d) The manufacturer of the pieces of wood operates a 'just-in-time' system.
Give one advantage and one disadvantage associated with this system. [2]

(e) What does CIM stand for? [1]

(f) Give one advantage and one disadvantage associated with a manufacturer using 'bought in' assemblies. [2]

CCEA GCSE Technology & Design Specimen Paper, Unit 3, Product Design, 2011, © CCEA

3. A toy kangaroo is shown in Figure 3.

Figure 3

(a) The kangaroo is made from MDF.
Suggest a suitable finish for the toy and give a reason for your choice. [2]

(b) (i) Name a suitable hand tool that could be used to cut out the parts of the toy in a school workshop. [1]

(ii) Name a suitable machine that could be used to cut out the parts to produce small quantities of the toy. [1]

4 (a) The production manager of a company which manufactures, assembles and distributes mobile phones has sub-contracted the manufacture of the circuit board for the mobile phone.

(i) Outline what sub-contracting means. [1]

(ii) Give two reasons why the company may wish to sub-contract the manufacture of the circuit board. [2]

CCEA GCSE Technology & Design Past Paper, Unit 3, Product Design, Summer 2011, © CCEA

SOCIAL RESPONSIBILITY OF PRODUCT DESIGN AND MARKET INFLUENCES

When designing a product you must be able to confidently demonstrate how you have been socially responsible with the design proposal. This means designing products that will not harm people's health, lives or the environment by considering issues such as consumer protection and health and safety. You need to be aware of how all aspects of your design will use energy and affect the Earth's resources. For example, are the materials you have chosen sustainable or will your finished product be recyclable? As a product designer you must also consider the ethical and moral implications associated with the design, manufacture and use of products, and be able to demonstrate an understanding of the influence that trends can have on the design and eventual success of a product. This section will give you the information you need to be a socially responsible product designer and help you understand the importance of marketing a product to a target market.

CONSUMER PROTECTION

Design briefs are driven by what a customer needs or wants. Manufacturers are dependent on customers, as without them there is no need for a product. Customer satisfaction is their main aim, and a customer will be satisfied when the product:

- works as intended.
- is good to use.
- is good value for money.

If a manufacturer does not produce a safe and reliable product for the consumer, they could be prosecuted under one of the following acts:

The Trades Descriptions Act: This act makes it illegal to make false claims about products. For example, if a manufacturer claims that their product is waterproof, this must be true.

The Consumer Safety Act: This act is concerned with the safety of products such as toys, electrical goods and electrical products. It enables the government to ban or restrict the sale of dangerous products.

The Sale of Goods Act: This act ensures that a product is fit for its intended purpose, that it works as it should and lasts a reasonable length of time.

These laws give the consumer protection from poor quality goods that could be dangerous or do not work as intended.

HEALTH AND SAFETY

The main purpose of safety standards and safety labelling is to give the consumer confidence in a product, reassuring them that it is of a high quality and safe to use. Official labels are awarded by the **British Standards Institution (BSI)** to show the consumer that standards have been met for quality, safety or design. The British Standards' label is the **Kitemark** and when a product is to be sold in the European Union the product must have a **CE mark** to show it has met the Central European Standards. Safety labelling also informs the consumers about its use, maintenance instructions and safety instructions, which all ensure the consumer is kept safe when using the product.

Products can also undergo a **risk assessment**, which is a procedure to identify if there are any potential risks to the consumer and to ensure any potential dangers are minimised. Risk assessment can also be used to identify and minimise any potential risks of using equipment, machinery or chemicals. These are the types of questions that need answered in a risk assessment:

- What is the potential hazard?
- Who could be harmed and how?
- What can be done to prevent it from happening?

The potential risks are assessed and the level of precaution has to be justified. In school, the T&D teacher or technician would do a risk assessment on the workshop and justify what precautions they need to put in place to minimise the risk of anyone being hurt or injured when using the workshop. This may include displaying the correct health and safety signage or ensuring machine guards are all in place.

When designing a product think about the safety of the consumer at all times.

The product must not injure or cause damage to the user in any way.

- It should be designed and manufactured to meet legislation such as CE and BSI.
- You should use standard components that you know have undergone extensive safety testing by the manufacturer.
- Containers for drugs and medicines should be designed to have childproof lids.
- Windows of high rise buildings should be designed to only open so far.

When designing children's products, think about specific safety features relevant to them.

- The corners of the product need to be smoothed.
- Ensure small components are firmly attached to avoid choking hazards.
- Use non-toxic surface finishes, especially on toys that can end up in a child's mouth.

ACTIVITY

- List five other products that have been designed to ensure the safety of the consumer.
- Explain how each product has been designed to ensure safety at all times.

SUSTAINABILITY OF RESOURCES

Sustainability of resources is meeting the needs and demands of society without harming natural cycles or depleting resources for generations to come.

Every action we take has an impact on the environment so as a product designer you must consider the sustainability of the Earth's resources. Consider using renewable materials that are grown from plants or animals rather than those from non-renewable sources, such as fossil fuels. Fossil fuels are taken from oil, ores and minerals, which are finite, and can only be found in limited amounts.

Sustainable hardwood and softwood plantations

Sustainable hardwood and softwood plantations are a recent development in forest production. They are planted in areas were no natural forest originally existed or to restock forests that have become depleted as a result of deforestation (the clearance of trees from an area to make room for another land use such as agriculture or urbanisation). In these plantations young trees are planted instead of waiting for natural seedlings to replace felled timber. They produce more uniform growth and can be more easily controlled. Ireland had its forest cover reduced to less than 1% at the turn of the century, but it currently stands at 10%, due to the establishment of plantations.

Ireland, Britain, New Zealand and South Africa all have widespread plantations. There are also schemes of managed natural forests and plantations being implemented in France and Germany in an attempt to increase forest cover, while the USA are replacing natural forests with plantations to speed up the rate of tree reproduction. The tropics are experimenting with plantations (their forests are not fully established yet) but in some areas there are plantations growing species of both softwoods and hardwoods. The main role of plantations in the twenty-first century is to conserve the reducing natural forest resources. People today are very aware of the positive effect forests can make to climate change.

Timber is a renewable resource so its future is assured. The proper management and maintenance of forests in the world would ensure that virtually all the tree species that provide the wide range of timbers we use could be available to timber users for as long as there is a need for them. Therefore, it is vitally important that the renewability of the timber resource be maintained worldwide. Industrial wood production is roughly 70% coniferous and 30% non-coniferous.

CHECK YOUR LEARNING

1. Explain the term 'sustainable resources'.
2. How can a product designer consider the sustainability of the Earth's resources?
3. Describe what a sustainable plantation is and its main role.
4. What type of resource is timber?
5. Why do forests need to be properly managed and maintained?

REDUCE, REUSE AND RECYCLE

It is important as a designer to consider the environmental impacts that using raw materials can have on the environment, and to dispose of products responsibly. You should try to:

Reduce: Cut down the amount of material and energy you use as much as you can.

Reuse: Use a product to make something else with all or parts of it. This reduces the processing needed, reducing cost and making the product more environmentally friendly.

Recycle: Reprocess a material or product and make something else from it.

Rethink: Do we make too many products? Consider people and the environment when designing.

Refuse: Do not use a material or buy a product if you do not need it or if it is bad for people or the environment.

Repair: Fix a product when it breaks down or does not work properly.

You must also consider how the design of products can influence the problem of wastage. Reducing packaging and designing products that can be reused or recycled will potentially reduce the waste that goes into landfill sites. Some products contain chemicals that can cause serious problems if they get into the water system or soil, so there are laws about what can be disposed of in landfills and what must be recycled or made safe with special treatment. It is also beneficial to assess how much packaging a product really needs to see if a reduction can be made to limit the amount of waste created. For example, in recent years the packaging of chocolate Easter eggs has been reduced significantly. By considering ways of reducing wastage during the design process, designers can reduce their carbon footprint.

─ WORD BOX ─

CARBON FOOTPRINT

A carbon footprint is the amount of carbon produced by any human activity and its effects on the environment. It is measured in units of carbon dioxide.

Various symbols are used on most products and packaging, and can inform the user:

- that it can be recycled.
- what material it was made from.
- how much of the product has been made from recycled material.
- how the product should or should not be disposed.

The environmental benefits of recycling

Recycling is the process of turning the useful parts of a product into a new product, which conserves the consumption of resources, energy and landfill space. If an old product has come to the end of its life cycle and has been disposed of in an environmentally way, often parts of it can be recycled or sometimes even the entire product can be used to manufactured a new item. For example, old car tyres can be recycled into rubber mats used to cover hard surfaces in children's play parks or roof tiles. Currently the UK has a low recycling rate of only 11%.

Recycling can save energy: as it often takes less energy to process recycled materials than to create new materials from scratch. For example, the energy required to recycle paper is less than that required to cut, pulp, wash, bleach, dry and press wood to create new paper from trees.

Recycling can conserve natural resources: such as wood, water, oil, ores and minerals. Some of these resources are non-renewable and cannot be produced at the rate that they are being consumed. Recycling reduces the consumption of these resources, which would be used to make new products from scratch. This helps the environment, as less pollution is generated by the manufacturing plant producing the new product.

Recycling can reduce pollution: Manufacturing creates air pollution, as the factories give off harmful emissions when fuel is burned for energy. Pollution can be reduced and global warming lessened if non-biodegradable waste is recycled rather than burned. Air pollution and greenhouse gasses such as carbon dioxide CO_2, methane and nitrous oxide all cause damage to the ozone layer. The ozone is the layer above the Earth that absorbs ultraviolet light from the sun, which can damage life forms on Earth. Recycling products can help to save energy and reduce the harmful emissions given off when fuel is burned in factories during manufacture.

Recycling can reduce waste: by reusing products that are no longer useful and would otherwise have been thrown out. This reduces the pressure put on landfill sites, where non-biodegradable waste is usually disposed of, which can only hold a limited amount of waste. Also, as it often takes less energy to process recycled materials than to create new materials, less waste is produced in the manufacturing process.

Recycling can save money: Products that are made from recycled materials are often more affordable than products made from fresh materials. There are also organisations that will pay you for your recyclable materials.

ACTIVITY

Use the Internet to research companies that are helping reduce the problem of overfilling landfills by offering other options for disposal of waste products. Record your findings.

CHECK YOUR LEARNING

1. How could a designer consider the environmental impacts of using raw materials and dispose of products responsibly?
2. List six environmental benefits of recycling.

Energy efficiency

As a designer you need to be able to appreciate the advantages and disadvantages of different forms of energy efficiency:

Energy efficient lighting

Energy efficient lighting saves money and energy, helping reduce your carbon footprint.

Regular light bulbs: run electricity through a resistive filament to create light. The filament glows and produces visible light with a warm yellow or plain white colour as it heats up to a very high temperature.

Advantages:
- Most light fittings are still designed to hold regular light bulbs.

Disadvantages:
- Light bulbs are not very energy efficient, as 98% of the energy required to give of light is lost as heat.
- These light bulbs will only last about 1,000 hours.

Fluorescent light bulbs: pass electricity through mercury vapour to produce ultraviolet light. A phosphor coating inside the lamp absorbs the UV light causing it to glow.

Advantages:
- Fluorescent bulbs are slightly more efficient than regular bulbs, as less heat is generated.
- Their life span is longer than regular light bulbs at around 10–20,000 hours.

Disadvantages:
- Fluorescent bulbs are 5–6 times more expensive than regular bulbs.
- They are not compatible with dimmer switches.
- Many people find the quality of light harsh and bright because fluorescent bulbs do not have a broad band of frequencies.
- Energy is still lost in generating UV light, as the light needs to be converted into white light.
- Mercury exposure can occur if the lamp breaks.

LEDs: LEDs provide the option of using a light source that is energy saving, with very few disadvantages.

Advantages:
- LEDs are available in a range of colours and are produced without the need of a filter.
- They are more energy efficient than regular and fluorescent bulbs. From a one watt device over 100 lumes (visible units of light) can be produced.
- They are available in small sizes and as rows, rings, clusters or individual points.
- They are very durable, with a life span of 50,000–60,000 hours. This is much more than the life span of a regular light bulb which is approximately 1,000 hours.
- LEDs can be dimmed so colors can be mixed if LEDs of different colors are used.
- LEDs contain no hazardous materials such as mercury or halogen gases.

Disadvantages:

- LEDs are not suitable in applications that need a direct beam of light.
- The intensity of the light emitted from blue and white LEDs is above the level for eye safety so they should not be looked into directly.
- LEDs are sensitive to changes in voltage so resistors need to be used to protect them from damage.

Energy saving light bulbs: use less power and last up to 10 times longer than regular light bulbs. Since 5% of most home energy bills is due to the use of lights, this is very useful.

Advantages:

- Regular light bulbs use two thirds more power than energy saving bulbs.
- They last up to 10 times longer than regular light bulbs (about 10,000 hours).
- They save money on purchasing as they need replaced less frequently.

Disadvantages:

- They are more expensive than regular light bulbs, so the short-term investment is larger.
- Some people find they do not give off bright enough light.
- They are difficult to dispose of at the end of their life due to their mercury content, as they cannot end up in landfills.
- They may have to be posted back to the manufacturer for safe disposal.

Source: Armin Kübelbeck

ACTIVITY

From what you have studied in this section, produce a table listing the advantages and disadvantages of energy efficient lighting.

Fuel efficiency in vehicles

When driving, it is important to ensure your car is running efficiently. This can be achieved by simple vehicle maintenance and changing your style of driving:

- Ensuring tyres are inflated properly will save fuel and give more miles to the gallon. This saves money and reduces the CO_2 emissions produced by a vehicle.
- Driving fairly cautiously, accelerating slowly and moving into a high gear as quickly as possible can all save fuel. Driving in a lower gear than necessary wastes fuel, but driving in a high gear on hills and corners will make vehicle engines overwork.
- Driving at a reduced speed can save fuel. For example, fuel consumption can rise by 20% if you cruise at 75 mph compared to 55 mph.
- Turning off engines that are going to be stopped for more than 30 seconds can save fuel. An engine running idle without the vehicle moving wastes fuel and increases CO_2 emissions.
- Using air conditioning sparingly can reduce fuel consumption.
- A regularly serviced engine will use less fuel and produce less emissions than a badly tuned one. Clean air filters and oil can also give better fuel efficiency.
- Avoiding carrying excess baggage can help improve vehicle fuel efficiency.
- Reducing travelling miles will reduce the fuel consumed. Planning any journeys can assist with this.

Home insulation

Home insulation is an effective way to improve the energy efficiency of a building, making it more comfortable to be in. Insulation in an empty loft will keep a building warmer in winter and cooler in summer, and will pay for itself in just over a year by reducing heating bills. Insulating both walls and lofts can save a household around £200 every year in heating costs. It also helps lower CO_2 emissions as less fuel needs to be burned to heat a building.

Insulation has various uses and is available in different densities and formats, such as granules that can be injected as insulation into cavity walls, slabs for walls, rolls for roof space insulation, pre-formed and faced pipe sections, ceiling tiles and acoustic panels. Fibreglass, cellulose and rigid foam board are common types of insulation used in homes.

Expanding foam insulation is a more recent development in insulation, with the specific advantage of being able to stop nearly 100% of heat loss from your home compared to fiberglass and cellulose. However, it also has some disadvantages:

- It is highly flammable and when it burns it gives off toxic fumes. When used it needs to be protected with a fire protective coating, which is expensive.
- It is more expensive to install than other forms of insulation, mainly because it needs to be installed by professionals.
- Damage can occur if it over-expands, as it can split wood and bend aluminum, which can damage windows and doors.
- Some expanding foam insulation contains harmful chemicals that can result in skin irritations and lung cancer.
- Its effectiveness as insulation is reduced over time if air has not been used to expand the foam. If gases have been used to blow the foam these can gradually escape, making the insulation not as effective.

ACTIVITY

Produce a page of images that show a range of environmentally friendly designs. Annotate the page to explain how each product is environmentally friendly.

CHECK YOUR LEARNING

1. Explain how simple vehicle maintenance and changing your driving style will help to ensure your car runs efficiently.
2. What is home insulation and how can it improve the energy efficiency of a building?
3. What are the disadvantages of expanding foam insulation?

ETHICAL, MORAL AND SOCIAL CONSIDERATIONS

As a designer, you must consider the ethical, moral and social considerations associated with the design, manufacture and use of products.

Ethical considerations

Ethical consumerism: is when a consumer intentionally buys a product or service that they believe has been made ethically. This means that no humans, animals or the environment have been harmed or exploited in the manufacturing of a product. There has been a rise in the mass market of consumers making ethic-based decisions when purchasing products or services. Some consumers even engage in a 'moral boycott', which is when they avoid buying a product because it has been manufactured in a way that is unethical. This has led to many large manufacturers marketing themselves and their products as ethical and improving the ethical standards of their industry.

The FAIRTRADE Mark: is an independent consumer label that can be displayed on products as a guarantee that disadvantaged producers in the developing world are getting a better deal. Fairtrade ensures that companies pay producers a fair, stable and sustainable price, which never falls beneath the market price. It also gives producer organisations extra money, which is invested in economic or social development projects.

ACTIVITY

- Research ways that a manufacturer can design and manufacture a product ethically.
- Make a list of products that display the FAIRTRADE logo.

Moral considerations

The word 'moral' concerns human behaviour, especially the distinction between right and wrong based on conscience.

Product designers must consider morality when designing and making products. The way that products are designed and manufactured affects the safety, comfort and well being of the people who come into contact with them. Therefore, the morality of thinking and decision-making has an impact on every aspect of design work and on the people who will use the products. Morality considerations exist within all of the following stages:

1. The design opportunity
2. The design specification
3. The design
4. The choice of manufacturing materials
5. Recycling materials
6. The use of energy
7. The manufacturing processes
8. The choice of manufacturer
9. Quality
10. Health and safety
11. Transport
12. Sales
13. After sales

The design opportunity:
By identifying a problem or design opportunity the designer can do something about it. The moral issue for the designer is what to do. Should they do something that will benefit them even if it will be negative for others? Should they do something that will benefit others even if it is difficult or may be negative for them? Will other people perceive their design as negative or positive?

The design specification: The design specification is a detailed list of everything a product should do or have. A designer writes a specification for a product so it is suitable, of good quality and safe for the people and environment it is designed for.

The design: A good design will mean that its finished product does exactly what it was intended to do. However, this does not necessarily mean that the way that the product is going to be used is morally good or right. For example, a hand grenade is a small bomb, designed to damage whatever it is thrown at upon contact. It is designed to detonate upon impact or after a set amount of time, so as not to harm whoever throws it. This is a good design, which fulfils its intended use, but is it morally good? No, because a design's intended use affects its morality. To be morally good, designs should be inclusive, which means they need to be useful to the widest possible audience, *without* any harmful effects. However, every design cannot be useful to every person in the world, so designers will also need to make alterations to meet the specific needs of individuals. Ultimately, a designer's morality and decision making skills will determine how much society will benefit from a design.

The choice of manufacturing materials: Designers should consider the origin of their materials when deciding which to use to manufacture their product. Many of the world's resources are diminishing and there is a moral argument that people should use them respectfully, carefully and with as little waste as possible. Designers may, for example, decide to use timber from sustainable forests if creating a wooden product. Other designers may decide to use fabric rather than plastic in the manufacture of shopping bags, providing the consumer with reusable, durable shopping carriers. Both of these products may be popular with consumers when marketed as 'environmentally friendly'. Many materials used in manufacture come from animals, such as leather, fur and bones. However, some consumers consider it immoral to kill animals to create these materials and will not buy goods that have harmed animals in their production.

Recycling materials: As the world's resources are being used up faster than they can be replaced and in some cases are finite, there is a moral argument that the recycling of materials is good. Designers should consider how they will dispose of a product at the end of its lifecycle and if it can be recycled.

The use of energy: Energy use is unavoidable as it is essential for industry, development and a comfortable human existence. However, there is a moral argument that we should reduce our consumption of energy to limit the depletion of our finite fossil fuel resources, and reduce increasing levels of greenhouse gases and global warming. Designers should limit their energy use during production and try to design products that use less energy.

The manufacturing processes: The three main moral issues relating to the manufacturing process concern its workers, its product and its waste.

1. One of the largest expenses in the manufacturing process is labour costs; its workers. It may be more cost effective to outsource work to a country where wages are lower. However, working conditions in that country may not be as good as those in the UK. If conditions are not as safe, the hours are longer or children are employed, designers may decide it would not be morally good to have the products manufactured there.

2. Designers will have to consider how well their products are being manufactured and assembled, as this will affect the quality of the finished product. This is discussed under the 'Quality' section on page 161.

3. Waste is the final moral issue. As mentioned in 'Recycling materials', designers should consider how they will dispose of a product at the end of its life. Products that use non-organic materials such as metals, plastics and chemicals will not decompose or break down in a landfill site. Also they could potentially leak chemicals or toxins into the soil and water ways in the surrounding area, which could be unsafe for local residents or animals. The safe disposal of products

at the end of their life cycle is thus important and recycling can provide an alternative and safer means of disposal for many products than landfills. Also products made from recycled materials generally produce less pollution than new products. This is because it takes energy to run the industrial plants that make products, and it takes more energy to create a product from scratch than from recycled materials. Fuel has to be burned to create this energy, which emits greenhouse gases such as CO_2 as a waste product. These gases are damaging to the environment and create air pollution.

The choice of manufacturer: As mentioned above, one of the largest expenses for a manufacturer is labour costs. The other is the cost of premises. It is often more cost effective for manufacturers to process their work outside of the UK. In some countries labour costs, rates, rent and overheads are considerably lower but, as mentioned, there may be moral issues regarding working conditions. It may also be seen as morally wrong to outsource work if unemployment rates are on the rise in the UK.

Quality: The quality of products must be suitable for their intended purpose. If a product fails on quality the manufacturer has a moral obligation to recall all of the products for inspection and replacement if necessary.

Health and safety: When designing a product the designer must put safety first at all stages of the design, production, storage, marketing, distribution and use of a product. Any decisions they make will affect the risks encountered by the manufacturers and end users. A good designer will be able to identify the possible hazards of a design and know how to avoid them. Designers have a moral obligation to:

- identify hazards.
- assess risks.
- take actions to reduce or prevent health and safety risks to people.

Transport: The designers and manufacturers have a moral obligation to ensure products are transported safely and without being damaged, and that people, wildlife and the environment are not damaged by the transportation process.

Sales: Making profits from selling products is an essential part of designing and manufacturing. For the sales process to be considered moral, potential consumers must be informed correctly about the product for sale. What the product does, who it is intended for, the age range of the user, the instructions on usage and assembly all need to be clearly described either on the packaging or within instruction manuals accompanying the product. The seller must be able to confidently explain to the consumer everything they may need to know or want to know about the product. To omit information is unfair and the Government body Trading Standards Institute would be supportive in challenging manufacturers and sales people if a product is sold wrongly. Consumers have rights and products must be:

- of satisfactory quality, free of any defects and last for the time you would expect it to.
- fit for purpose, which is the use described and any other specific uses made clear to the consumer by the trader.
- as described, matching the description on packaging or what the trader told the consumer.

After sales: Consumers will have confidence in a brand or product and will trust the manufacturer if they can give guarantees, good after sales care and support.

Social considerations

Social considerations need to be taken into account by designers, as they have a responsibility to design products that will be accepted by society. They need to design products that can be used by consumers without injury and ensure that no one is damaged during its manufacture. The social considerations when designing a mobile phone, for example, can be both negative and positive. Negatively, more text messages may reduce the physical contact people have with others and if used inappropriately, such as when driving, the product could cause accidents. However, positively, people are given more freedom of choice, can keep in contact more easily and regularly, can access the Internet on the go and people can gain employment through the manufacture of the product in factories. Designers must consider all the affects a design will have on society.

> **ACTIVITY**
>
> Can you think of any social considerations that are associated with products aimed at children?

> **CHECK YOUR LEARNING**
>
> 1. What does the term 'moral boycott' mean?
> 2. What is the FAIRTRADE Mark?
> 3. What does the word moral mean?
> 4. How can a product be designed to be morally good?
> 5. What are the three main moral issues associated with the manufacturing process?
> 6. List any other moral issues a product designer must consider.

MARKETING

Marketing is the promotion and selling of a product or service to place it in the reach of potential customers. Marketing will make a business be seen and identify potential customers. Marketing a product you have designed and made is essential, as you have to be able to sell it. To do this you need to understand the importance of market research and your product's target audience.

Market research

Market research is the gathering of information about markets or customers in an organised way. It is essential for discovering what people want, need, believe or how they act. The research can be used to decide how the product will be marketed. Market research can involve using questionnaires, surveys and focus group discussions.

Target audience

The target audience or market is the group of customers a company has decided to aim their marketing and product at. Knowing your target market can be enhanced by collecting market information and market segmentation.

Market information

For your marketing to be successful, you will need information about what is happening in the market you want to get your product into. This market information will help you establish the supply and demand situation, and the prices of the different raw materials being used in the market. Information about the markets can be obtained from different sources, and in different varieties and formats, such as published statistics, surveys or questionnaires.

Market segmentation

Your marketing efforts may be enhanced if you are aware of how the market is segmented into subgroups of the population with similar motivations. The subgroups could be based on people with geographic differences, demographic differences, use of product differences, social class, lifestyle or personality differences and gender differences.

Market trends

Market trends are the upward or downward movement of a market, during a period of time. The market size is more difficult to estimate if you are launching a completely new product into a market than if you are launching a redesigned or repackaged product. In the case of a new product, you will have to derive the figures from the number of potential customers or customer segments.

Advertising and publicity

Advertising and publicity are important factors when trying to get a product to sell by increasing consumer awareness.

Advertising: aims to influence people and convince them to buy a product. This can be achieved through various forms of media, such as the Internet, email, bill boards, mail, radio, cinema, television, newspapers and magazines.

Publicity: is the deliberate attempt by a company to manage consumers' perception of a product. It is part of the promotion of the product, ensuring it is marketed well, which encourages consumers to buy the product, resulting in profits.

ACTIVITY

- Describe an advertising campaign that influenced you to purchase a product.
- Describe a publicity event you have seen to persuade consumers to purchase a product.

The life cycle of a product

Products have a life cycle just like humans. They pass through various stages such as birth, growth, maturity, decline and death. The stages are related to a product's life in the market, with respect to costs and sales. To say a product has a life cycle is to say:

- its life is limited.
- the sales of the product will go through distinct stages, and the seller will be presented with different challenges, opportunities and problems.
- that different strategies for marketing, finance, manufacturing, buying, and human resource at each stage of the product's life cycle will be necessary.

The main stages of a product's life cycle are shown in the flow diagram below:

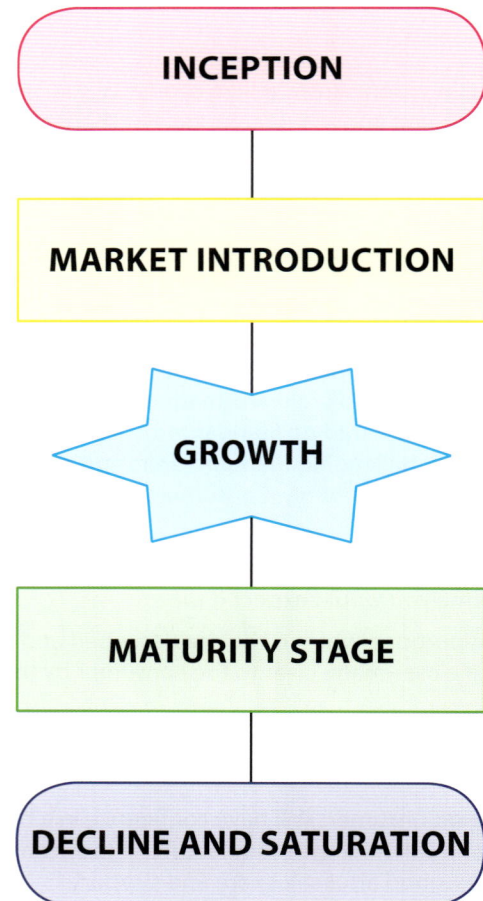

INCEPTION

MARKET INTRODUCTION

GROWTH

MATURITY STAGE

DECLINE AND SATURATION

Inception: is when an idea for a product is manufactured.

Market introduction: is when a product is first presented to the market. Costs are very high and the volume of sales is generally slow until a demand is created. Customers have to be encouraged to try a product and no money is usually made at this stage. There is little or no competition occurring.

Growth stage: is when the public becomes more aware of the product and the volume of sales increases significantly. Production increases and costs reduce as profits start to rise. Competition begins to increase causing product prices to decrease.

Maturity stage: is when sales peak and the market becomes saturated. Costs decrease as the volume of production increases, and prices fall because of the fast growth of competing products and the increase in competitors entering the market. Brand differentiation and features have to be promoted to maintain or increase market share, which results in reduced profits.

Decline and saturation: is when costs are not at their best and sales volume declines or stabilises. Making profit becomes more challenging when trying to achieve a balance between production and distribution efficiency.

Once a product has reached its maturity stage it is time for the manufacturers to try to find ways to extend its life. They will let it continue into the decline stage. To extend a product's life the following extension strategies may be tried:

- **Price reductions** – discounts or sale campaigns.
- **Repackaging and redesigning of a product** – products are changed slightly to make them seem new and attract fresh attention.
- **Launched into new markets** – the product is promoted to a different target group or it is launched in another country.

- **Promotions** – new advertising campaigns are engaged in to remind customers about the product in the hope of increasing demand for a little longer.

If a product is no longer as successful as it was or an upgrade is not going to be launched, the manufacturers will not invest time and strategies to keep sales up.

ACTIVITY

Think of products you have bought that:
- have been reduced in price. Name the product and give reasons why you think it had to be reduced.
- have been repackaged and redesigned. State the products and give reasons why you think this happened.
- were promoted in a way that made you buy it. Explain how the product you bought was promoted so you were tempted to buy it.

CHECK YOUR LEARNING

1. Why is market research necessary?
2. Explain the difference between advertising and publicity.
3. What does it mean to say a product has a life cycle?
4. Explain each stage of the product life cycle.
5. Explain four extension strategies that could be used to extend the life cycle of a product.

KEY WORD CHECK

Below are some key words, explain what each means. Remember to add these words to your glossary.

- **Consumer protection**
- **The Trades Descriptions Act**
- **The Consumer Safety Act**
- **The Sale of Goods Act**
- **Kitemark**
- **CE mark**
- **Risk assessment**

- **Sustainability of resources**
- **Energy efficiency**
- **Reduce**
- **Reuse**
- **Recycle**
- **Ethical consumerism**
- **Marketing**

- **Market research**
- **Market information**
- **Market segmentation**
- **Market trends**
- **Advertising**
- **Publicity**
- **Product life cycle**

Complete the following past paper questions to help consolidate your learning and practice your exam skills.

1. **Figure 1 shows some typical houses. Increasingly, efforts are being made by householders/consumers to reduce energy wastage.**

   (a) Give one advantage and one disadvantage associated with energy efficient lighting in the home. [2]

   (b) Consumers rely on products such as energy efficient lighting being safe to use.

   Explain how the Government protects consumers from the sale of products which are dangerous. [2]

   (c) State two areas of a house where insulation can be used.

   (d) (i) What is BSI/CE labelling? [1]

   (ii) Give one example of a household item which may be labelled with BSI/CE. [1]

Figure 1

CCEA GCSE Technology & Design Specimen Paper, Unit 3, Product Design, 2011, © CCEA
For copyright reasons the image in Figure 1 has replaced the one from the CCEA past paper.

2. **Using an annotated sketch, design a wall mounted toothbrush and toothpaste holder which will satisfy the following specification points:**

   • Hold four typical toothbrushes and one tube of toothpaste securely. [4]

   • Should be ergonomically comfortable to use. [4]

   • Must be easily installed on a wall. [4]

   • Be aesthetically pleasing. [4]

   • Use as little materials as possible. [4]

   • Should be long lasting. [4]

   Use the following information to help you:

   The toothbrush holder is intended to be used by male and female children aged between 3–11 years in a typical domestic bathroom.

   The toothbrush and toothpaste holder **must not** be larger than 300 mm x 300 mm x 100 mm.

   A typical toothbrush is approximately 200 mm x 20 mm x 20 mm.

   A typical toothpaste container/tube is approximately 160 mm x 50 mm x 50 mm.

   Your answer should include all necessary dimensions.

CCEA GCSE Technology & Design Specimen Paper, Unit 3, Product Design, 2011, © CCEA

3. **Consumer demand for mobile phones has continued to grow at a fast rate.**

(a) Give **two** specific technological reasons and **one** specific social reason for the growth in consumer demand of mobile phones. [3]

(b) The huge growth in consumer demand for mobile phones has resulted in a large number of older mobile phones being disposed of.

Discuss why mobile phones should be recycled rather than disposed of in landfill sites. [2]

CCEA GCSE Technology & Design Past Paper, Unit 3, Product Design, Summer 2011, © CCEA

4. Figure 2 shows a seesaw for pre-school children.

(a) (i) Give one ergonomic factor which should be considered when designing the seesaw. [1]

(ii) A risk assessment is carried out on the seesaw before it is marketed.
Explain what is meant by risk assessment. [1]

(iii) Suggest two factors which should be considered in the risk assessment of the seesaw. [2]

Figure 2

(b) The company manufacturing the seesaw is considering adapting the existing seesaw for use by older children.

Produce freehand sketches with notes to illustrate your ideas for possible modifications to the seesaw to enable it to be used by older children. [4]

CCEA GCSE Technology & Design Past Paper, Unit 3, Product Design, Summer 2011, © CCEA

5. Using annotated sketches, design a holder for pens, pencils and an eraser. Your solution for the holder should consider the following specification points:

• Must be freestanding and stable to sit on a desk or table. [4]

• Hold two pens, two pencils and an eraser in an efficient and effective manner. [4]

• Efficient use of material. [4]

• Ergonomic factors. [4]

• Aesthetic factors. [4]

• Material(s) selection and justification for their use. [4]

Using the following information to help you:

The holder is intended to be used by children aged between 3–11 on a desk or table.

The holder **should not** be larger than 200 mm × 200 mm × 80 mm.

A typical pen is approximately 150 mm × 10 mm diameter.

A typical pencil is approximately 180 mm × 8 mm diameter.

A typical eraser is approximately 35 mm × 20 mm × 7 mm.

Your answer should include all necessary dimensions.

CCEA GCSE Technology & Design Past Paper, Unit 3, Product Design, Summer 2011, © CCEA

UNIT 4

DESIGN ASSIGNMENT
CONTROLLED ASSESSMENT

DESIGN ASSIGNMENT CONTROLLED ASSESSMENT

*This unit is **compulsory** for all students. In this controlled assessment you will be assessed on your knowledge, skills and ability to:*

⟳ **Plan and carry out research**

⟳ **Produce sketches to illustrate your ideas**

⟳ **Design a product under controlled conditions**

⟳ **Evaluate your work**

ASSIGNMENT GUIDELINES

Students are advised to spend **approximately 15 hours** on the assignment.

The assignment enables students to demonstrate their capability to design a product under controlled conditions.

CCEA will issue **up to three** comparable tasks each year, in September of the first year of study. Centres select the task that is best suited to their needs.

By the end of the assignment, students should have compiled three A4 research sheets and four A3 design sheets for submission. These sheets **could** be put together using the following structure:

Research sheets	Design sheets
1. Problem statement and research on existing products	1. Concept 1
	2. Concept 2
2. Consumer research	3. Concept 3
3. Manufacturing and materials needed	4. Final idea

Examples of some these research and design sheets are shown on pages 167–171.

Research sheets

Your main aim in these pages of research is to gain maximum marks by producing appropriate, high quality research material. Begin by writing a **statement**, a couple of sentences long, about what the problem is, to articulate in your own words that you understand what you have been asked to do for this unit of controlled assessment.

1. Existing products

Product analysis is an important part of product design. In this section you should research other designers' products to discover what makes them work. You could analyse six existing products, deciding what makes the design good and if there is anything that could be improved. You will need good quality images and well written notes to explain the features of the product and your own opinion about the design. Some of these words may help you analyse the product: function, materials, size, cost, assembly, attachment, usability, aesthetics, manufacturing and safety.

166

It is important to be succinct with your notes but include technology enriched vocabulary.

- Do not copy and paste product information directly from web pages.

RESEARCH

This is the first page of my research into bicycle mirrors. The aim of this page is to look at existing products, comment on them and take inspiration from them, so I can design my own bicycle mirror that will help make cyclists more aware of rear view traffic and assist in safe cycling for all.

Example 1
This bicycle mirror is compact which makes it very neat. As it is compact, it isn't awkward or in the persons way. It has been very well attached to the bicycle. Simple, but effective. The attachment has been moulded to fit securely on the frame of the bike. It has simply been strapped on.
The mirror is adjustable which is useful because it can be adjusted to adapt to the size of the person.
Although, I think the mirror seems to be blocked by the person riding the bike, as it is very close to the frame of the bike.
The mirror has rounded edges which makes it completely safe for the young or in the event of a fall.
The colour, black, is slightly bland and the mirror doesn't really seem to be aimed directly at a particular target audience.

Example 2
This mirror is very cleverly designed. The attachment isn't very well considered. It is simply taped on with strong black tape. The mirror can be adjusted by simply extending the stem, according to your positioning. This stem has the same principle as a television aerial. The mirror head is very small. This decreases the rear view but, if made larger, would leave the goggles very unstable. This mirror doesn't look very good because of the attachment and the goggles. Not many people would buy this product.

Example 3
This mirror isn't designed for a bicycle, although I think it is extremely effective. The use of a bicycle wheel is a very eye catching design. This mirror will really inspire my ideas for my final design. The mirror is a reasonable size, although could be made larger for a wider view of rear view traffic. The design would attract everyone and would be extremely popular.
The mirror could be adapted even more to be suited for the road; this could be done by adding reflectors around the age. This would then let the mirror become safe for traveling at night. The plastic used could be easily shaped by the laser cutter. The mirror could also be changed to shatterproof, again this would increase the safety. Overall I think this is an extremely effective mirror and will definitely have an influence on my final design.

Example 4
This bicycle mirror isn't very well designed. The reason for this, is the attachment to the handle. This only suits one width of handle. The fitting doesn't adjust to fit different handlebars. The attachment is also not very strong. It could slip off at any second as the wind blows against it while cycling.
The mirror can be adjusted easily to suit different heights of people. Whether it is used for young children, adults or the elderly, it is easily adjusted by simply turning by hand.
It is black in colour which doesn't aim specifically at any target audience, although anyone could use it.
It has a very nice shiny finish, from emery paper and polishing. It is made from plastic. This is a very suitable material as it is easily moulded, quite strong and produces a very nice finish. Overall this mirror su ts its function quite well.

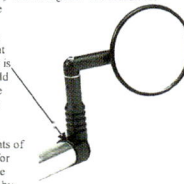

Example 5
This mirror is quite easily attached. It could be a problem for elderly as the small screw may be inefficient and awkward. The attachment is suitable for any bike handle bar as it can be adjusted. The more the screw is tightened, the smaller the hoop around the handle bar becomes. This is a strong attachment and won't break easily. The attachment also won't slip easily if it is screwed on tightly. This is good as the mirror won't move when cycling.
The mirror is easily adjusted by a flexible plastic stem. This is an important factor as the mirror needs to suit people of different heights.
The mirror is just a circle and plain black in colour. There is no target audience.
The mirror is most likely to be made from shatterproof glass. This is to ensure, in the case of an accident, the mirror won't break or hurt anyone.
The mirror is a reasonable size. It is big enough to see past. You don't block it. Although it is small enough to not get in your way or distract you when you're cycling.

Example 6
This mirror is very unusual. It has a long hollow stem which fits around the handle bars of the bike. It is easily attached by simply sliding it over the handle bars. Anyone could do it. If the bike had gears, this type of mirror would not suit its purpose as the stem would be unable to slide over the handle bars.
The mirror can't adjust very much. Just very slightly. This is not good as it wouldn't suit people of all heights.
The mirror is very small. This is good as it is neat and compact, but also is bad as you can easily block the mirror with your body or, it simply isn't big enough to see a clear view of what is behind you.
The mirror is made from plastic which is good as it won't rust when rain hits it and it is also easily cleaned.
The mirror has no main target audience, but in general could suit anyone.

2. Consumer Research

In this section you should explain what consumer research is and how you intend to use it to help you generate ideas for a new design of product. Consumer research will give you an insight into what potential users want from a product, or the features they like or dislike about similar, existing products. This type of research will help you generate possible concepts for the new product you have to design.

When you have selected a range of similar, existing products to research, it is important that you analyse and evaluate them. You may wish to comment on some of the following features: function, materials, size, cost, shape, assembly, usability, aesthetics, manufacturing and safety.

One way of collating consumers' comments on the features of existing products is to draw a table listing each product against the features they are to be scored on (see example on page 168). Score the features for each product out of 10, then add up the total score for each product. The important part of this research is to analyse your findings. Comment on the products that scored highest and the lowest, including the reasons and features the consumers liked best. Discuss how you think the product has been fabricated. Explain how you will incorporate these findings into your design concepts.

This research page shows the popularity of each bicycle mirror in the certain areas scored below. This gives me a clear idea of how I could adapt these popular factors into my own design.

Product	Function	Materials	Adjustability	Attachment	Compactness
1	7/10	8/10	3/10	9/10	8/10
2	8/10	8/10	6/10	8/10	9/10
3	9/10	8/10	10/10	7/10	6/10
4	7/10	7/10	4/10	2/10	7/10
5	8/10	8/10	10/10		5/10
6	5/10	5/10	5/10	4/10	7/10

Explanations

The reasons for the scores for product 1: This product scored high for attachment as the plastic was shaped to fit securely on the metal frame of the bike. Then it is just tied down with a strip of plastic. I scored the adjustability low as the mirror doesn't really have any movement.

The reasons for the scores for product 2: This scored this high on compactness as it is very neat looking on the bike and is also big enough to shine the light brightly. Again this product was scored low on adjustability as it doesn't have very much movement

The reasons for the scores for product 3: Product 3 scored 10 for adjustability as the flexible stem a has a lot of movement. It scored 6 for compactness as it is very big and awkward looking and would disrupt your cycling quite a lot.

The reasons for the scores for product 4: Product 4 scored low on attachment as the attachment would only suit one type of handle bar thickness. It scored high on materials as plastic is quite strong, easily shaped and has a nice finish

The reasons for the scores for product 5: Product 5 scored high on adjustability as the flexible stem can be moved in any position easily to suit the cyclist. Although, it scored low on compactness as it is large and not very neat looking. It would also disrupt your cycling

The reasons for the scores for product 6: Product 6 scored highest on compactness as the mirror head is small and neat and also big enough to get a clear view of behind you. It scored low on attachment as it isn't easily attached and only suits one thickness of handle bar.

Now, because of this research, I know how to make my own mirror help make cyclists more aware of the rear view traffic and will assist in safe cycling for all.

Mirror Head

My mirror head is going to be shaped like a tyre. It will be an adapted version of this mirror, which I evaluated on the first page of my research.
The dimensions of my mirror head:
It will be 100mm in diameter
It will be 8mm in width.

- Easily shaped
- Lots of colours
- Cheap
- Nice finish
- Can snap quite easily when force is applied.
- Strong
- Durable
- Can rust
- One colour, but can be painted
- Not easily shaped
- Nice finish

I chose acrylic as it was the most suitable material because of the above reasons. I could shape the plastic with either the:

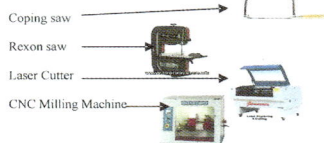

Coping saw
Rexon saw
Laser Cutter
CNC Milling Machine

I will use shatterproof glass for my mirror. This glass breaks but doesn't shatter. This is because of interlayer between two pieces of glass, that is held in place. This glass is relatively cheap.
Ordinary glass would not be as suitable because in the case of an accident the cyclist could get hurt by the broken glass, especially children.

Adjustment

Option 1

Option 2

- Quite strong
- Plastic easily shaped
- Easily cut to suitable size
- Easily adjusted
- Easily cleaned
- Very flimsy rubber
- Easily cut
- Not very durable
- Not rigid

I chose the plastic flexible tube for my mirror because of the above reasons.
This flexible tube would be extremely difficult to make so I think the tube would have to be bought.

I would attach the mirror head to my flexible tubing in a similar way to this mirror. It would be simply melted together and it could be filed down and made smooth so you wouldn't even notice the joint.

Another possibility is:
This is attached by a ball which is a very weak attachment.

Some other examples of flexible and moving parts are:
This chain is a brilliant example of flexibility and moving links. Although this definitely would not be suitable for a stem for my mirror as it would be too flimsy and not stable enough. Also, it doesn't look very nice.

Size
My flexible stem would be 150mm long and 20mm in diameter. Ay bigger would make awkward on the bike and any smaller would make it difficult to see behind you.

Attachment

Plastic

Metal

- Easily shaped
- Not very strong
- Variety of colours
- Nice finish
- Strong
- Not easily shaped
- Can rust
- Can be painted

I chose plastic for my mirror because of the above reasons. I like this style of attachment as it is strong and easily used.

This is another possibility for the attachment, but it isn't as easily used, isn't as compact and doesn't look as nice.

Manufacturing

I would bend the plastic into a round shape using the line bender. I would then file down the rough edges on the plastic. I would then cross file, draw file (using a flat file), use emery paper, then wet and dry and then polish it.

Line bender   Flat File

My attachment would be 50mm in diameter. Although, this can be varied when the nut is tightened which leaves it appropriate for any width of handlebar.
The size of an average handlebar is 25mm.

* My whole mirror will be made of waterproof, durable and lightweight materials

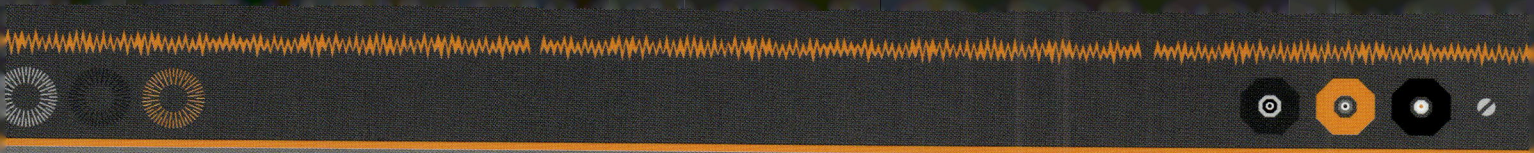

3. Manufacturing and materials research

In this section you should research possible materials and manufacturing processes that could be considered for your concepts. At this stage you are not making any definite decisions about what you will use, instead you are showing that you have researched and considered a range of possibilities. This page of research should include explanatory text and images of possible materials, tools, equipment and machinery that you have considered.

You might find it useful to use a template similar to the one below to get you started. It breaks the product into three sections and looks at the materials and processes that could be used to manufacture each section. This will focus your research. The example is for the design of a new bicycle mirror but could be adapted for any design brief.

.... **Template: manufacturing and materials research** ....

Write a statement explaining what you are going to research and why.

Mirror head	Adjustment	Attachment to bicycle
Shape: List the possible shapes that would be suitable and state the reasons why they should be considered.	**Methods:** List two possible methods of adjusting the mirror head. Sketch or include images of each.	**Methods:** List three possible methods of attaching the product to a bicycle. Sketch and explain how each works.
Colour: State a range of possible colours and why you would choose them.	**Reasons:** State the reasons why you would you each method and why.	**Manufacture:** List a range of manufacturing techniques available in the school workshop that could be used to manufacture these types of attachments.
Size: Estimate the average dimensions (in mm) that the mirror head should be. Explain why you decided on this size.	**Other methods:** List any other possible methods of achieving flexibility and movement of the mirror.	**Size:** Estimate the average dimensions (in mm) that the attachment should be. Explain why you decided on this size.
Material (mirror head): List the various materials that could be used to manufacture the mirror head. Explain why each material would be suitable.		
Material (mirror): List the various materials that could be used to manufacture the mirror. Decide which one would be best and explain why.		
Manufacturing: List the various manufacturing methods that could be used to manufacture the product, including tools and equipment. Explain why each would be suitable.		

Now your research is complete, you must link it to your design work. The use of the research in your design work needs to be obvious as there are many marks available for using your reference materials as stimulus. You will need to write comments beside your concepts to demonstrate how the research has influenced, inspired or connects to the design proposals. If you can do this successfully you have the potential to achieve higher marks in this section.

Design sheets

Now that you have completed in-depth research on the problem, you should feel confident about starting to solve it. You should use these design sheets to sketch three different concepts that will solve the problem, using a variety of sketching techniques.

Concepts

In this section you should reference your research. You could insert pictures from your page on existing products, gluing them in beside your own ideas and labeling them 'stimuli' to show this is how your idea was inspired. You should include a range of graphical techniques in your design work, such as two dimensional, sectional view(s), pictorial and exploded views. The graphics and annotation should be completed to a high standard to communicate ideas and fabrication details. Sketching exploded views of the parts you design will show you have thought about how they could be fabricated, which is necessary to achieve top marks in this unit of work. Remember you are designing for manufacture so your concepts need to show evidence of how the parts are assembled and fit together. Also include appropriate materials that could be used for each concept. CAD must not be used for designing.

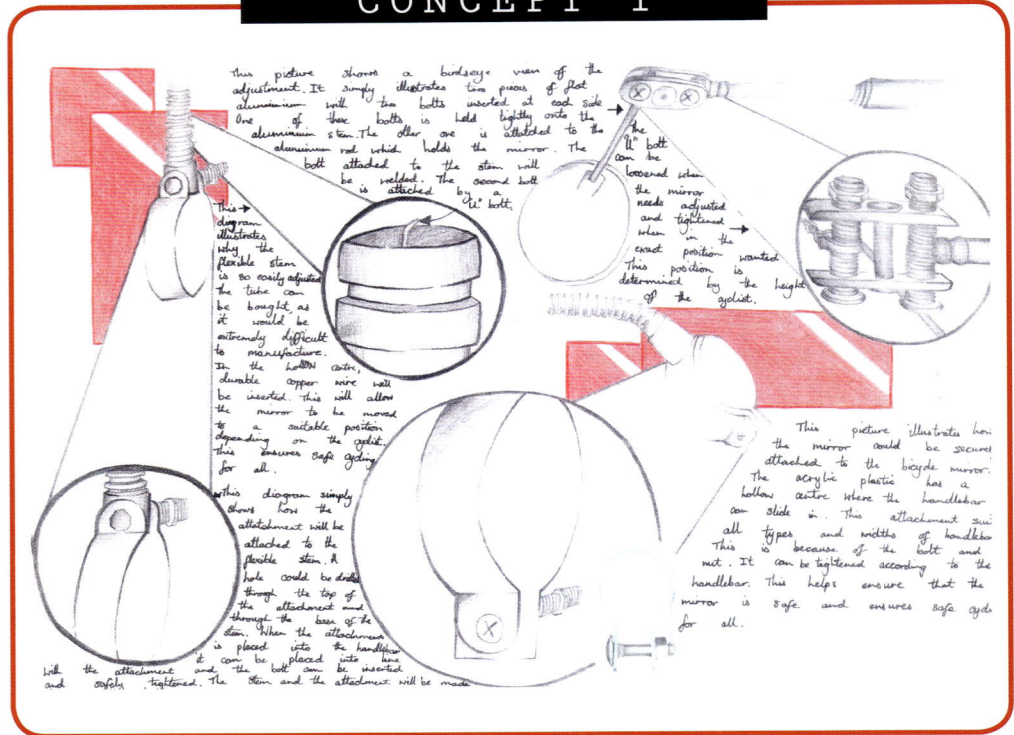
CONCEPT 1

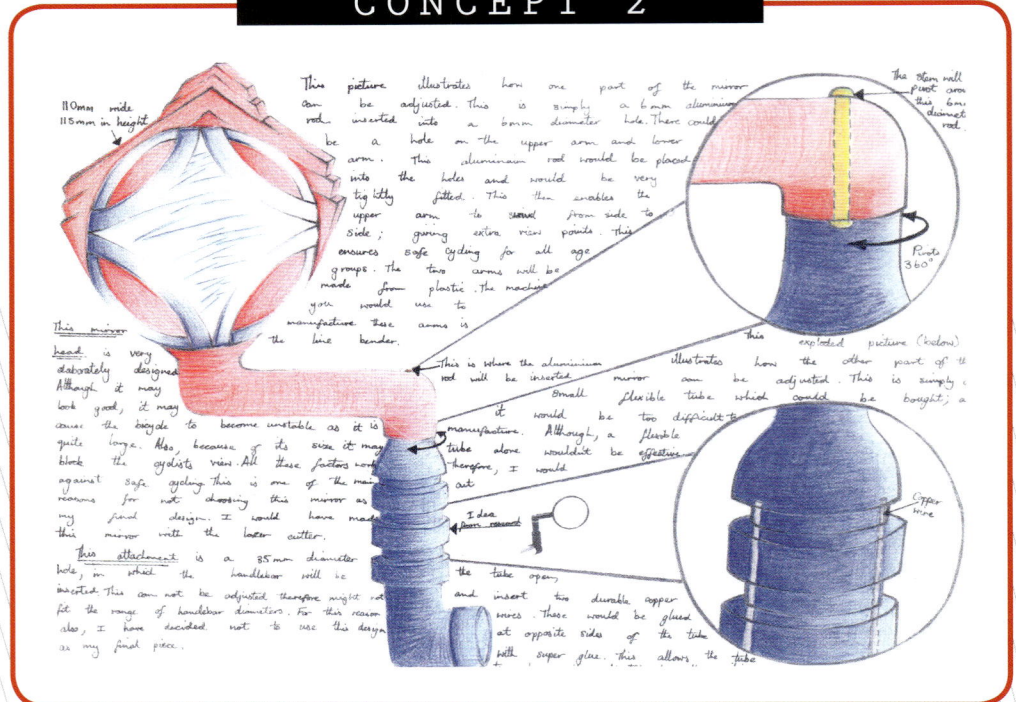
CONCEPT 2

Final idea

In this section you should develop your final idea. Begin with a simple statement about the concept you have chosen to develop as the final idea and give a brief explanation of why you chose it. You may want to consider the following factors: function, materials, size, assembly, attachment, usability, aesthetics, manufacturing and safety. You should also link your development to your research on these areas. You could include pictures to illustrate how your research has been used in your design, for example, images of different tools and processes.

The final idea must be justified and it is important that you show evidence of the following features to ensure your design pages are covering all the aspects of the assignment:

- The appropriate and good quality research materials you have used.

- How you used your research materials as a stimulus for inspiration.

- Your first ideas and concept sketches, including annotation.

- That you are designing for manufacture, using graphics and annotation to communicate ideas and fabrication details. It is not essential to write about the manufacturing process on your design sheets, however, students are expected to demonstrate their understanding, using illustrations, of how parts fit together.

- You need to demonstrate a good level of knowledge and understanding of the materials you selected and their properties, with justification for their use. You need to be specific, so the generic terms plastic, wood or metal are not precise enough to gain high marks. For example, if the material is plastic, make sure you state the exact types such as acrylic or polypropylene.

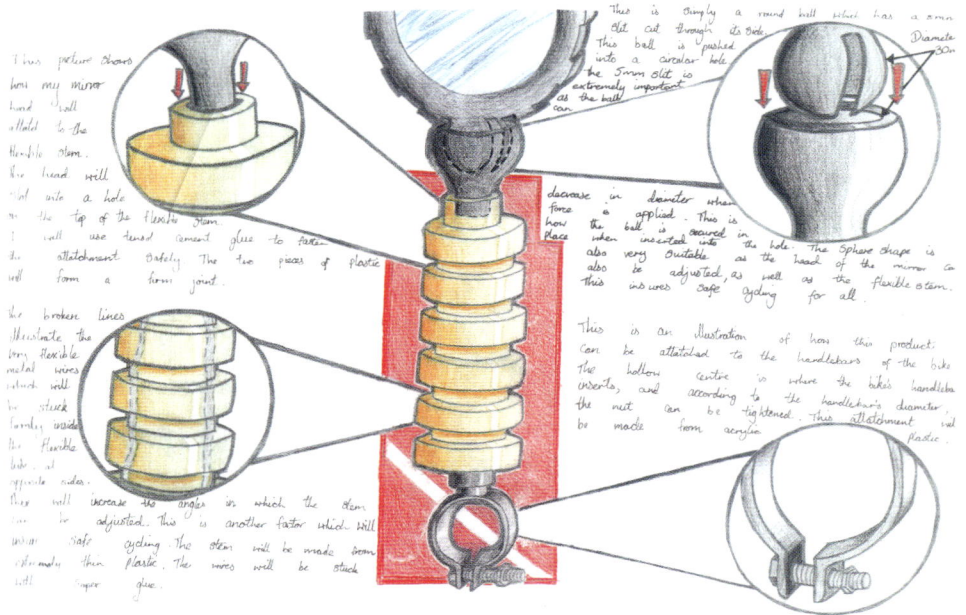

FINAL IDEA

DEVELOPMENT

You should refer to this list regularly as you complete the design assignment, checking you have shown the evidence required. You should also use each of these features to annotate your final idea. Refer to the theory you have learned throughout Units and 3 to improve your marks in this section.

Design briefs

The following are some of the design assignment tasks that have been set by the examination board over previous years.

Design brief 1: safe cycling

Context: In recent years *safe cycling* has become an important issue. In an effort to reduce annual death tolls and injury rates on roads you are asked to undertake research and design into the use of "bicycle mirrors".

Design opportunity:
Design a bicycle mirror that will help make the cyclist more aware of rear view traffic and assist in safe cycling for all.

Design brief 2: emergency LED light

Context: In situations of extreme weather conditions electrical power interruption is a reality in many cases. Power can also be interrupted when accidents happen or through a deliberate act of vandalism.

Design opportunity:
Design an emergency LED light to be used in an emergency situation. The light should be wall mountable and detachable.

Design brief 3: a sleeping aid

It is a common occurrence that children may not fall asleep easily when put to bed. In such circumstances they may need some kind of soothing device to aid the settling process.

Design opportunity:
Design such a device or system that could be attached to a cot or bed to help a young child fall asleep.

Design brief 4: a night time reading lamp

Research shows that good lighting reduces eye strain when reading or studying at night.

Design opportunity:
Design a lighting device for a teenage bedroom which provides appropriate and adjustable lighting when reading/ studying.

Design brief 5: Chewing gum disposal bin

There are more than 28 million gum chewers in the UK, disposing of over 3 billion pieces of gum per year. Discarded gum is one of the worst litter blights of the last 50 years, plaguing public areas all over the country with chewing gum deposits which do not decompose, are unsightly, unhygienic, and are a potential risk to pets and wild animals. According to a government report, currently about £150 million is spent annually by local authorities in the UK on chewing gum removal.

Design opportunity:
Design a chewing gum disposal bin for a school playground that would encourage students to use it. Consider the bin location and ease of attachment for discarding the contents and for cleaning purposes.

Design brief 6: disaster relief: lightweight emergency shelter

A safe and secure shelter makes getting through a disastrous situation a little easier, whether it's in an urban setting, or in the wilderness. To survive life in the great outdoors means being prepared for all situations.

Design opportunity:
Design a lightweight emergency shelter that will keep three persons dry, warm and safe in the event of an emergency.

Design briefs 1 & 2 taken from CCEA's Controlled Assessment Task, Unit 4: Design and Assessment (Summer 2011), 1, © CCEA

Design briefs 3 & 4 taken from CCEA's Controlled Assessment Task, Unit 4: Design and Assessment Summer 2012), 1, © CCEA

ACTIVITY

Select one of the design briefs and produce a research page on existing products. Make sure your page includes good quality images and high quality annotation that explains the product. Remember to consider the following factors: function, materials, size, assembly, attachment, usability, aesthetics, manufacturing and safety.

ACTIVITY

This activity will help develop your sketching techniques and the skill of annotating.

Sketch, render and annotate a range of solutions for one of the design briefs. Produce one A3 page of initial concept sketches and one A3 page with the development of a final idea on it that has good quality annotation.

TIME MANAGEMENT

Good time management is an important skill that is required during controlled assessment. With your teacher and class you might find it useful to work out the days and dates you will be working on the design assignment in school and at home. A visual aid such as this timetable below will keep you focused and ensure your time is used wisely to produce a quality outcome that will achieve maximum marks.

DAY	DATE	TOPIC	HOURS	WORK PRODUCED
Monday		Research	1.5 hrs	
Tuesday		Research	1.5 hrs	
Monday		Research	1.5 hrs	3 x A4 sheets of research and preparation completed in 8 hours
Tuesday		Research	1.5 hrs	
Monday		Research	1.5 hrs	
Tuesday		Research	0.5 hrs	
Research completed				
Monday		Design Work	1.0 hr	
Tuesday		Design Work	1.0 hr	
Monday		Design Work	1.0 hr	
Tuesday		Design Work	1.0 hr	4 x A3 sheets of design work completed in 7 hours
Monday		Design Work	1.0 hr	
Tuesday		Design Work	1.0 hr	
Monday		Design Work	1.0 hr	
Design work complete				
Total hours: 15				
Unit 4 Design Assignment to be submitted on:				

This chapter provides guidance on how to carry out your controlled assessment work, providing the requirements of the unit in a suggested format, which should ensure that you cover all aspects of Unit 4. However, this guidance must be used in conjunction with the direction and teaching you receive in your own school. The page layouts and presentation techniques need to show your own individual style but the information in this chapter should help get you started and provide a check list to keep you focused. Remember good time management is essential, so make sure you leave enough time to get everything covered.

UNIT 5

DESIGN PROJECT CONTROLLED ASSESSMENT

*This unit is **compulsory** for all students. In this chapter you will be completing one of the following units:*

Your school will advise you on your chosen element of study.

In this controlled assessment you will be assessed on your knowledge, skills and ability to:

Systems Design and Manufacturing

Product Design and Manufacturing

- Plan and carry out research
- Produce sketches to illustrate your ideas
- Design a product under controlled conditions
- Manufacture a product
- Evaluate your work

PROJECT GUIDELINES

This controlled assessment has an equal weighting of possible marks for the design portfolio and the manufactured product or system.

Students must complete their design portfolio under informal supervision, they should spend:

- approximately **15 hours** producing their design portfolio.
- approximately another **15 hours** producing their manufactured product or system.

If time is saved in the portfolio production, this time can then be used for manufacturing and visa versa.

CCEA will issue **up to three** comparable tasks each year, for each element, in September of the second year of study. Centres select the task that is best suited to their needs.

By the end of the assignment, students should have demonstrated their ability to design and manufacture a product in their chosen element under controlled conditions.

Design portfolio

The design portfolio is integral to the design project. Every design project will be unique, and therefore have its own characteristics and relevant processes. However every design portfolio should cover all the areas outlined in the pages that follow.

The CCEA specification states that the portfolio size cannot be more than ten A3 sheets (or equivalent). Text cannot be larger than the equivalent of a font size of 14 points using ICT. These sheets **could** be put together using the following structure. Quality of written communication (QWC) will be assessed in this task.

	Element 1: Systems design and manufacturing		Element 2: Product design and manufacturing
Page 1	Problem identification, theme/design brief and specification.	Page 1	Problem identification, theme/design brief and specification.
Page 2	Research/analysis and investigation appropriate to the System(s) including problem, existing solutions and circuit.	Page 2	Research existing solutions.
Pages 3–5	A range* of quality concept sketches that show creativity, knowledge and understanding of the system(s) including detailed annotation.	Page 3	Research, such as: • Produce a questionnaire for the client or end user • Investigate possible materials and manufacturing processes • Research relevant information on ergonomics and anthropometrics associated with a potential solution to the problem
		Pages 4–5	A range* of initial ideas for proposed product design that show a depth of knowledge and understanding of how the products may work. Use sketches and annotation to show how the research materials have inspired and influenced the concepts.
Page 6	Development of the proposed system(s) design.	Pages 6–7	Development of the chosen idea showing most of the assembly detail including fabrication details, material selection and justification.
Page 7	Good development of the chosen system(s) design showing detailed understanding.		
Page 8	Final concept of chosen system(s).	Page 8	Final idea: Produce a well sketched, rendered and annotated drawing or CAD drawing of your final idea.
Page 9	System development: Use drawings/models to explain how the system works, detailed drawings explaining the Input-Control-Output, and quality diagrams with annotation that fully explain how the system(s) work(s).	Page 9	Working drawing.
Page 10	Evaluation and suggested modifications.	Page 10	Evaluation and suggested modifications.

*Note: A range is considered as **two** concepts for Element 1 and **three** concepts for Element 2.

Design portfolio and manufacturing

The tables on pages 178–182 give some guidance on how you could to complete your design portfolio to accompany your manufactured product. However, this guidance must be used in conjunction with the direction and teaching you receive in your own school. The page layouts and presentation techniques need to show your own individual style but the information in the tables could be used as a reference guide as you progress through your design project. Examples of some of these presentation techniques are shown on pages 176–177. It would also be useful to engage in some self and peer assessment throughout the design process, to check you are on track. Sometimes it is useful to get other people's opinions on ideas or concepts, as designers rarely work alone and it may give you further inspiration, which will benefit your designing and manufacturing.

Examples of presentation techniques:

Initial ideas continued and evaluated

Note: Candidates are not expected to evaluate their concepts against every factor in the specification but the positives and negatives of each should be analysed.

DEVELOPMENT

- Here I have decided to develop both designs 2 & 3 further as I feel these designs combined will definitely reflect all the criteria I need to hit the specification.

SIDE VIEW — 180mm
ring of rubber
50mm
50mm
FRONT VIEW
200mm
180mm
Circular/oval shape
300mm

I considered using this layered, boat shaped design. But prefer to try keeping a design similar to my model.

- As my original design would have to be made using the vacum-forming process, to ensure

- I would like to keep my glass as design and take the idea of a curved glass moulded into my product.

will form its shape from several layers of acrylic pieces cut out to size on the lazer cutter.

plastic rods

This is a solid model made from polystyrene to figure out the general shape I would like to produce whilst making my product.

MODEL

- I convey my knowledge and skills within the manufacturing area. To do this I will want to use the lazer cutter to produce my product. Doing this I shall get a unique and modern shape and overall product.

This is my first design idea developed from my original design

plastic rods

Development continued

DEVELOPMENT

✱ I wanted my product to look as similar to my polystyrene model as possible

PART ① x1
PART ② x5
PART ③ x5

✱ So in order to do this, I have decided to make all my parts compact, by glueing them together with tensil cement. PART ①

(separated parts)

·For extra added asthetic appeal a clear acrylic lid or cover that opens or closes could be incorporated into my design

·A simple lid which can open and close easily like so... would be perfect.

·I would cut the amount and shape I desire for my lid on the laser cutter.

TEST PIECE

LINE BENDING

· Then some line bending will be needed.

This is the final design I have developed. It is a display unit which will display the latest IPOD in the entertainment section of my local supermarket. I feel the design meets all the spec points. The display unit is attractive and eyecatching and showed an increase in sales. It is a unique design with a novelty factor.

50mm
50mm
180mm
250mm

I POD ♫

300mm

TRIAL → FINAL DESIGN

The product has been designed to be portable so its easily moved to various locations with the entertainment section, e.g on to a shelf at a P.O.S (point of sale)

Note: Select the column in the table that shows your element of study. There is a ✓or a ✗ for each row to show what is required for your design portfolio.

Requirements for design portfolio	Element 1 Systems Design	Element 2 Product Design
Problem identification, theme/design brief and specification To begin the design portfolio you need to write a description of the problem identified, a theme/design brief and a specification: **Problem identification:** You need to state the theme that was issued by the exam board and describe the design opportunity you have been presented with. **Theme/design brief:** The theme/design brief should be written as a clear statement beginning 'Design and manufacture …' Remember from your study of Unit 1, a theme/design brief is a short simple statement about what you intend to do. For example: 'Design and manufacture an educational resource for young children in primary school.' or 'Design and manufacture a display unit for the entertainment section of a supermarket.' **Specification:** A detailed specification needs to be written identifying the key requirements of the product you intend to design and manufacture to fulfill the theme/design brief. Although you may present the specification on the first page of your design portfolio, it will be written after you have completed your research and investigation into the problem. Remember from your study of Unit 1, a specification is a detailed list of everything a product should do or have. It is also important to remember to justify your key requirements to gain high marks in this section. This means writing detailed explanations of the reasons why you think the product should do something or have this feature.	✔	✔
Research Research is an essential part of the design process so it needs to be documented in your design portfolio. Research will make the problem clearer and will help you when you start generating possible solutions. It will also help you decide on the specific key requirements for your product – its specification. Research is completed before any concepts are started. **General research:** This can take many forms including questionnaires to potential consumers of the product, information about different materials, manufacturing processes, ergonomics and anthropometrics. You may find it useful to incorporate some of this data into your concepts. Research on the problem may also include finding out more about why the problem exists. **Researching existing solutions:** This will make you aware of the similar products that already exist, and what possible materials and manufacturing processes are available. **Investigating existing solutions:** It is simple to find images of existing solutions and present them in your design portfolio but they will mean nothing if you do not do something with this type of research. You need to make it beneficial for generating your own concepts in the next section and to do this you need to analyse each product. You might find it useful to make clear notes commenting on features such as materials, design, form, appeal, function, safety and performance; and your own thoughts about the existing products such as likes and dislikes, and your reasons why. Remember to connect your research to the problem by noting how it is linked to or solves it. Mood	✔	✔

boards can be used as another possible method of research. They are made up of a variety of random thoughts, collections and pictures. Really anything can be presented on a mood board but it is only useful in this design portfolio if you can reference how each part of the mood board has influenced your thinking about the problem.

Research and investigation of circuit systems

If you are completing Element 1 it will be necessary for you to complete research on circuit systems relevant to the problem. Include some research on systems and systems environments,* for example, if an electronic system has been chosen consider research of casings, housings, displays, etc. For higher marks you need to demonstrate a depth of analysis of the research collated on systems, environments, materials, components, parts, etc.

Systems environment is interpreted as engineering solutions designed to support, encase, house, and or display the system.

Conceptual designs

Concepts are your initial design ideas sketched, rendered and annotated in detail with clear explanatory notes.

Creativity: Each concept should be different to show you have considered a range of possible solutions to the problem. They need to be creative, imaginative and innovative to gain high marks in this section, so do not copy existing products.

Good use of reference materials: Although your ideas need to be innovative, your research on existing products should have helped you. For example, you may have drawn inspiration from an existing product or alternatively decided against a certain design feature because you found it did not work well in practice. Reference this research and explain how it assisted you, as this will show how you used your research to good effect.

Knowledge and understanding: Write your annotation in a way that shows a depth of knowledge and understanding of how the products you have designed will work. To achieve this you need to explain the function of the product, how it will work and how it will solve the problem.

Graphical techniques: The concept pages of your portfolio need to display a range of graphical techniques to illustrate your ideas such as 2D, 3D, sectional, exploded, pictorial and scrap sketches showing details. Do not discard any ideas or thoughts at this stage of design but include everything you have considered, even if it is not used in your final concept. Remember you are a designer and will have many great ideas during this process.

For the concepts section of Element 1 only:
- Ensure you show a depth of knowledge and understanding of how the systems work, for example, explain the Input, Control and Output of each system designed.
- Use concept sketches to show appropriate environments for displaying, containing or supporting the system(s).
- Also include concept sketches presenting the system(s) in an appropriate environment.

Development of an idea and fabrication details

Development of a concept means taking the initial idea and thoughts further by

considering a range of possibilities for shape, form, style, materials, finish, colour, dimensions and manufacturing processes. The main aim is to produce a final idea by the end of the development by making design decisions throughout this process.	✗	✓

Designing for creativity: You could begin the development section with a clear statement about the concept you want to develop and perhaps a sketch of the concept or combination of concepts you are proposing to develop. You may also find it useful to state the reasons why this concept was chosen over your other concepts.

Knowledge and understanding: As part of your development deeper thinking skills are required that show attention to details of how the product will be assembled and fit the purpose for use. This is expected for projects achieving top marks, so show how parts fit together or possible assembly details through the use of graphics and annotation. Development should include further ideas or suggestions about the solution where appropriate to enhance your design(s).

Good use of reference materials: Throughout this section you must refer to your research. Including some relevant annotation or an image from your research will show how you used it to good effect. For example, if you are considering CAD/CAM as a manufacturing process in your development, perhaps note that you investigated the advantages of this process in your research and include an image of a CAM machine such as a laser cutter.

Designing for manufacture: Developing a concept will require you to look at a range of possible materials that could be used. Ensure that you identify appropriate materials for your design, and both explain and justify the reasons for their use. To clarify ideas, estimate dimensions, proportions, etc, of the product details you may find it beneficial to make card models and/or use 3D CAD where appropriate. Models could also be photographed and included in this section if they aid development and help you make design decisions.

You could end this section with a statement on the design decisions you have made, as a result of this development, which will be included in your final idea.

## Final concept The final concept is the product you have designed and developed that solves the problem, fulfils the theme/design brief and meets the keys requirements of the specification. This is the design you intend to manufacture. It can be presented as a 3D rendered sketch or as a 3D CAD model produced using a software package such as SolidWorks.	✓	✓
## System development To demonstrate an understanding of the system you need to: • show the development of the proposed system(s) design. For example, if an electronics system has been chosen for development, you could use graphics and annotation to show your understanding of how changing inputs and outputs can affect the system's characteristics or performance. • present concept sketches of the proposed system in an environment. For example, again if developing an electronics system, you would be expected to design appropriate housings, casings, displays, etc.	✓	✗
## Drawings/models In this section you are required to explain how the system(s) works.	✓	✗

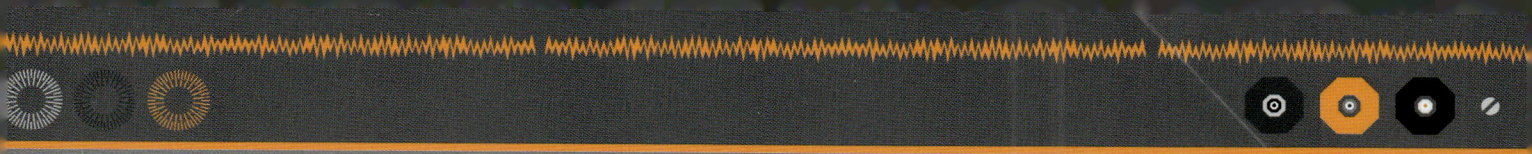

Drawings: You should include detailed drawings that will explain the Input–Control–Output of the system. Good quality diagrams using either freehand sketches or virtual CAD drawings, hard models, etc, combined with informative annotation, will help you to explain how the system(s) work. For example, if an electronics system is being developed you could choose to use software such as Bright Spark, Livewire, PCB Wizard, Circuit Wizard or bread boards.

Models: Then the final diagram(s) outlining the full system needs to be presented. If it is appropriate, you could model the system in card or use 3D CAD to clarify ideas. Dimensions, proportions, etc, of the system(s)'s environment can be estimated and shown as a sketch(es) of the proposed system, assembled in an appropriate environment.

Note: Candidates opting for Element 1: Systems Design do not have to produce a working drawing but if an Electronic Systems is manufactured then all PIC circuits should include pin layout of the inputs and outputs. Candidates should also include stage development of the program.

Working drawing

Orthographic drawing: You need to produce a detailed working 'orthographic drawing or drawings' in third angle using either a drawing board or by using 2D CAD. The drawing(s) must include:

- Elevations of all the main parts (drawn to BSI).
- The convention used for third angle.
- The scale that it is drawn to.
- All the key dimensions that are necessary to manufacture each part.
- A list of materials required.
- The key parts balloon referenced.

Also include the details necessary for manufactured templates, jigs and formers.

Evaluation and modifications

The evaluation is the final section of the portfolio and it documents what you and potential users think about the final product that has been designed and manufactured.

Constructive evaluation: An evaluation should be written that includes reference to your original specification and comments on how the product has fulfilled each of the specification's points. The key to making the evaluation constructive is to be honest. If the product does not fulfill certain points of the specification fully explain why it does not. For example, if your specification required a tabletop product of a certain dimension and your final design was much larger, state the reasons why. Perhaps the product required more space to fit in all the components or it needed to be larger for ergonomic reasons.

Testing: Testing features such as how well the product works or how safe it is for users is an essential part of the evaluation process. Make sure you document the findings of your testing and use them to write your constructive evaluation.

Modifications: In this section you should also suggest improvements or modifications that may be implemented to improve performance. These can be future developments of the product and it is considered good practice to include sketches, photographs and models as part of this section.

Note: Candidates do not have to provide photographic evidence of how the product is manufactured.

Requirements for design portfolio

Standard expected at GCSE level: When manufacturing your final product for either Element 1 or Element 2 you need to demonstrate manufacturing techniques that reflect the standard and complexity expected at GCSE level. To achieve this, try to think of simple products you manufactured when you were studying the subject at Key Stage 3 – this level of manufacturing skill would not be good enough for a GCSE project.

Manufacturing skill and quality: The final product you manufacture needs to do the following to achieve top marks in this section:

- Use appropriate materials, processes and techniques.
- Demonstrate precision and accuracy of fabrication techniques.
- Show quality in the finishing, accuracy and attention to detail.
- Satisfy the design specification you wrote in your design portfolio.

Use of modelling: If you used any templates, jigs, formers, printed circuit board masks, etc, to assist you with the manufacturing processes, include these in your portfolio. Either take a photograph of the modelling used and explain how it assisted you, or mention it in your evaluation section.

If studying Element 1: Systems Design, and an electronics system is used, the following elements are necessary to achieve top marks:

- A good quality printed circuit board.
- Components should be positioned accurately and soldered to a high standard. Where appropriate, heat shrink or sleeving should be used.
- Wires should be neatly positioned and the printed circuit board, battery, switches, and all other components must be secured accurately in their housing.
- The housing, environment or casing must be manufactured to a high standard, with a good quality of finishing.

Note: Although the examples in this section focus on electronics, the systems design is NOT restricted to electronics and candidates may also consider: mechanical, electrical, pneumatic or computer control, or a combination of these systems.

This chapter provides guidance on how to carry out your controlled assessment work, providing the requirements of the unit in a suggested format, which should ensure that you cover all aspects of Unit 5. However, this guidance must be used in conjunction with the direction and teaching you receive in your own school. The page layouts and presentation techniques need to show your own individual style but the information in this chapter should help get you started and provide a check list to keep you focused. Remember good time management is essential, so make sure you leave enough time to get everything covered. As with your design assignment in Unit 4, you might find it useful to use a timetable to plan when you will be working on the design project (refer back to page 173 for guidance).

COPYRIGHT

Picture Credits

The following photographs are included with kind permission of the copyright holders. The numbers denote page numbers.

CCEA

33-35 (All), 55-56 (All), 57 (bottom), 58, (top), 64 (All except Robot), 68 (bottom), 69-70 (All), 87 (top), 88 (top), 89-91 (All), 107-110 (All), 134 (top), 135 (bottom), 152-153 (All), 165 (top). See also copyright acknowledgement on previous page.

Dassault Systemes SolidWorks Corp. All associated trademarks are attributed to Dassault Systemes SolidWorks Corp

22 (All)

Drumragh Integrated College

117 (right), 167 (top), 168 (top), 168 (bottom), 170 (top), 170 (bottom), 171 (top), 171 (bottom), 176 (top), 176 (bottom), 177 (top), 177 (bottom)

Emerson Power Transmission Corp

49 (left, 3rd image)

iStockPhoto

9 (2nd from top), 9 (middle), 10 (top), 10 (bottom), 11 (bottom), 13 (right, 5th image), 15 (left, top, left), 15 (right, 3rd, right), 28 (bottom), 37 (left, 2nd image), 47 (left, bottom), 47 (right), 48 (left, bottom), 48 (right, bottom), 49 (left, top), 49 (left, 5th image), 51 (left, 3rd image), 51 (left, bottom), 53 (left, middle), 53 (left, bottom), 53 (right, top, left), 53 (left, 2nd image), 57 (top), 59 (right, middle), 77 (left, top, left), 77 (left, top, right), 94 (right, 2nd image), 94 (3rd from bottom, left), 96 (right, top), 95 (left, 2nd image), 100 (right, bottom), 106 (left, bottom), 106 (right, top), 106 (right, 2nd image), 112 (left), 112 (right, bottom), 113 (right), 117 (left, bottom), 119 (left), 120 (left, top), 121 (bottom), 125 (left, top), 125 (right, top), 125 (right, middle), 126 (top), 126 (2nd image), 127 (left, bottom), 128 (left, bottom), 131 (bottom), 132 (right, 2nd image), 132 (right, 4th image), 133 (middle), 136 (right, bottom), 136 (right, top), 138 (right, top), 139 (left, top), 139 (right, bottom), 140 (left, bottom), 140 (right, bottom), 142 (left, top), 143 (left, top), 143 (right, 3rd image), 145 (left, top), 145 (left, middle), 145 (left, bottom), 146 (right, top, left), 146 (right, bottom), 164 (top), 57 (top)

James Dyson Foundation www.jamesdysonfoundation.com

27 (bottom)

Malcolm Johnston

9 (2nd from bottom (top))

New Media Learning Ltd

61 (left, top), 61 (right), 85 (left, bottom), 85 (right, bottom), 86 (left, bottom)

Suzanne Hagan

14 (left, 5th), 25 (bottom), 37 (left, top), 60 (right, bottom), 83 (right, top), 85 (right, top)

TechSoft UK Limited www.techsoft.co.uk dd

21 (All)

Wesley Johnston

9 (2nd from bottom (bottom)), 158 (right, bottom)